TOURISM

Marketing and Operations

Tourism
Marketing and Operations

Harish Bhatt
B.S. Badan

CRESCENT
PUBLISHING CORPORATION

[The responsibility for the facts stated, conclusions reached and plagiarism, if any, in this book is entirely that of the Author. And the Publisher bears no responsibility for them, whatsoever.]

Tourism : Marketing and Operations

First Published : 2006

ISBN 81-8342-007-9

Published by :

CRESCENT PUBLISHING CORPORATION
4831/24, Prahlad Street,
Ansari Road, Darya Ganj,
New Delhi - 110002
Ph. : 23272541, 23257835
Fax : 91- 011- 23257835
e-mail : campusbooks@hotmail.com

Typesetting by :

Arjun Computers
Delhi - 110051

Printed at :

Roshan Offset Printers
Delhi

Preface

Marketing is an important activity for any business that wishes to become and remain competitive and successful. This is certainly the case in the rapidly changing tourism industry, and therefore tourism destination marketers must constantly review and revise their marketing goals, images, strategies and plans. The tourism industry encompasses many businesses, such as accommodations, attractions, transportation, and restaurants, each of which may undertake marketing efforts. That is, there are different scales at which marketing can occur, from large-scale marketing of individual businesses or attractions, to small-scale marketing of regions or entire countries.

Marketing is one of the main ways for destinations to inform and entice potential tourists and to gain competitive advantage. It also can be used to protect the environment, improve quality of life, and help society as a whole. Marketers can use demand management to increase, decrease, or shift demand for a product or service either temporarily or permanently.

Today's tourists are more selective and demanding, and more educated, experienced, independent, conservation-minded, respectful of cultures, and insistent on value for money. This paradigm shift within the tourism industry must be taken into consideration when marketing tourism, in order to ensure that the needs and wants of the new tourists are met. Tourism destinations that adopt a modern marketing philosophy "that focuses on the satisfaction of tourist needs and wants while respecting the long-term interests in the community" will benefit not only themselves, but consumers, the environment, and society.

This book analyses the new trends in tourism marketing and operations. The role of new technologies in revolutionising all business processes, the entire value chain as well as the strategic relationships of tourism organizations with all their stakeholders are elaborately discussed. Besides students and teachers of in business, tourism and hospitality management, researchers and practitioners will find this work of utmost use.

Harish Bhatt
B.S. Badan

Contents

1

Marketing Operations

Over the past twenty years, the tourism industry has evolved dramatically. Changes in the environment, economics, technology, and tourists' beliefs and activities have caused the mass tourism which dominated the 1970s and 1980s to give way to the "new tourism," involving new tourists, new technologies, and new management practices.

Marketing is an important activity for any business that wishes to become and remain competitive and successful. This is certainly the case in the rapidly changing tourism industry, and therefore tourism destination marketers must constantly review and revise their marketing goals, images, strategies and plans.

Importance of Marketing in Tourism

The tourism industry encompasses many businesses, such as accommodations, attractions, transportation, and restaurants, each of which may undertake marketing efforts. That is, there are different scales at which marketing can occur, from large-scale marketing of individual businesses or attractions (such as a horse-and-carriage tour operator, a hot dog stand, a whale watching business), to small-scale marketing of regions or entire countries. The focus of this research is on the small scale marketing of destination regions, because it is at the regional, or community, level that "successful tourism planning is likely to take place" and at which "most of the impacts of tourism, both positive and negative, occur".

Tourism is the largest industry in the world. It is a very competitive industry with a highly volatile product. Destinations in vogue today often are out of fashion tomorrow. Marketing is one of the main ways for destinations to inform and entice potential tourists and to gain competitive advantage. However, many service industries such as tourism have traditionally used marketing less than manufacturing firms, as they felt it was too expensive, time-consuming, unnecessary, and unprofessional, relying primarily on an established reputation to attract business.

There are still those who consider marketing unprofessional, particularly within the area of advertising. Such detractors hold on to the belief that marketers will do anything to sell their products or services, with their number one goal being the making of a "quick buck." They are seen as having a complete lack of respect for customers' opinions, desires and intellects, and the environment or society as a whole. But this is an unfair view of many of today's marketers, because in a true marketing philosophy, customer satisfaction is key.

Marketing also can be used to protect the environment, improve quality of life, and help society as a whole. Marketers can use demand management to increase, decrease, or shift demand for a product or service either temporarily or permanently. In the case of tourism, demarketing can be particularly useful, as it can be used to even-out demand (i.e., increase off-season visits, and limit high-season visits, thus reducing congestion, crowding and environmental impacts), to restrict access to sensitive areas, and to inform and educate tourists about problems facing various areas.

Tourism destinations that adopt a modern marketing philosophy "that focuses on the satisfaction of tourist needs and wants while respecting the long-term interests in the community" will benefit not only themselves, but consumers, the environment, and society. This is corroborated by Poon who believes that "[n]ew tourism can play a leading role in providing and promoting more sustainable patterns of development and in saving Planet Earth." Thus, tourism marketing can and should assume an important role in education and conservation, because in the tourism industry, there is much more to gain (or lose) than just profits.

In these days of increased amounts of leisure time, higher standards of living, greater quality of life, higher expectations, and increasing choices (at least in so-called "developed countries"), tourism destination marketers must work harder to provide tourist satisfaction and to ensure they obtain and retain their share of the market. But tourism marketers should be sensitive to the new situation in which they are marketing. They must realize that tourism can and does have a sizeable impact on the environment, and tourism should not be promoted without full knowledge and understanding of that fact. Certainly not all regions are ready or willing to accept and develop tourism. Nor should they, as tourism does not always have a positive effect.

But in many areas, tourism marketing can make a significant contribution to the quality of life of residents and tourists alike. Destinations that have chosen to embrace or at least accept tourism as a valuable industry must find a way to compete and succeed, and to protect the environment from the negative impacts of tourism. Adoption of a marketing philosophy is the key to success, and tourism marketers that adopt the societal marketing concept will be better off in the future, as consumers are becoming more educated and concerned about choosing products and services that benefit rather than harm the environment.

Basics of Marketing

Marketing is defined most simply as "providing the right products [or services] at the right price in the right place and promoting them in a way that will appeal to the target market". More specifically:

> "marketing is a managerial process involving the setting of organizational goals and objectives, analysis, planning, and implementation. It is a set of activities that results in the formulation of plans and programs. Through these activities an organization seeks to bring about a voluntary exchange of values by providing benefits to its clients and potential clients and, through this, benefits to the organization and its constituent parts or members".

Marketing can be visualized at three levels.

Firstly, any "exchange" of products or services in order to satisfy needs and wants is considered marketing.

Secondly, marketing is a "system," which includes the providers of goods and services (i.e., the industry), those purchasing the goods and services (i.e., the market), and those responsible for delivering goods and services from the producers to the consumers. The marketing system also encompasses the flows of money, communications, and information between the industry and the market, and the surrounding environment in which these flows occur.

Thirdly, a marketing "management philosophy" is one of five management philosophies, including the "production concept," the "product concept," the "selling concept," the "marketing concept," and the "societal marketing concept", that may be adopted by organizations involved in exchanges with consumers.

Organizations that focus on providing their products and services in the most efficient manner possible are said to have a "production" orientation, whereas organizations that concentrate their efforts on producing the best product possible have adopted a "product" orientation. The "selling" philosophy involves "large-scale selling and promotion effort[s]" in order to stimulate purchases.

A "marketing philosophy" involves "determining the needs and wants of target markets and delivering the desired satisfactions more effectively and efficiently than competitors do". Some companies go further by adopting a "societal marketing concept" in order to "deliver the desired satisfactions more effectively and efficiently than competitors in a way that maintains or improves the consumer's and society's well-being."

According to this philosophy, marketers should make every effort possible to find out what it is that consumers really want and need, and then endeavour to provide these products and services in an ethical and socially-responsible way. One example of the societal marketing concept for tourism can be seen in the case of bike tours of Africa.

The tourist experiences the outdoors, improves his/her well-being by obtaining exercise, learns about the history, culture, ecology, and economics first-hand, all the while avoiding the pollution and environmental damage that would be produced by renting a vehicle.

The marketing system comprises many complex, interrelated elements and processes. Despite the fact that the individual, specialized elements in a marketing process vary, and the order in which the steps should be followed is flexible, there is a general consensus on the process to be followed regardless of the product or service being marketed.

Strategic marketing planning is the first step in the marketing process, and involves developing the business portfolio, creating the mission statement, determining goals and objectives, and designing functional strategies for each department of the business (e.g., human resources, accounting, purchasing). A business portfolio is "the collection of businesses and products that comprise the company".

The mission statement is a statement of a company's overall reasons for doing business, and provides guidance for all the various departments, products, and services which make up the company. Goals and objectives are set in order to help the company and its various departments fulfill the mission statement, and to provide direction for every aspect of the business. Functional strategies are plans which help each business unit to achieve its goals and objectives.

Another major step in the marketing process is the selection of the target market, defined as the group of consumers sharing similar characteristics or needs that the company has chosen to satisfy. This in turn is made up of four steps:

— demand measurement and forecasting;

— market segmentation;

— market targeting; and

— market positioning.

Demand measurement involves determining whether or not there exists a market for the product or service at the present time, and forecasting is used to estimate the demand for the product or service in the future. As it is nearly impossible to satisfy every consumer with a particular product or service, market segmentation is performed to identify "distinct groups of buyers with different needs, characteristics, or behaviours who might require separate products or marketing mixes".

The selection of the particular markets to be satisfied by the company's product or service is called market targeting, and is followed by marketing positioning, which involves determining the distinctive position (e.g., most luxurious, most economical) the product or service will occupy in the market relative to competing products or services.

The development of "competitive marketing strategies" requires the examination and evaluation of competitors so as to discern "areas of potential advantage and disadvantage". This is followed by the development of the "marketing mix," which is "the set of controllable tactical marketing tools - product, price, place, and promotion - that the firm blends to produce the response it wants in the target market". The marketing mix is of great importance as "[i]t determines how the marketing budget is allocated, forms the foundation of the marketing plan's strategy, and provides the marketing manager with the techniques to optimise his [sic] budgetary expenditure". "Product" refers to the product or service that the company has chosen to offer to its target markets, and the "price" is the amount that consumers will have to pay to obtain the product or service. "Place" refers to the physical location in which consumers may access the product or service, and encompasses the distribution of the product or service. Lastly, "promotion" involves the activities that the company undertakes in order to make consumers aware of its products and services.

Businesses also must undertake the management of their marketing efforts, which includes analysis, planning, implementation and control. Marketing analysis involves "complete analysis of the company's situation . . . to determine which opportunities it can best pursue".

Through the process of marketing planning, a company develops a marketing plan, which "will help the company attain its overall strategic objectives" and includes an "executive summary, current marketing situation, threats and opportunities, objectives and issues, marketing strategies, action programs, budgets, and controls".

The third step in marketing management is implementation, which involves "turn[ing] marketing strategies and plans into marketing actions to accomplish strategic marketing objectives". Lastly, marketing control is used to evaluate the performance of the plans and strategies against preset goals. In this way, marketers may analyse the performance of their plans, and then take "corrective actions" in order to improve future performance.

The preceding description of the marketing process highlights the fact that marketing is a complex, time-consuming, and expensive undertaking, made even more so because it occurs in an environment that is constantly changing, and involves competitors that are trying to gain competitive advantage. Businesses (and tourist destinations) must realize the importance of their marketing efforts, and continually monitor and modify their marketing strategies and plans in order to survive in this competitive environment.

Marketing Process

Marketing involves the creation of an image of a product or service. In the case of tourism marketing, the product is "the destination itself", or "an experience of place (location and people) at a particular time". Thus, the purpose of tourism marketing is to create a desirable image of the tourism destination in the minds of potential tourists, with the goal of enticing tourists to select the destination for their next holiday. As Ashworth affirms:

> "the demand for holidays emanates from a consumer reaction to perceptions of anticipated tourism experiences which are inextricably place-bound . . . the tourism product is a set of such experiences packaged as a destination place and marketed largely through images of that place."

Murphy agrees, stating that "tourism is built upon imagery." However, a desirable image is not enough. Kotler et al. stress that destination images must also be simple, appealing, distinctive, believable, and above all valid, as deceptive or unrealistic images can lead to tourist disappointment and dissatisfaction, loss of repeat business, bad "word-of-mouth" advertising, and a poor reputation. Thus, the formation of a desirable and realistic image of the tourism destination is of the utmost importance in tourism marketing.

Despite the unusual nature of the product, the principles of tourism marketing are the same as for the marketing of other products and services, however, "differences occur in the *application* of the theory". Tourism is a service, and must be marketed accordingly. Services are "products purchased through an exchange transaction that does not confer ownership but permits access to and use of a service at a specified time in a specified place". Hence the four special characteristics of tourism: "intangibility," "perishability," "inseparability," and "heterogeneity".

Middleton discusses three other important characteristics of tourism services, namely "seasonality and demand fluctuations," the "interdependence of the tourism product" and the "high fixed costs of service operations."

Demand for tourism products and services varies on a daily, weekly, monthly, and yearly basis (termed "seasonality"), mainly as a result of varying climatic conditions and the patterns of the school and business year. "Interdependence" occurs because when tourists visit a destination their experience is made up of several services, such as accommodation, transportation, and attractions. Tourism services have "high fixed costs," meaning that in order to perform a tourism service, the fixed costs are practically identical regardless of how many people use the service. For example, to operate a hotel, overhead costs are virtually the same, regardless of whether there is 30% or 70% occupancy on a particular day.

Wheeler describes the tourism industry as "volatile," because it is "affected by world events and the health of national economies." The horrible incidents of September 11, 2001 are an extreme example of the tourism industry's volatility. The terror attacks significantly impacted tourism in New York, which suffered a loss of almost $1 billion, and in the entire travel sector.

Due to the preceding factors, the tourism "product evolves over time to become . . . a totally different product". This has been described as the "non-standardization" of tourism. When marketing tourism, the marketing mix (which includes the variables of product, price, place, and promotion - the "4 Ps") must be applied appropriately and may be expanded to include "people" and "physical evidence".

Within tourism marketing, the marketing mix elements are important because they communicate to consumers what type of tourists particular destinations are trying to attract. The marketing mix is closely related to the "scale" of tourism to be marketed, as each of the marketing mix elements will vary depending on the scale of the tourism product being marketed. Obviously, the overall marketing mix, including such things as price and promotion will differ greatly, depending on the scale of the tourism product.

The "product" of tourism is different in nature than other products. The product of tourism is "a satisfying experience at a desired destination" and "a bundle of benefits", and is intangible, inseparable, perishable, and heterogeneous. Furthermore, "the tourist travels to the destination area where the product is experienced". More generally, the product of tourism is space and place, and tourism destination marketers can be considered "place marketers", or "experience" marketers.

The "price" of tourism is highly variable due to the interdependent and seasonal nature of tourism services. Heath & Wall state that, "[u]nderstanding the composition of and interrelationships among regional tourism products is . . . an important prerequisite to the development of an effective pricing strategy." Variable pricing strategies play an important role in demand management, as lower prices can be used to attract tourists to various destinations during their "off-seasons." In the same way, higher prices can be used to limit visitors in peak seasons.

The element of "place" in the marketing mix refers to the distribution of the product, and includes "the location of all the points of sale which provide prospective customers with *access* to tourist products". As discussed earlier, tourism services are perishable, and cannot be stored for sale at a later date. This affects the distribution of tourism services, as they must be marketed in a way that minimizes lost capacities (e.g., empty seats on an airplane, vacant rooms in a hotel).

The fourth 'P' in the marketing mix refers to "promotion," which is the most visible element in the marketing mix, because "advertising and other promotional activities are the primary means of communication with tourists in target markets". Promotion consists of personal selling, sales promotion, public relations, and advertising."People" refers to staff who deal with customers, and the customers (or tourists) themselves. "Physical evidence," the sixth marketing mix element, includes "physical characteristics" that influence "a company's atmosphere, image and identity and can affect consumers' judgments and perceptions about the service product they receive and about the service organisation itself".

Integrated marketing communication should be used to coordinate all direct and indirect contact that consumers will have with a company's message. In integrated marketing communication, the "4 Ps" become the "4 Cs" - consumers (rather than products), cost (rather than price), convenience (rather than place), and communication (rather than promotion).

The above discussion highlights the complex nature of the tourism marketing process, and perhaps provides reason for the claim that "good marketing practice is rare". In fact, "[m]any communities, including those whose economies are dominated by tourism, do not have tourism plans, marketing plans, or even tourism or marketing components in a general plan". Failure to recognize the importance of a dynamic tourism marketing plan and to implement it will lead to the loss of (or failure to attain) competitive advantage, tourist dissatisfaction, and possibly environmental degradation.

Promotional Materials

The most visible tourism marketing materials are those involved in the process of promotion, as its purpose is to create and increase awareness of a business' products or services and involves communicating with prospective clients. Promotion encompasses the areas of personal selling, direct marketing, sales promotion, public relations, and advertising and of these, advertising is usually the most obvious as it is conducted on a larger scale than the other four.

Personal selling consists of one-on-one interactions between a company's salespersons and their prospective clients, and is one form of direct marketing, which involves communicating with potential customers, usually by direct mail and telephone, and measuring the response. Public relations involves "building a good reputation and image", and "handling or heading off unfavourable rumours, stories, and events". Sales promotion includes "short-term incentives to encourage purchase or sales of a product or service", such as rebates, coupons, or contests.

Advertising can occur through a number of different media, including print materials (such as brochures, magazines and newspapers), direct mail (flyers, announcements), television commercials, videos, radio advertisements, window displays, and through the newest communication channel: the Internet. These advertisements usually consist of pictures, graphics, drawings, videos, maps, animation, and text, in varying amounts depending on the advertising channel employed.

Consumers access marketing materials by either seeking them out, coming across them while pursuing other activities, or receiving them directly from the company undertaking the advertising effort. Once discovered, they can choose either to ignore the information, to express interest, to request further information, or to put the information to use (e.g., to make comparisons, to help with decision-making, for fun or educational use, for personal interest or armchair travel, or to book a holiday). In addition, marketing may be either direct or indirect. Direct marketing is that which attempts to make a sale immediately, whereas indirect marketing is aimed at making a sale eventually.

Images of space and place play a prominent role in promotional materials, as their goal is the creation of a desirable image of the destination region, with the hope of causing consumers to seek further information and eventually select the destination as the site for future tourism experiences. Images are created through textual description, pictures, drawings, graphics, maps, music, audio, video, and animation.

Even the overall "look and feel" of the promotional materials, the choice of promotional methods, and the communication channel used, may influence the image of a destination. However, there are other factors which may influence images of place. Indirect influences (both positive and negative) on place images include movies, television shows, web sites, books, magazines, clothing, sporting events, music, posters, myths, rumours, stories, legends, and word-of-mouth from family and friends.

Tourism advertising materials are used to communicate images of tourism destinations to potential tourists. As humans are mainly "visual beings" these materials usually contain many pictures, maps, animation, and video. Textual descriptions are rich in adjectives and adverbs, and sounds or music elements are used to complement the images created by the visual elements.

Print advertisements include those in magazines and newspapers, and tourism brochures and flyers.Television commercials also endeavour to create desirable images, and due to television's visual nature are largely focussed on video images and pictures of the destination. Music is played, and while text is minimal, verbal descriptions and commentary are common. Most commercials provide a toll-free telephone number which you can call to obtain a brochure, and many recent commercials also refer watchers to their web site.

Radio commercials for tourism are less common, mainly because radio is a "nonvisual" form of communication, thus making it harder to create an image of the destination. Radio advertisements are more commonly used to announce current specials or promotional offerings by various tourist agencies and transportation carriers, rather than to promote destination regions.

The Internet is the newest and perhaps most powerful tool available to tourism marketers. The World Wide Web, the graphical interface through which users may navigate the Internet, has multimedia capabilities and, therefore, is a valuable device for creating images of tourism destinations. Tourism destination web sites may consist of pictures, videos, sounds, animations, graphics, maps and interactive maps, charts, text, games, and even programs, such as distance calculators and currency converters.

The tourism industry is highly competitive, and tourism marketers must constantly review and revise their marketing goals, plans, strategies, and images. Knowledge of the special characteristics of tourism, and how these affect traditional marketing methods is crucial.

The communication of a desirable and realistic image of the tourism destination to potential tourists is crucial as nothing will convince potential tourists to visit a destination unless they possess a desirable image of that destination.

Since 1995 and the demise of the U.S. Travel and Tourism Administration, the United States has been the only western industrialized nation without a national tourism agency to market the country as an international tourism destination.

During this period, the U.S. share of the global tourism market has slowly but steadily declined. Since 9/11 the decline has accelerated and international visitors to the U.S. have fallen about 20%. This has meant lost revenue and lost jobs to the U.S., made even worse by the fact that international visitors typically stay longer and spend more on their vacation trips than do Americans.

In February, 2003, in response to this problem, as part of the Omnibus Appropriations Act of 2003, Congress established a $50 million campaign at the Department of Commerce to increase the number of international visitors to the U.S. For nearly twelve months, the Department of Commerce planned and prepared to implement this campaign, with the help and advice of a 15- member industry advisory committee. In January, 2004, as part of the Omnibus Appropriations Act of 2004, before any implementation of the campaign, Congress rescinded $40 million of this funding.

In every southeastern state, international visitors comprise a substantial portion of their total tourism business. The decline in foreign visitors has been especially damaging to the economies of international gateway cities such as Atlanta, Miami and New Orleans. Both the travel and tourism industry and the Administration are exploring options for recovering from the rescission of 80% of the funding for the aborted international tourism marketing campaign.

Leaders in Congress have indicated they will try to restore all or most of rescinded $40 million. The outlook is further muddled by the immediate threat of losing a portion of the remaining $10 million due to budget cuts at the Department of Commerce. For more than six months, the industry has also been developing legislation to establish a permanent U.S. national tourism office, but no action is likely until the status of the international marketing campaign at the Commerce Department is resolved.

The Southeastern Tourism Society strongly supported the 2003 $50 million marketing campaign and opposed the rescission. The STS, while cooperating with other industry organizations to develop legislation that would establish an adequately funded, permanent national tourism office, is also striving to ensure that the interests of rural tourism in general and the Southeastern states in particular are included in any international tourism marketing program for the U.S.

Tourism Marketing and Business

Marketing is an essential part of running a business. New tourism businesses need to undertake at least some basic marketing initiatives to be successful. The best hotel, tour or attraction in the world will not succeed without a planned approach to marketing. The good news is that effective marketing does not need to cost a lot of money.

Tourism is a complex industry that involves a wide range of businesses working at different levels - from service stations and newsagents to hotels, motels, tour operators and travel agents. Tourism is about providing experiences which involves a number of steps:

— People need to be motivated to travel People need to know what their holiday options are and what different destinations offer

— Bookings need to be made for accommodation, travel, tours etc. and

— Service providers (eg. tour, transport and accommodation operators etc.) need to deliver their product.

Each party in the chain contributes to the overall holiday experience of the customer. They form part of a network of wholesalers, retailers, and providers of tourism products and services that together deliver a complete travel package. If one party fails to deliver, the total travel experience of the customer could be ruined and reflect badly on all the other service providers, even if they did nothing wrong. Tourism is a 'big picture' business - understanding where your organisation fits into the network will help you to manage it successfully.

Like many industries, tourism has its own language. Some of the more commonly used terms include:

Product - this includes the broad spectrum of tourism services provided by an operator ranging from day tours, package holidays, services and facilities at a hotel, motel or resort and so on.

Operators - businesses that provide tourism services such as tour and transport operators, hoteliers, restaurateurs, and attraction and souvenir shop proprietors etc.

Retail agents - retail travel agents and similar outlets (eg. RAC Travel Centres, Western Australian Visitor Centre, local visitor centres etc.) that sell holidays and travel products on a commission basis.

Wholesalers - businesses that package the different components of a holiday eg. accommodation, day tours, travel, and sell them to customers via retail agents on a commission basis.

Inbound tour operators - businesses that organise the ground components of tour packages for retail agents based in other parts of Australia or overseas.

Tourism operators will find it useful to be familiar with the following characteristics of the tourism industry: Western Australia's active international markets are the United Kingdom, Continental Europe (consisting of Germany, The Netherlands & Switzerland), Singapore, Malaysia, Hong Kong, Japan, China, New Zealand, South Africa and the United Arab Emirates & Gulf States.

Tour products appeal to different types of people or markets, each with varying tastes and budgets. These include people wanting to stay in up-market resorts that pamper to their every need, to backpackers who are more interested in discovering the flora and fauna of Australia than luxury accommodation. The expectations of these two different markets are very different and the success of any tourism business will depend on knowing who their markets are and developing products that meet the needs of those markets.

Seasonal fluctuations have a major impact on tourism, eg. weather conditions, school holidays or the presence of a particular animal or feature at certain times (eg. whale sharks at Exmouth, wildflowers). Periods of high demand are called 'peaks', periods of low demand are known as the 'off season', whilst the remainder are known as the 'shoulder' periods. Tourism businesses need to consider seasonal fluctuations and make their business decisions based on annual trends and not only the good times. A good operator will develop marketing tactics to attract customers during 'shoulder' and 'off season' periods such as special offers (eg. stay two nights, get one free etc.) to attract business.

Tourism is about creating and selling experiences. These are mostly 'intangible', or difficult to capture in words, making it difficult for operators to promote their product as customers can't generally sample or see the product before they buy. Brochures are widely used as one way to visually represent a tourism product to customers. Websites are also popular and can be a very effective method of promoting a tourism business to a global market. Whatever method is used, aim to help potential customers visualise and understand the experience that you are offering.

There is a number of government, government funded and industry bodies involved in tourism. In Australia, the Department of Industry, Tourism and Resources through its Tourism Division aims to develop, implement and deliver policies and programs which:

— encourage the development of tourism, sport and recreation in Australia
— identify opportunities in tourism, sport and recreation
— reduce barriers to industry development
— provide information to the tourism, sport and recreation industries to assist in decision making.

The focus of the Department is largely in the policy area, and it is not generally involved in marketing activities - this is the responsibility of the Australian Tourist Commission. The Tourism Division publishes some tourism research information and updates the industry with a monthly newsletter called Impact.

The Australian Tourist Commission (ATC) operates within the portfolio of the Commonwealth Department of Industry Science and Resources and has a primary role of promoting Australia internationally as the world's best tourism experience for the benefit of all Australians. The ATC promotes Australia to consumers, the travel industry and corporate sector in more than 40 countries around the world from a head office in Sydney and overseas offices located in Auckland, Bangkok, Frankfurt, Hong Kong, Kuala Lumpur, London, Los Angeles, Seoul, Shanghai, Singapore, Taipei and Tokyo.

Working with the tourism industry and State and Territory tourism organisations, the ATC's activities include television, print and online advertising; media, public relations and information programs; and co-ordinating Australian tourism industry participation in international trade events. The ATC plays a role in retail travel agent education programs overseas, as well as providing input to government and industry policies that affect inbound tourism.

'International ready' operators need to be listed on the ATC's Corporate Database, also known as the Marketing Information Database (MID) to receive corporate communications and information on the ATC's co-operative marketing activities. The database is used in all ATC offices, Aussie Helpline service (telephone enquiry service), international media relations and is the source for the travel directory on the ATC's website www.australia.com.

The ATC conducts strategic research into key international markets to determine the propensity and interest in travelling to Australia for leisure purposes. The reports, which can be purchased from the ATC, outline the key characteristics of the markets, target demographic groupings, origin areas, the drivers which encourage international travel and other factors involved in the decision making process of travellers.

The Australian Bureau of Statistics (ABS) collects and publish tourism information through a number of surveys. The Survey of Tourist Accommodation provides 'supply' data regarding the number and amount of certain types of accommodation throughout Australia, at a local level. Other surveys provide varying types of data. Details of data is available from the ABS' Directory of Tourism Statistics.

The Bureau of Tourism Research (BTR) is funded jointly by state and federal governments, and is an agency that collects, analyses and disseminates information about the Australian tourism industry to the general public, government and industry. The BTR produces a wide range of publications and research information and is responsible for two major surveys:

The National Visitor Survey (NVS) is a survey based on interviews with more than 80,000 Australian residents aged 15 years and over. This survey provides details of Australians travelling in Australia such as visitor characteristics including origin, as well as details of their trip including accommodation, purpose of travel, transport, expenditure, and activities. Trips by Australians overseas are also surveyed.

The International Visitor Survey (IVS) is the most comprehensive source of information available on the travel patterns of visitors to Australia. Interviews are conducted with 20,000 visitors per year departing from major Australian airports following their experiences in Australia. The IVS covers visitor profiles (eg. age, sex, reason for visit, place or origin), travel in Australia (including regions visited, accommodation, expenditure etc.). There may be a charge for information provided by the BTR.

The Western Australian Tourism Commission (WATC) is a State Government agency whose role is to:

The WATC is overseen by a Board of Commissioners and is divided into the following operational areas:

1. Marketing and Communication
2. Industry Development and Visitor Servicing
3. Eventscorp
4. Corporate and Business Services
5. Executive Services

The Marketing and Communication division promotes Western Australia as a tourism destination intrastate and in core interstate and international markets using Brand WA image and cooperative advertising campaigns. The Western Australian Tourism Commission (WATC) focus' its destination campaign strategies on building consumer awareness and desire to visit the State by leveraging the Australian Tourist Commission's (ATC) marketing campaign initiatives. This includes a strong focus on the ATC's Visiting Journalist Programme (VJP) which is supported by WATC media publicity campaigns.

Tactically, the WATC works with selected influential tour wholesalers, airlines and direct sell operators to drive visitation to the State. The WATC is driving the adoption of on-line campaign initiatives in all marketing campaigns.

A shift from a mass media approach to a one-to-one marketing premise is the most efficient and cost effective means of working in market.

The Long Haul Markets consist of: .

— *United Kingdom* - The State's largest international source market, the United Kingdom is a growth market for Western Australia and has remained resilient during recent difficult times. It has a high VFR/leisure mix, with the traditional mature visitor segment being underpinned by a growing young adventure travel market which includes backpackers.

— *Continental Europe* - Made up of Germany, The Netherlands and Switzerland, these three markets collectively represent a significant proportion of the 4 in 10 European inbound travellers to Australia seeking an adventure holiday. The strength of the "adventure traveller segment", our product and destination fit with this segment, the high dispersal rate of 77%, length of stay and yield presents real opportunities for the State to grow market share.

— *United Arab Emirates &Gulf States* - Made up primarily of high yield traffic from the Arab Families and Western Expatriates market segments. The Commission is working in market to dez market opportunities with influential trade partners. There are currently daily, non-stop, direct flights between Dubai and Perth with planned expansion of services in 2004.

— *South Africa* - Significant VFR traffic to Western Australia drives leisure tourism, however, the strongest opportunity for growth is based around leveraging major sporting and cultural events such as Rugby World Cup, Tri-Nations and the Perth International

Arts Festival. The WATC will focus primarily on a trade led strategy working with influential outbound operators.

— *Japan* - The third largest international source market with 81% of visitors travelling to Western Australia for a leisure holiday. Recent global events have highlighted the volatility of this market, with Japanese travellers reluctant to travel when events occur. Despite this, the potential for growth in this market is high.

SHORT HAUL MARKETS

Due to their geographical location, the short haul markets have the ability to respond quickly to market issues and trends. With this in mind, the Western Australian Tourism Commission (WATC) will concentrate all marketing efforts on Brand/Tactical consumer campaigns in conjunction with influential cooperative partners. The WATC will use on-line initiatives in all of their consumer advertising. Other than New Zealand, there will be a shift from a mass media approach to one-to-one marketing, working with wholesalers, airlines and product partners.

Short Haul Markets consist of:

Australia (Interstate) - Western Australia's second largest source market, making up 12%of all visitors, with the bulk of visitation emanating from Sydney and Melbourne. The WATC has three field offices on the east coast. Based in Melbourne, Sydney and Brisbane, these offices service the core markets of South Australia, Victoria, New South Wales, Queensland, Tasmania and the ACT.

These offices work closely with wholesalers and transport providers to maximise opportunities to promote the State through cooperative advertising, joint promotions and involvement marketing campaigns. The WATC is interested in participating in cooperative marketing opportunities with these industry partners to raise awareness of Western Australia as a holiday destination. Destination training seminars, familiarisations and workshops are conducted for travel agents and airline staff to increase their knowledge about the State's nature-based assets. Support is also provided to WA operators to promote their products to key agents in Eastern States markets.

New Zealand - Represented by a strong leisure /VFR travel market with Australia having 56%of the total outbound travel market. Recent research by the Australian Tourist Commission identified high desire and propensity for experiences offered by Western Australian product.

Singapore -Western Australia's second largest international source market however a market facing significant challenges. 80%of all travellers are repeat visitors and there is a decline in first-time visitors. The segment which shows potential for Western Australia is the growing 50+segment.

Malaysia - Western Australia has had marginal growth over the last 10 years and the broader market is not responsive to market spend. The market is not homogenous which presents challenges to our marketing efforts. As such, the WATC will focus on identified niche segments, including the education market, to drive new business to the State.

Hong Kong - Consumer confidence is returning following the dramatic effects of SARS on the economy, however, high unemployment will affect outbound travel.

Hong Kong is a major outbound gateway for Chinese holiday makers. The Commission will work closely with the Australian Tourist Commission through its Visiting Journalist Program to build awareness of WA and will participate in cooperative campaigns to drive incremental business.

China - Potentially a significant source market for Western Australia, with strong growth forecast to Australia over the next five to ten years. The Western Australian Tourism Commission is committed to having a market presence in mainland China by the end of 2004 to capitalize on this significant market opportunity. The primary focus will be on trade led strategies.

Media and Communication

The Destination Communication and Familiarisation unit promotes Western Australia as a world class holiday destination by providing public relations support to media and trade. This process includes writing travel features, providing images, and supplying destination and tourism product information to a range of stakeholders.

The unit also manages the international and domestic media and trade awareness program (familiarisations). This program brings members of the media and trade to Western Australia to sample destinations and showcase tourism product. This generates favourable publicity for WA as a tourism destination; enhances the product knowledge and motivation of the retail trade in selling WA tourism product; demonstrates to wholesalers and inbound operators that WA has a broad range of saleable product; and creates positive attitudes towards WA as a tourism destination.

The Media Centre is on the WATC corporate website www.westernaustralia.com and offers information about the marketing and corporate activities of the WATC, as well as new product and destination material. A team of media and public relations professionals provide regular updates on the latest marketing projects, breaking news and tourism issues. A comprehensive database of new product, travel articles and destination photographs is also available. The unit also produce In Touch - an industry newsletter which is released every week. You can register to receive this newsletter online.

The Industry Development unit works in partnership with the tourism industry to encourage, promote and facilitate the development of new tourism ventures throughout WA and to improve existing tourist services and facilities to meet visitor needs. WATC staff liaise closely with tourism operators, developers, state and local government agencies as well as regional tourist organisations to assist with innovative ventures that reflect market demands and enhance the State's tourism assets.

The four broad objectives of Industry Development include:

— Providing strategic marketing information, consultancy and interpretation of market intelligence to the tourism industry.

— Providing planning and strategy advice on identified tourism issues and identifying new infrastructure requirements for the tourism industry.

— Encouraging the development of new tourism product, infrastructure and facilities which meet market demands.

— Identifying and working to remove impediments to tourism development.

Industry Development assists by:

— Accessing market intelligence for proposed tourism projects for prospective investors and developers.

— Negotiating with the Department of Land Information on matters concerning land releases and changes in pastoral leases to provide for tourism development.

— Making representations to Main Roads WA and local governments on road signage matters.

— Providing input to Federal, State and local governments on matters relating to tourism developments, town planning schemes and rezoning appeals.

— Providing expertise in securing additional funds for tourism projects through grants.

— Providing consultative advice to various regional bodies concerned with tourism.

Industry Development maintains a comprehensive tourism development database called the Tourism Development Register which tracks new tourism developments from the planning stage through to completion. The Register is updated in June and December of each year and published on the WATC's website the following month.

The tourism regions of Western Australia each have a Regional Manager who focuses on improving existing tourism products, nurturing new tourism products and assisting in their region by fostering industry professionalism, education and quality assurance mechanisms to ensure an enhanced tourism industry.

Industry Development produces a series of five Destination Development Strategies, one for each of the five tourism regions. These strategies assist the tourism industry to focus attention on developing tourism infrastructure and product where market analysis has identified unmet demand. Industry Development works in partnership with the Tourism Council Western Australia ensure that all visitors have access to high quality tourism product and services through operator participation in the National Tourism Accreditation Program.

Brand WA is a cooperative marketing strategy that has developed a strong identity, or brand, for Western Australia by creating a complementary range of images (icons) that represent regions, localities, individual businesses, and more, to form a strong and consistent brand image for the State.

Becoming a Licensed User of Brand WA entitles businesses and organisations to use the Brand WA trademarks and icons in promotional and advertising material. If you are a premium member of the WA Tourism Network then you automatically become a licensed user of Brand WA. The WA Tourism Network is an industry initiative that provides a practical framework for creating and sustaining tourism business within Western Australia. It clearly defines the roles of key stakeholders which include the Australian Tourism Commission, Regional Tourism Associations and Visitor Centres to deliver a high level of visitor servicing.

This includes a range of functions which include electronic promotion and booking of destinations and tourism product at local, regional, state, national and international level, a coordinated brochure racking strategy, publishing of statistical and research information, use of Brand WA logo, the virtual call centre and a recognisable network of professional visitor centres around Western Australia. The formation of a fully integrated Network of

Visitor Centres across Western Australia is undertaken within a broader WA Tourism Network initiative to standardise the delivery of visitor servicing. The WA Tourism Network reduces the need for tourism businesses to join as many different tourism bodies (eg. Local visitor centre, Regional Tourism Organisations (RTO's) etc).

As the retail arm of the Western Australian Tourism Commission, the Western Australia Visitor Centre operates as a travel agency specialising in the promotion and sale of Western Australian tourism product to markets across Australia and overseas. The Western Australian Visitor Centre also plays a vital role in providing a significant proportion of Western Australia's tourism operators with marketing assistance and advice, as well as being a point of distribution for their products. The Centre operates five and a half days per week. The Western Australian Visitor Centre also operates a nation wide call centre five days per week.

Sustainable Product Development

This unit is responsible for nature based and niche tourism product development including indigenous, culture/arts, wine/culinary, education, cruise shipping and backpacker based tourism. Nature based tourism has been recognised as one of the most rapidly growing tourism markets in the world today. The distinctive Western Australian environment is a major drawcard for both domestic and international visitors. The diversity of attractions, that include climate, plants and animals, scenery, wide open spaces and unspoiled landscapes, are found in higher proportions in Western Australia than elsewhere in Australia, and arguably most other places in the world.

The Sustainable Product Development unit produces a range of projects including the development of indigenous tourism businesses, research into sustainable low impact accommodation in remote areas and a range of environmental tourism packages throughout the State. These environmental packages allow visitors to participate in activities that have a positive impact on the natural environment. This involvement can be 'active' for example by having a hands-on role in activities such as collecting seeds, spotting and recording wildlife and revegetation work, or 'emotive' whereby visitors make an emotional connection related to the environment such as 'adopting' an animal as part of an animal reintroduction program.

Eventscorp

Eventscorp is a unit of the WATC that attracts major events to Western Australia and manages selected events that provide significant economic benefit to the State. It also uses events to broadcast images of Western Australian throughout the world. Eventscorp also operates a regional events unit based in Bunbury. This unit provides event development assistance across all of regional Western Australia.

Corporate and Business Services

This division coordinates significant WATC procurement, contract advice, risk management advice and asset management. It also manages the accounting and financial services and the human resources of the WATC.

Executive Services

The Executive Services unit manages the development and

provision of advice and support to the CEO. Chairman and Executive Management Team, as well as management of the executive planning and (non-financial) accountability processes, communication and liaison with the Minister's Office, Cabinet and Parliament and management of cross-agency responses to issues and initiatives as required.

Industry Organisations

Regional Tourism Organisations (RTOs)

A network of Regional Tourism Organisations (RTOs) operates in Western Australia, each with the aim of promoting tourism in their region. Each RTO is managed by an elected Board and employs a Chief Executive Officer or Senior Marketing Manager who develops and implements marketing strategies for the region.

Tourism operators are encouraged to become members of their local RTO in order to access cost-efffective consumer and travel trade marketing opportunities. The RTOs participate in consumer and trade events, work with the WATC in developing media and trade familiarisation programs, produce and distribute annual regional holiday publications and undertake co-operative advertising and promotional activities. The RTOs also provide a forum for tourism operators to network with other industry stakeholders.

Australian Tourism Export Council (ATEC)

Formerly known as the Inbound Tour Operators Association, the Australian Tourism Export Council (ATEC) represents the interests of inbound tour operators and acts as a lobby group to governments, industry and the wider business community. Its membership comprises inbound tour operators and suppliers of tourism products. ATEC organises an annual workshop in conjunction with the WATC which attracts eastern states 'sellers', and also organises national and regional workshops to link inbound tour operators with suppliers of tour products with the aim of developing new tourism products.

Tourism Council Western Australia (TCWA)

The Tourism Council Western Australia (TCWA) is the peak tourism body in Western Australia. It lobbies the government on issues identified by tourism operators, encourages the adoption of State policies that facilitate travel and create business opportunities and promotes a wider understanding of travel and tourism as a major industry that contributes substantially to the economic and social well being of Western Australia.

The TCWA aims to unify the tourism industry and is an advocate for greater tourism training and recognition of excellence. It operates the National Tourism Accreditation Program in Western Australia and organises the Western Australian Tourism Awards and the State Tourism Conference.

Perth Convention Bureau

The Perth Convention Bureau - a not for profit member-based company formed in 1972 is the peak industry organisation responsible for marketing Western Australia as a convention, exhibition and incentive travel destination (incentive travel is a performance based reward offered by companies to their staff or clients, usually to encourage increased productivity and product sales).

Membership is based on a six-tiered benefits driven system and is open to any business that obtains commercial benefit either directly or indirectly from the business tourism sector. A key marketing tool is a confidential calendar which provides members with a list of confirmed conventions, exhibitions and events booked for Perth and other regional locations.

Other benefits include the distribution of sales leads, the opportunity to network with fellow members and access to e-marketing via the Bureau's website. The Bureau publicises and promotes the facilities, services and products of its members to national and international association and corporate meeting planners and incentive travel buyers.

The meetings sector alone is estimated to be worth more than $630 million annually to the Western Australian economy. In 2002-2003, the Bureau was responsible for securing convention and incentive travel business worth nearly $72 million in direct delegate expenditure.

Future Trends

Research shows that businesses that have a business plan have a greater chance of staying in business than those without a plan. Developing a marketing plan goes hand in hand with developing a business plan, but it is possible to develop a marketing plan as a stand alone document. A complete business plan will also address the financial (budgets, cash flow) and operational (business premises, staff, equipment, etc) functions of a business. Assistance in developing business plans is available from the Small Business Development Corporation Business Enterprise Centres and business advisers and accountants.

Many people often think that marketing is selling. Although selling is one function of marketing, there are many other aspects that need to be considered.

One definition of marketing is:

> 'Marketing means selling your products and services at the right price, with the right promotion, to the right people, at the right location.... at a profit'.

A breakdown of the major components of marketing is as follows:

— Knowing who your customers are and what they want

— Developing products that meets their needs at a price that they are prepared to pay, and

— Promoting the product by a variety of means so that a purchase can occur.

In general, marketing activities fall into two general categories:

— Researching your market - discovering who your potential customers or markets are, and determining what they want, and

— Reaching your market - developing a program of activities that puts your product in the market place and making sure that customers know about it.

These are the steps that need to be undertaken to develop a marketing plan:

1. *Business background*: What is your business about? What is your business mission, your goals competitive advantage?
2. *Situations Analyses*: What are the internal and external factors that will impact on your business industry

trends, competitors, the economy, your financial resources, etc.

3. *Target Markets*: Who do you want to sell your product to and what are their needs?
4. *Marketing Mix*: Putting it all together - the 'Ps' of marketing
5. *Action Plan*: A summary of marketing initiatives that identifies who will be responsible for each initiative, how much they will cost and timeframes.
6. *Evaluation*: Evaluating the impact of marketing activities and modifying as required.

The Marketing Plan

The Business Mission is a simple statement that describes what a business does or will do. This will also help to describe your business concept to others. The Business Mission can change as circumstances change - be prepared to review and modify if necessary.

Business Goals is important to identify achievable objectives or goals for a business. These help to provide direction for decision making, measure the success of a business and provide a focus for staff. Objectives are more helpful when they are quantified ie. include figures or other measures. Some examples of business objectives could be to:

— increase the net return from the business from 10 per cent to 15 per cent; or

— increase the average number of passengers on each tour from 12 to 15; or

— increase room occupancy from 50 per cent to 60 per cent; or to

— increase business by 20 per cent during shoulder periods.

Goals will be more valuable if they relate to a specific time-frame eg. 'to increase the average annual occupancy rate from 45 to 55 per cent within two years'. You may wish to add personal objectives for your business. These could relate to your financial security, how much time you wish to spend with your family, paying off your house mortgage etc.

A competitive advantage is the 'point of difference' that sets a business apart from its competitors. Every business needs a competitive advantage. It gives you an edge over your competitors and provides a focus for marketing activities. One way of determining your point of difference is to examine your competitors in areas such as quality of products and services, location, price, etc. If you are unable to determine a competitive advantage by looking at your competitors, you may need to develop a feature that will give your business its marketing edge. Examples of competitive advantages include:

— offering a unique product

— developing a product for a niche market

— offering superior facilities and/or services

— offering a more efficient service than your competitors

— offering a price advantage

Businesses don't operate in isolation. There are factors both within the control and beyond the control of businesses that can affect its success. These include the state of the economy, the general state of the tourism industry, the value of the Australian dollar, international events, what competitors are doing, etc. A full analysis of your business needs to consider the internal and external factors in terms of strengths, weaknesses, opportunities and threats.

External factors are factors beyond your control that could affect the business eg. the economy, technology, trends affecting the tourism industry, legal and political issues, competition, the environment etc. These factors can have a major impact. For example, when the economy is in recession, or when interest rates and unemployment levels are high, people have less money and less demand for goods and services such as tours, accommodation etc.

External factors are generally beyond the control of a business. But by being aware of these factors it's possible to make decisions that minimise possible negative impacts and maximise opportunities that may arise. For example, the current interest and publicity surrounding nature based tourism presents an opportunity for tour operators that can develop products to suit this market.

Internal factors are those over which you have some control, eg. equipment, financial resources, staff, etc. Depending on the nature of your business, there will be a number of areas that need to be considered, for example, your physical resources - buildings and equipment. Are they being fully utilised? Can they cope with expansion?

Then there are the financial resources of the business. Is your cash flow sufficient? Do you have access to additional funds to finance any growth activities? Is a lack of finance impeding your growth?

Finally, you need to look at the experience and expertise of your staff. Are they motivated? Are they being used to the best of their ability? Is there any training available that could improve the efficiency and service offered by your business? The answers to these questions will assist you to understand what your business is able to achieve.

S.W.O.T

A common way of summarising strengths, weaknesses, opportunities and threats is in a table format.

Use the table to:

— Build on your business strengths whenever possible. They should be exploited and reinforced to give your business an edge over competitors.

— Only correct weaknesses that are holding the business back - don't address minor areas which have little impact on the business.

— Maximise your business success by taking advantage of opportunities.

Competitor Analysis

It is unlikely that you will operate a business that does not have competition. It is important that you identify who your competitors are, what their strengths and weaknesses are, how much of the business or market share they have and how much of the market share you have or want to have.

We have already referred to the need to consider your competitors to determine your competitive advantage. You can also use a competitor analysis to maintain your advantage and seize opportunities that may arise from the actions of your competitors.

Market Identification

Successful marketing is based on understanding who you wish to sell or market your product to. You can help to determine your market and understand more about their characteristics by undertaking market research. There are various ways of identifying different customer groups, or target markets. These include:

— Demographics - age, gender, income, family size, and structure, education, occupation etc.

— Origin - where they live

— Socio-economic class - professional, non-professional

— Lifestyle - 'pleasure seeker', 'achiever', etc

Put another way, you need to ask yourself questions about who your likely customers will be:

— What age groups best describes your market?

— Is your product aimed at males, females, or both?

— Will it suit singles, couples, or families?

— Is your product aimed at a specific group of people and if so what group? eg. bird-watchers, tennis players, etc.

By identifying your target market/s you will be able to develop a customer profile - which will tell you how your target market thinks and behaves - what newspapers/ magazines they are likely to read, when are they likely to travel, etc. This information will be useful in developing promotional strategies to reach potential customers.

Marketing Mix

The marketing mix is the way that you put together the factors under your control to satisfy the needs of your customers. These are often known as the 'P's' of marketing - Product, Packaging, Placing Yourself in the Marketplace - (or Distribution), Promotion and Price.

There are many factors that affect the way that you develop your product or service. You first need to identify exactly what your product is - what it includes and where the value is in what you are offering. Whilst this may appear obvious, there are many failed businesses that did not fully understand what their product was. As part of identifying your product, you need to consider where it fits in the market place ie. its position in relation to other operators. For instance, some accommodation operators position their property at the top end of the market, while others will develop their product to meet the needs of budget travellers.

You also need to develop an image that is appropriate for your product and its position in the market. Your image will be communicated through your business name, brochures, letterhead, business cards, signage, and advertising. It will also be represented by the appearance of your premises and staff. Associated with image is branding, which makes your product or service distinctive by the use of slogans, logos, distinctive colours and graphics. Well chosen brand names and logos can add value to a product or service and can be used with great effect to gain customer loyalty.

Each product or service that enters the marketplace has a distinct life cycle. This is not difficult to understand when you consider how often fashion tastes change and how cuisines that are in vogue one year, are unheard of the next. The same occurs with holiday destinations and tourism products. There are four stages to the product life cycle:

1. *Introduction* - The product is introduced into the market. Sales are slow as the product becomes known. Nil or very low profit is experienced due to the expense of developing and introducing the product.

2. *Growth* - A period when the product is accepted by the market place which results in growing sales and profit.

3. *Maturity* - Sales slow as the product achieves acceptance by the majority of potential buyers. Profits stabilise or decline. Increased marketing is required to attract sales.
4. *Decline* - Sales show a strong decline and profits drop.

By considering the above cycle you can plan changes to existing products or introduce new products as they reach the maturity stage to maintain business growth.

Packaging is the way that associated products and services are put together to package deal. A motel operator may develop a package that includes transport, to a local concert and evening meal as part of a total package. The operator benefits ensuring that guests dine in-house, while customers don't have to spend time considering their options.

Packaging offers great opportunities to target specific markets and explore new particularly during shoulder and off season periods when business is slow eg. 'book nights, get two free, plus a fruit basket and chocolates on arrival!'.

Operators in regional areas can work together to develop attractive deals that will encourage visits to their region. Not only does each individual operator benefit arrangements, but the region in general benefits by greater visitor numbers and increased expenditure.

Once you have a clear understanding of what your product is, you need to make accessible to the public. It is likely that you will be targeting your product to markets in other parts of Western Australia, interstate or overseas. To reach these markets you may use the services agents, or intermediaries to act on your behalf and take bookings.

Intermediaries include travel agents, travel wholesalers and inbound tour operators. Using intermediaries is the most common way of broadening the distribution base your product and are usually necessary if a business is to expand.

Travel agents are generally paid 10 per cent of the retail price as a booking fee, although this rate does vary and can be as high as 20 per cent. It is most important that agents and operators charge the same price. Travel agents will not make bookings for operators who sell their products at a lower price to customers direct. Operators need to be able to guarantee the rates that they provide to retail agents.

It is the responsibility of tourism operators to ensure that travel agents are familiar with their products. Retail agents are able to book many destinations and products making it difficult for them to be up to date with every tour product. Operators can use some of the following ways to keep travel agents informed:

— Make sales calls

— Provide special rates to people working in retail agencies to encourage staff to experience their product

— Offer agents a familiarisation of your tour/service

— Send regular newsletters or other direct forms of communications (email, fax)

— Ensure that agents have current brochures and rates

— Participate in wholesale programs

Above all, tourism operators must be able to respond to travel agent enquiries and bookings promptly.

Not all retail travel agents book individual tourism operators. Many agents specialise in international holidays or only book fully inclusive packaged Australian holidays, which offer high commission payments. Other agents, particularly those in large networks, have a 'preferred' range of products that they sell and operators may need to offer heavily discounted rates to be included in this list.

The Western Australian Visitor Centre (WAVC) is the WATC's retail centre and information centre. It is located in Forrest Place, Perth. It provides advice and information, in addition to taking bookings on behalf of Western Australian tour operators and accommodation outlets. The WAVC has staff that deal directly with the public. Staff respond to over 380,000 requests for information each year, and during peak periods, can assist up to 1 500 visitors in a day. The WAVC is a good avenue to promote the tourism business of Western Australian Tourism Network (WATN) members.

Royal Automobile Club of WA (RAC) has 11 travel branches in Western Australia that operate as retail travel agents. The Perth branch, located in Adelaide Terrace, helps a high volume of tourists plan their holidays in Western Australia and is an important outlet for local operators. The RAC distributes a comprehensive touring and accommodation guide. The guide is available for a small cost to 500,000 RAC members and is also sold to non-members. The RAC also maintains a database for accommodation properties in the State.

Wholesalers package tour programs including travel, accommodation, and tours that are sold to the public via retail travel agents. Wholesalers do not sell directly to customers. Wholesalers link individual tourism operators with retailers. They consider what type of tour program would appeal to a particular market and package the program accordingly. Wholesale packages are usually priced lower than if the consumer was to book each component direct. Wholesalers are able to achieve this price advantage because of the volume of business and exposure they generate. Major wholesalers of Western Australian tourism product are Great Aussie Holidays, Qantas Holidays and Discover West Holidays.

Benefits to Operators of being included in a Wholesale Program:

— A brochure is produced and distributed to travel agents in Australia, and often overseas.

— An industry launch is usually held to promote the program.

— The wholesaler's representatives will conduct sales calls on retail travel agents to promote the program and operators in it.

— Wholesalers have computerised reservation systems to record bookings. Many of these are global systems allowing travel agents worldwide to book products in the program.

— Familiarisation visits for the retail industry are conducted to give front-line sales staff an opportunity to experience the product first hand.

— Familiarisation visits by the media are conducted to generate publicity for the program.

— Wholesalers generally undertake advertising campaigns aimed at both consumers and retail travel agents.

Customers benefit by the ease of booking through a retail agent and the knowledge that the tourism products are of good quality - wholesalers will rarely include a product in their brochures that don't have a proven track record.

Every wholesaler will have a different cost structure for operators to participate in their programs. In most cases, wholesalers aim to produce a brochure that is funded by participating operators, ie. operators pay for space in the brochure. While this rate will vary, it is generally reasonable in comparison to the cost that operators would have to pay to produce and distribute their own brochure. Wholesalers usually charge a 25 per cent commission, but this can be as high as 30 per cent. This covers the travel agent commission, which is generally 10 per cent, plus a margin of 15 to 20 per cent to the wholesaler.

Wholesalers will request a net rate from tourism operators which needs to be at least 20 per cent less than the operator's own rack rate - or the advertised selling rate. This rate needs to be honoured for the life of the brochure, usually a one year period from 1 April to 31 March the following year. Wholesalers are an important intermediary and have the potential to provide 'top up' business. There are two ways of reaching potential clients:

— Directly - advertising, brochure distribution, website
— Indirectly - using retail travel agents, wholesalers and inbound tour operators

There is a cost attached to both methods that needs to be considered in your financial feasibility assessment and the cost of tourism products. Tourism operators do find difficulty in justifying the commission required by some agents, yet the costs in accessing these markets are generally way beyond the reach of small operators and the cost of paying commission is often balanced out by the number of bookings received direct by the business, which don't incur a commission. It is important that you keep a record of all sales and identify the source of all bookings - direct, travel agent, wholesaler etc. as this breakdown could influence the future selling price of your product.

Inbound tour operators act on behalf of national and international tour wholesalers to organise the 'land/ground' content of a tour program in Western Australia. For example, a wholesaler in Germany wishing to package a tour program to Western Australia would use the services of a Perth based inbound tour operator to book accommodation, tours, and transfers as opposed to making the bookings from Germany. Inbound tour operators act as intermediaries between wholesalers and tourism operators. They are usually able to negotiate better rates due to the volume and regular use of the tourism products they book.

Inbound tour operators put together different tourism products to create packages to suit the needs of different inbound markets. These include:

— The individual traveller, known as the 'fully independent traveller' or FIT. This market buys from a wholesaler's brochure or buys a specially tailored itinerary.

— The group traveller, known as the 'group inclusive tour' or GIT. They can also buy from a wholesaler's brochure or have a specially tailored itinerary created to suit their needs.

— Incentive traveller. Many businesses reward performance by providing travel rewards to employees as incentives. These travel arrangements usually require a tailor made product that is at the top-end of the market.

— Convention traveller. Conventions involve the movement of large numbers of people and inbound operators can develop pre- and post-convention tours.

Inbound tour operators conduct a number of activities to attract the interest of overseas wholesalers and retail agents and to make them aware of the services and products in Western Australia.

The benefits of working with an inbound tour operator include:

— They create individually tailored packages eg. farm-stay, self-drive, nature-based tourism, special events, etc

— They attend trade workshops, missions and shows

— They provide international exposure for your product

Operators of tourist attractions or accommodation establishments may also wish to consider attracting business from coach tour operators. Attracting the interest of a coach operator may take time. Each year coach companies receive hundreds of requests from tourist attractions and other businesses to be included in their itineraries.

Send coach operators an introductory letter, brochure and invitation to visit your business or perhaps offer to host a lunch or overnight stay, if relevant. After these initial approaches, maintain regular contact.

The issue of setting rates is a complex one, and needs to be part of a detailed and objective financial feasibility for your business. It is not the purpose of this Guide to discuss the process involved in setting rates that will result in a profit for your business. In the context of marketing, however, varying the cost of your product can be used as a sales promotion tool. You can consider various sales tools such as discounting, cash back vouchers and give-aways. Often, reducing the price is seen as the only way to beat the competition, but beware - reducing your price could reduce your profit.

You need to consider how discounting will affect the willingness of consumers to purchase your product and how great the effect will be. In developing a price strategy you need to look at what your competitors are charging. Before entering into a price war you need to consider whether this will affect the perception of your product by consumers. It is possible that products offered at lower prices will be perceived as having less value. An option to price discounting is to 'value add'. This can be achieved by offering extra services which will be perceived by the consumer as a bonus, but which do not add a major cost to you.

So far, we have been considering the 'behind the scenes' elements of the marketing process. The next stage in the marketing process is to promote your product to potential customers and generate sales. There are many useful promotional tools available. Unfortunately, many operators are tempted to try too many of these at the one time.

Advertising includes mass media such as newspapers, magazines, radio, television and billboards. It can reach many people at once and the same message can be repeated many times. There are advantages and disadvantages to advertising. It can be very expressive and emotional in its appeal and can reach a large audience. On the other hand, it is expensive and impersonal - it is one way communication. There are many opportunities for cooperative advertising where several businesses or organisations work together to produce and pay for a joint advertisement. These are often coordinated by RTOs, the WATC and the ATC.

It is sometimes possible to arrange editorial in publications in which you advertise. This is when the newspaper, magazine or other mediums produces a feature article about your business (often on the basis of information you provide) that supports your ad. This is often call 'advertorial' and can be effective as it appears to be more objective and have more credibility than advertising.

One form of advertising that can be cost-effective for tourism operators is newspaper advertising. There are two main types of newspaper ads:

— Display ads - these can appear in the travel pages or in the general news section of a newspaper.
— Lineage ads - 'line ads' are so-called because you are charged on a per line basis. Line ads may be. placed in the classified section or a special classified section in the travel pages.

Display ads are much more expensive than line ads, however, this means of advertising is often an important source of business for small operators.

Direct marketing

Direct marketing means contacting - by mail, telephone, fax or email - potential customers. It also includes coupon advertising where potential customers send in a coupon asking for more information. Direct marketing usually involves sending messages (brochures, letters) to a database, which is simply a list of potential customers that have been collected because of common characteristic eg. occupation, income level, postcode or by business type or interest such as travel agents, inbound tour operators, bowling clubs, ornithological associations etc.

Databases are available in different formats including mailing labels, computer disks, and lists. They are available from a variety of sources including firms that specialise in compiling databases. An advantage of direct marketing is that it is more personal, however, it does not have the same penetration as general advertising. The success of any direct marketing activity will be determined by the quality of the database and the quality and impact of the message or offer.

Trade shows provide the opportunity for tourism operators/RTOs to promote their business/region to the travel industry. Trade shows are organised by the WATC, RTOs, ATEC, TCWA and the ATC amongst others. Exhibitors, called 'sellers', usually book a space or booth. Appointments are made with 'buyers', who, depending on the type of trade show, could be retail travel agents, inbound tour operators and/or tour wholesalers. Appointments are usually 10 to 20 minutes long, during which sellers give a presentation on their product.

Trade shows are a cost-effective means of servicing a large number of agents in a short period of time. It is possible to share a booth at some shows with another operator, preferably one that is not in direct competition to your business, to reduce costs. The success of your participation will depend on having effective, good quality promotional materials and a package and/or product that buyers can sell.

It may take up to two years to gain results from participating in a trade show as wholesalers usually prepare their packages two years in advance. To maximise the value of participating in trade shows, it is important to follow up with buyers after the show either by letter or email. Your hard work and investment can be wasted if you do not maintain contact with, and the interest of, buyers. Trade show organisers generally set selection criteria for each show to ensure that a high standard of tourism product is presented. Most shows are organised well in advance and participants are generally required to book at least six months in advance.

Consumer Promotions

Consumer promotions or shows provide tourism operators with the opportunity to promote direct to consumers - ie. the general public. Consumer promotions can vary greatly and target different market segments. They can include caravan and camping shows and holiday and travel shows. Space is allocated to tourism operators and RTOs to promote their products. Booth costs are determined by size and/or location. Many shows are held on the weekend, however, some shows run up to seven days.

Consumer shows provide operators with the opportunity to talk personally with potential customers, conduct market research by talking to the public and to network with other operators. You will generally have the opportunity of selecting a site from a floor plan of the exhibition area. Good site selection will help to ensure the success of your participation. Good sites include corner locations on main aisles; main aisles as opposed to secondary aisles; sites leading to/from restaurants, toilets and entrances; and in the instance of multi-hall venues, sites in the main hall. These locations will generally attract greater traffic flows than other areas.

When participating in consumer promotions you are competing with many other tourism operators and destinations. To maximise your involvement, make sure that your stand is attractive and eye-catching and that you have plenty of brochures available for distribution. Consider having a competition relating to your product or other 'catches' such as giveaways to attract attention. Tour operators can draw attention to their business by being 'newsworthy' and gaining free publicity in newspapers and magazines.

Large businesses may employ a public relations (PR) professional to generate news stories and media releases which are distributed to the media. While smaller operators may not be able to employ the services of a PR professional, you can derive great benefits by maintaining a close liaison with your local media and travel writers of State newspapers. Keep them informed of new developments that might be of interest and have a go at writing your own media release.

Tourism operators that participate in famils need to observe some general guidelines that will maximise the benefits from their involvement and contribute to the success of the visit. Where there are a similar range of products, preference is generally given to Tourism Network members and accredited operators. There are opportunities to promote your tourism product using television and radio. These include interviews, donating prizes for competitions, or using community service announcements to promote an achievement or activity of your business. Holiday and lifestyle programs also offer excellent promotional opportunities.

An important way of selling your product is by personal sales calls, generally to retail travel agents, but also to inbound and coach operators and tour wholesalers, depending on what is appropriate for your business. Sales staff may also represent your business at trade and consumer shows, and participate in promotion activities of the Western Australian Tourism Commission. Many small operators are not able to employ sales staff or sufficient sales staff to service all markets eg. the eastern states and overseas and may engage the services of a sales representation company to cover specific markets.

Marketing is an ongoing process. Plans need to be monitored and reviewed regularly. Evaluating your marketing plan will also help you to prepare more realistic and achievable plan in the future. Ways of measuring the performance of your marketing plan include changes to sales figures, market share, and profit. This will require keeping accurate figures to monitor where business is being generated and if it can be directly attributed to marketing initiatives.

2

Potential Marketing

Markets have the potential to enhance lives in a sustainable framework through providing wealth creation, choice, innovation and competition. The travel and tourism industry contains these four elements that enable it to be a dynamic market force for sustainability in the future. It has the capacity to increase exports, bring in capital investment, boost an economies GDP and create employment. Travel and tourism generates jobs throughout the economy, both in companies directly involved in the business and in related supplier industries such as retail, construction, manufacturing and telecommunications.

World Travel and Tourism (WTTC) estimated that travel and tourism generated 203 million jobs - over 8% of all jobs worldwide—in 2000, rising to over 207 million in 2001. Within a decade, this is estimated to increase to over 260 million jobs or 9% of all employment. These jobs employ a significant proportion of women, minorities and young people and are predominantly in small and medium-sized enterprises (SMEs). SMEs make up the majority of the travel and tourism sector, although the exact percentage is unknown. SMEs encourage entrepreneurs, provide many diverse job opportunities and enable low skills entry for emerging countries.

Successful human resource management, in the shape of training and education, is crucial to achieve the economic prosperity, for both SMEs and the larger multinational companies that can be accrued through tourism. Highly competitive destinations are realising that quality of services and facilities are vital to ensure a consistency of tourists to the destination. On the other hand the fragmentation of the industry and the high proportion of SMEs has led to unconstructive training and protection for employees. Given the number of low-skilled workers in the sector, the industry has been criticised for offering nothing more than 'hamburger flipping' jobs that contribute little to the sustainability of an economy or society. The travel and tourism industry is renowned for its high turnover, anti-social working hours, low pay, seasonal employment, instability and low job status. However, this does not tell the whole story.

Travel and tourism is reliant on a human service, yet is increasingly using technology to facilitate the sector in competitive pricing. The growth in tourism forecast for the next ten years, will lead to a greater dependency on information technology, which will become more important in the future as the industry copes with rapid expansion and sophistication of the tourism and hospitality supply. While tour operators have a limited number of staff in some of their receiving countries, a huge network of activities and jobs across the economy depends upon delivering the demand for tourism.

The tour operator industries reach many areas of the economy such as hotel and infrastructure development, transport services, agriculture, information technology, restaurants and entertainment and media, education and training, consumption of pharmaceutical products, clothing, equipment, and medical services. The hospitality industry contributes to the important process of job creation. As a labour-intensive industry, it employs large numbers of wage earners, whose taxes and disposable income add to gross domestic output and help to create further employment opportunities.

Given that each hotel room typically requires one member of staff, every hotel room built has the potential to create an additional job. The industry provides the opportunity to travel, free medical care and upward mobility, particularly for women from developing nations. Some of the major obstacles to this growth are the lack of infrastructure, environmental degradation and fragile linkages that weaken a country's tourism potential. One way to address these barriers is for the sector to foster tourism investment through public-private sector partnerships that not only enable a country to grow economically, but retain the essential social, cultural and environmental assets that make each country a unique product.

Public-private sector co-operation and planning are also essential to creating sustainable employment in the tourism industry, and to this end the private sector has fought for recognition of its true contribution to job growth and economic development. Hitherto, the industry had been disadvantaged by a lack of data reflecting its full economic impact. Only recently has the methodology known as Tourism Satellite Accounting (TSA), pioneered by WTTC, WTO/OMT and others, been developed and accepted by governments as a means for fully measuring travel and tourism's contribution as an economic activity.

TSA is based on a 'demand-side' concept of economic activity (i. e. the economic activities of visitors and travel companies), as tourism does not supply a homogenous product or service. Unlike traditional industries (agriculture, electronics, steel, etc.), travel and tourism is a diverse set of industries offering a multitude of products (consumer and capital durables and non-durables), and services ranging from airline and cruise ship fares and accommodations, to restaurant meals, entertainment, souvenirs and gifts, immigration and park services, recreational vehicles and automobiles, aircraft manufacturing and resort development. By using input/output modelling, TSA is able to differentiate between travel and tourism industry supply and economy supply, including that portion of supply which it imports from abroad.

Additionally, it breaks down the supply side accounts into direct and indirect impacts and the individual elements of GDP (wages and salaries, transaction taxes, operating surplus, depreciation and subsidies) . These data ensure governments have a broader understanding of the impact of travel and tourism, in particular the implications of policy for the travel and tourism economy. TSA data a reiterates the fact that travel and tourism has the potential to be a catalyst industry for emerging countries to kick-start their economies, offering many opportunities that are not available in other industries. For example, the rise in cultural, heritage and wildlife niche market tourism, in developing countries, is becoming a viable alternative for communities that want to move away from mono-culture farming, which can not only destroy sustainable patterns of agriculture and traditional fertility cycles but has been associated with negative changes in social structures and economic relationships.

The hotel industry has considerable growth potential in those nations and regions that are just beginning to develop their economies and improve their performance, because the total output of the hotel industry is closely tied to the variables associated with economic development. These variables include basic infrastructure and levels of gross domestic output, employment, and education of the workforce. The hospitality industry also produces a 'multiplier effect' whereby money spent by hotel guests travels through a community generating further revenue. The cruise line industry is a significant economic contributor worldwide and particularly to the United States economy, leaking into industry, agriculture, airlines, travel agents, food and beverage suppliers and other service sectors.

A 1999 report Sustainable Tourism and Cultural Heritage published by the World Bank underscores the symbiotic nature of the relationship. The mutual dependence that exists between tourism and cultural heritage is becoming more evident. While culture heritage creates a foundation for tourism's growth, tourism has the power to generate funds that make conservation possible. Cultural heritage loses much of its meaning without an audience, and a society participating in and benefiting from it. Without sustainable management, tourism loses its potential for growth. With the growing interest in culture and community, tourism is finally being recognised as an industry that can boost rural economies, create entrepreneurs and jobs and help preserve indigenous cultures.

A multi-stakeholder dialogue process was adopted including all private and public sector voices. The outcome was that local groups have the potential to add diversification to a primarily wildlife destination and the private sector has the key for effective marketing and business development skills. Following the trends already mainstream in other economic sectors, social responsibility and corporate citizenship are expected to become in the future issues of strong concern requiring a response from the tourism industry as a whole, as well as at corporate level.

The concept of 'corporate citizenship' is now being adopted by many of the key leaders in the private sector of travel and tourism and is emerging as a central issue for business companies. Corporate citizenship recognises the need to create a balance between all stakeholders' needs, society's different interests and the sustainability of the natural environment with a greater focus on governance and accountability. It is about taking responsibility for, and doing as well as possible in terms of social, environmental and economic performance given competitive opportunities and constraints.

The business case and corporate citizenship have become joined in current debate about the changing role of business in society. The Award for Responsible Capitalism 2001 - sponsored by First Magazine was presented to Marilyn Carlson Nelson, chair and CEO, Carlson Companies and highlights the importance of corporate citizenship for multinationals. Profit can serve many functions, and within travel and tourism modern business leaders are using it for good purposes. Multinationals can help contribute to the wealth and welfare of us all, and increasingly leading players in the travel and tourism industry are recognising the importance of the contributions they can make to the communities within which they work. Corporate citizenship balances the interests of the economy with those of public policy-makers, individuals and groups in civil society.

Within travel and tourism, corporate citizenship is becoming an increasingly important concept for the private sector. *Tour Operators Initiative*: The Tour Operators Initiative (TOI) launched in March 2000 is a network of tour operators that have joined forces to improve their practices, as well as raise the awareness of the industry. TOI acts as a platform to develop ideas and projects to address the environmental, social, economic and cultural aspects of sustainable development within the tourism sector.

As a major component of travel and tourism, the hospitality industry has a vested interest in protecting the environment - its key resource - and most hotels are likely to take a multitude of environmental actions that extend beyond the control of any single monitoring agency. Self-regulation appears to be the most viable course of action for this industry, whether in the form of in-house environmental audits, the adoption of an environmental management system, and/or application for eco-certification. The travel and tourism industry has come far since the Earth Summit in Rio de Janeiro, in 1992, when the impact of industries on the environment was high on the political agenda.

The increasing numbers of travellers and the rise in package tours during the 1980s were causing a valid concern among environmentalists. WTTC, with WTO/OMT and the Earth Council, in response to the scrutiny with which tourism was judged, collaborated and produced Agenda 21 for the Travel & Tourism Industry. This public-private sector effort was designed to ensure that as travel and tourism grew globally, its influence would not have an undesirable impact on the environment.

Indeed all areas of travel and tourism have over the last decade implemented many individual environmental schemes and programmes, not for-profit funds and foundations all over the world. Recently there has also been an increase in conferences on the environment hosted by governments and by private sector companies, which are highlighting the responsibility of both the public and private sector to protect natural and cultural heritage and emphasise the importance of environmental sustainability.

If tourism is not planned and managed carefully, it can overwhelm the very assets with which it attracts visitors to the destination. With the rise of mass tourism comes the threat of destruction of fragile eco-systems and coastal regions, local culture, and the depletion of natural resources. Conversely, tourism can generate the necessary revenue to protect and preserve biodiversity and act as a force for environmental protection especially in developing countries. Game parks and nature preserves are centres of institutional strength and can act as a focus for tourism development in rural areas.

Tourism helps generate resources to maintain these protected areas, as illustrated by the Royal Chitwan National Park in Nepal, the Masai Mara in Kenya and the rainforests of Costa Rica . Not only can it help to preserve the environment, but profits have a greater potential to reach local and rural communities, compared to other sectors. The new concept of eco-tourism or nature tourism is experiencing faster-than-average growth.

Eco-tourism alone contributed $154 billion in receipts in 2000 and is growing 20% annually compared with just 7% for tourism overall in an already booming industry, and reflects those consumers who are aware of the issues facing travel and tourism. There are indications that consumers are also beginning to influence businesses, as they become more aware of the choices available to them, and of this rapid growth in the eco-tourism niche market. Dialogue between stakeholders in both the private and public sectors, has led to the establishment of global voluntary initiatives throughout the last decade. These initiatives have taken various forms and represent all sectors of the travel and tourism industry.

Although there has been an encouraging explosion of such schemes, adoption of them by the industry is as yet limited. It has proved particularly difficult to encourage SMEs to participate in sustainable good practice. A number of private sector travel and tourism companies, as well as industry associations, present annual awards in recognition of outstanding actions on behalf of the environment.

The fundamental infrastructure issues such as airport congestion, air traffic management, sources of capital investment, regulation and political support, and institutional reform facing the sustainable development and growth of travel and tourism, concern both the private and public sectors. Governments are beginning to take a more dynamic role in developing sustainable and economically-successful tourism, but there urgently needs to be more proactive participation from government. With effective networking processes, legitimate policies, planning and development from government, tourism can alter its adverse environmental image to one of sustainability and stewardship. The many and varied voluntary industry initiatives, ranging from education to certification, are an important and imperative part of the ongoing process working towards sustainable development.

As well as these initiatives, the industry is already doing much to improve its performance in terms of sustainable development. Tour operators are looking at implementing strategies that combat both the indirect, as well as direct, impacts that tour operations have on the environment and the communities within which they operate. Direct issues that are being addressed include better information to consumers, ensuring that sustainable development concepts, procedures and practices are included in training programmes, and greater adherence to tour operator codes of conduct.

Indirect impacts being addressed are the monitoring of subcontracted suppliers in environmental performance and having more involvement with other stakeholders in the sustainable development process. Hotels from all geographic regions are successfully implementing strategies in favour of sustainable development. Key areas of progress include rising levels of awareness that using resources in an efficient and environmentally-sensible manner can positively impact the bottom line, and the recognition that transparency and reporting make for good business practice.

Through public-private sector alliances ICCL devises solutions to all of the challenges facing the cruise lines sectors, and works in partnership with a number of public bodies and environmental agencies to find productive solutions to the issues that confront the industry on a daily basis. The need to maintain a sustainable travel and tourism sector is now becoming an urgency. WTTC wants to share a vision of the world where travel and tourism benefits everyone, making a positive, growing and sustainable contribution to the prosperity, understanding and well-being of people, shared by those who travel and the communities they visit, and their social, cultural and natural environments. WTTC believes the way forward to achieving sustainable development for industry leaders is to lead by example and to practise corporate citizenship and responsible capitalism.

For the industry sector to implement sustainable development initiatives successfully there needs to be a multi-stakeholder process whereby all stakeholders take responsibility for the future of travel and tourism. The outbound tour operator has emerged in the past 50 years as a useful means of distributing leisure air travel and accommodation services to consumers. Consumers in one country wishing to visit another require information and want to book travel arrangements in advance. Tour operators obtain information, make contracts with suppliers of services, and publish their holiday offers in brochures, which are distributed directly to consumers or by travel agents.

Tour operators judge overall demand and the expected demand for each destination and seek to satisfy that demand if it can be accomplished profitably. Present in substantial numbers in Europe and in the United States, Canada, Japan, South Korea, Russia, Australia, New Zealand, South and Latin America, tour operators remain small in number where tourism is less developed. Globally, they represent around 12% of international arrivals, while in Europe they account for 35% of leisure air holidays.

The marketing efforts of tour operators are what the suppliers of services and governments look for. Tour operators can have a significant impact upon economies. Whereas the Balearic Islands were the poorest province in the whole of Spain in 1950, by the year 2000 it was the richest – almost entirely due to organised tourism. The Maldives is no longer to be classified as a 'lesser developed country' thanks to the economic impact of tourism, operator industry particularly organised tourism. Cancun in Mexico had a local population of 600 before tourism arrived. It now provides income for 600, 000 and support for ten times that number through organised tourism from North and South America, and Europe.

In Turkey, tourism revenues reach 30% of total commodity exports, most attributed to organised tourism. Foreign exchange received by countries through tour operators takes the form of payments to hotels and ground handlers as well as taxes, duties and charges. In addition, consumers spend money outside the hotel on the 'complementary offer'. This amount can vary from 150% of the hotel cost in countries such Spain to virtually zero in those developing countries that offer little to see, do or buy. Outbound tourism demand is affected by confidence in economic conditions and security as well as perceptions of discretionary income.

Leisure outbound travel has been growing at around one and a half times the growth in GDP and is not highly volatile, unless there are safety concerns. Fluctuations tourism revenues in receiving countries are more marked due to consumer perceptions of the relative safety and attractiveness of destinations, as well as changes in relative price.

By far the most positive influence of tourism has been on the citizens of the receiver countries, where the foreign influx has provided income for much greater social choices than have hitherto existed and accelerated the process of modernisation and openness. As local people have become richer through tourism, countries dependent on international tourism have found themselves generating a greater number of domestic tourists. The effect of this phenomenon in Spain, for example, has been the restoration of a strong Spanish identity – both cultural and culinary – which had been weakened.

Tour operator distribution has created jobs in originating countries, particularly for women in travel agencies, airlines, airports and hotels as well as for tour operators themselves. Negative social consequences have been felt in a number of different and significant ways. The 'homogenisation' of global products and services devoid of local identity has been exacerbated by tourism movements. There is no doubt that people brought for a short time to another country seek to retain their own habits and practices – while host communities adapt to satisfy visitor tastes in order to make money from them. Those with vulnerable cultures are likely to suffer most and local disaffection is most keenly felt where there are high densities of tourists.

Reaction tends to come from regional, religious or cultural entities attempting to preserve key features that provide a manifestation of a local identity. Overall, the opportunity for jobs in tourism and tourism-related activities in receiving countries have been very positive, as has the opportunity for training and development. However, a major market failure has been the inability to develop and diversify the complementary offer (things to see, buy or do outside the hotel) that would provide extra jobs and income in the community and allow monies to be distributed more widely and deeply This remains a significant opportunity to alleviate poverty in some developing countries.

In countries where the money economy is limited and unemployment high, tourism can be seen to benefit the few who are directly involved in tourism, leaving workers in the informal economy marginalised and disaffected. Tour operators have many sub-contracted suppliers that are expected to deliver quality services under some form of supervision. They rely upon close relationships with people working in the destinations – at airports, hotels, restaurants, excursion venues, public administrations, medical authorities, etc. – for without them, holidays could not be delivered.

Tour operators act as a bridge between suppliers, customers and the country visited, providing information about the destination, safety and cultural sensitivity (dress codes, etc) . With smaller guided tours, customers often seek greater detailed interaction and are very aware of their social and cultural responsibilities. The International Federation of Tour Operators (IFTO) acts as the spokesperson for tour operators (and their clients) with municipalities, regional and national governments and international organisations such as the WTO/OMT, UNCTAD, WHO, UNESCO, UNEP, and the EU. Issues range from the broadest level to the narrowest dealings with the public administration involve ministries of foreign affairs, home affairs, public works, environment, transport, tourism, education, health and finance. the private sector, all the actors in tourism and related to tourism are involved in discussions.

As tourism is a horizontal activity, co-ordination, consultation and partnerships are essential for it be successful. Developed nations have the technical and financial resources to monitor and enforce environmental standards in tourism development and, in many cases, the political to act as well as a body of planning regulations. In these circumstances, should a problem arise a basis for negotiation exists between the governing authorities and the local tourism actors together with IFTO. Developing countries may have priorities that are more pressing than sustainable development in tourism. There may be neither the political will nor the technical or financial resources to monitor environmental performance.

Airports have been extended as a result of consumer demand – larger aircraft are now used. Tour operators seek out the lowest seat mile costs – this requires in turn, high-density seating and fuel-efficient modern aircraft operating at high load factors. The resulting emissions of noise, CO_2 and NO_x per passenger are lower than for other forms of aviation, but nonetheless would not have occurred had customers stayed at home. Customers are usually transported from the destination airport to the hotel by modern diesel-engined or gas-powered coaches which can carry up to 58 people and have low seat/mile CO_2 emissions. These vehicles reduce the incidence of car traffic by more than 25 times.

In beach destinations where movement outside hotels is limited to excursions, consumption/emissions during a two-week stay are likely to be much less than staying at home. The huge majority of tourists fly from colder to warmer climates in countries with beaches nearer the equator, which get less rain and have less available water. Although tourism uses very little water compared with agriculture, there is a significant increase in the consumption of water as a result of tourism. Desalination plants have been installed in some areas of high-density tourism where there are water shortages. Hotels pay for water consumption by volume and this is reflected in prices to consumers.

Many hotels employ systems to reduce consumption of water and energy consumption and waste, but this remains a major issue in much of the developed and developing world. Sewerage systems are expensive and 'high tech' systems are required to avoid contamination of seawater. These may be funded through central/local government and through multi-lateral sources. Huge investments have taken place in coastal areas of high tourism density, but much remains to be done. Likewise, solid waste is a major issue for many municipalities operating in tourism areas.

Many tour operators seek to monitor the environmental performance of sub-contracted suppliers and destinations. They support countries and regions in implementing the development processes of local 'Agenda 21s' and actively promote the harmonisation of local, communal and regional needs in tourism development plans. They support measures that help in visitor management and make their own staff aware of sustainable development needs. Strong governance and institutional frameworks have helped to manage flows of tourism through tour operators in most developed nations, although more could be accomplished. In the developing world this has been less effective with the exception of low volume specialist destinations, which have benefited from responsible management policies of tour operators.

It is in the few developing countries with volumes of tourists that are not appropriate for the habitat or current infrastructure that problems can arise. It should be emphasised that multi-stakeholder involvement in receiving countries/destinations can only be effective if tour operators are included as active partners.

Worldwide there are many thousands of incoming tour operators. In developing countries, in particular, these local businesses compete to represent tour operators and those that fail resent that all the business of the outbound tour operator goes through one local business. The incoming tour operator attempts to create a range of offers to attract consumers that are practical in terms of logistics and the environment and provide the right price/value to consumers and profits to themselves.

From the perspective of the suppliers in the receiving destination, the incoming tour operator forms part of their destination network for which they are prepared to pay. The outbound tour operator can also play a role in that distribution to customers. The coach companies play a crucial role in the batch distribution of customers from airport to hotels and on tours to excursion venues. Their fleets are, in the main, very modern and well maintained. The rent-a-car companies usually provide new or nearly new vehicles for hire.

The economic value of rent-a-cars for tourism is that customers can reach destinations not accessible without motorised transport. The major attractions act as magnets to tourists providing the motivation for visits and leading to increased use of hotel rooms, roads, airports, rail transport as well as the land use for the attraction itself. They can provide a major drive for increased local employment. Major attractions depend on very high visitor throughput. The incoming tour operators can, and do, lay down clear policies and procedures for subcontracted suppliers to follow to protect the environment and to support enlightened social policies.

However, these local businesses are run on local labour law, regulations, custom and practice. In some developing countries, the custom and practice may not meet the standards demanded, for example, by International Labour Organization (ILO) . Outbound tour operators can have influence over how their passengers are handled by the incoming tour operators/suppliers, however, they have no influence on how the incoming tour operator arranges for the majority of their work with their suppliers that takes place with individuals on independently organised groups. The incoming tour operators recognise that they have a significant role to play in tourism development. Their decisions on excursion venues and planning of trips can have strong impacts on particular communities.

These communities are in competition with each other for offering attractions to tourists who have limited time. Tourists will often go to one craft market, but not two, so decisions by incoming tour operators count heavily. The obligation of the coach companies is to ensure that the vehicles are safe and secure and emit the lowest emissions possible with the use of local fuels. Their social obligations relate to conditions of work, particularly drivers' hours, as well as driving and parking procedures.

Hotels and restaurants also contribute to the important process of job creation. As a labour-intensive industry, hospitality employs large numbers of wage earners, whose taxes and disposable income add to gross domestic output and help to create further employment opportunities. Given that each hotel room typically requires one member of staff, every hotel room built has the potential to create an additional job. Furthermore, for every dollar spent by a guest in a hotel, one additional revenue dollar is generated for the community: Referred to as the 'multiplier effect', this concept is used by economists to explain how money spent by a hotel guest travels through a community to purchase the goods and services required to meet the guest's needs.

In the United States, for example, the multiplier effect is approximately two; that is, for every dollar spent by a guest in a hotel, one additional revenue dollar is generated across a wide range of businesses. The total output of the hotel industry is closely tied to the variables associated with economic development such as basic infrastructure and levels of Gross Domestic Product (GDP), employment and education of the workforce. This relationship is worth noting since it can be expected that the hotel industry has considerable growth potential in those nations and regions that are just beginning to fully develop their economies and improve their performance in each macro-economic variable. Of particular concern to the hospitality industry in high-income countries are current demographic trends - notably declining birth rates and ageing populations - which put further pressure on an industry characterised by high turnover and a shortage of qualified labour in both developed and developing countries .

These problems are exacerbated by constraints on the international mobility of workers as a result of visa restrictions and national immigration quotas. Although no data is currently available as to the actual extent of the labour shortfall globally, it can be anticipated that trade associations will lobby for a more flexible job market on a global scale, and that in order to help combat the labour shortage hotels will have to embrace a training culture in their businesses and employ people from an increasingly wide cross-section of cultures and backgrounds. By providing many young or unskilled people with their first job experience, the industry also effectively offers them an entry into the labour market. The industry's labour-intensive nature puts it in a prime position to draw upon all sectors of society to meet its workforce needs.

Given its key contribution to gross global output and employment generation, and the social consequences this may have, hospitality industry leaders are being challenged to demonstrate greater levels of social responsibility and will be increasingly called upon to address the gap between the so-called 'haves' and 'have-nots'. In this spirit, some hotel companies have signed agreements with trade unions, which focus on issues of trade union rights, skills training and equality in the workplace.

Hotels increasingly recognise the need for measures to protect 'frontline' employees given the higher-than-average extent of direct contact between customers and staff. One response to this need has been the publication of the Guide for the Hospitality Industry on dealing with HIV/AIDS in the Workplace produced by IH&RA in collaboration with UNAIDS. This gives guidance to hotels on introducing an AIDS policy and AIDS education in the workplace and details essential safety measures. The commercial sexual exploitation of children in tourism – commonly referred to as child sex tourism – is a further area of social concern with implications not just for hotels worldwide, but for the tourism industry as a whole.

Rules for Successful Marketing

Tourism is an important economic activity because it brings in dollars from outside the community. It continues to be a fast growing sector and is typically included among the top three industries in the country. In addition, tourism provides a "front-door" to non-tourism economic development efforts such as business recruitment. Many of rules apply to the tourism marketing efforts of small city downtowns and business districts.

1. Success Begins With a Good Plan

Creating a Tourism Development & Marketing Plan is the first rule for successful tourism. The plan should include several details like product development, upgrades and improvements, repositioning and/or branding, attractions and events, visitor amenities and services, marketing and public relations, public/private partnerships, recruitment, funding and budgets, and organizational responsibilities. The plan should integrate existing comprehensive plans and economic development and Main Street efforts.

2. Importance of Front-line Sales

Your front-line employees can be your most valuable sales team. This is because they establish the first contact with the customer. The front-line employees should be knowledgeable about your community and should promote other stores, attractions and amenities to visitors to keep them in the area longer.

3. Critical Mass

In order to attract and keep visitors in your community, there must be several retail and dining establishments within walking distance. Shopping and dining in a pedestrian setting is one of the top activities for visitors. An average rule of thumb for rural communities is to have nine retail stores and four dining/treats establishments within two or three blocks.

4. Turn Negatives Into Positives

Almost every community and attraction has its challenges. Think creatively on how to convert these negatives into positives. You can then attract people to your area using clever promotional tactics. For example, when an article in the Washington Post labelled Battle Mountain, Nevada the "Armpit of America", the town took a positive spin on that title by having an annual event sponsored by Old Spice drawing thousands of visitors.

5. Be Unique

In order to be successful, you must be worth the trip. A visitor must be able to differentiate you from the competition and you must strive to be creative and set yourself apart from others. Being unique will make a visitor travel the extra distance.

6. Telling Stories

Museums and interpretive centres should always tell stories, not just display artifacts. Stories can keep visitors in the area longer, which means additional spending. Visitors also remember stories, and captivating stories are told and passed on to others. More people pick destinations by word of mouth than any other method.

7. Four-Times Rule

People are willing to travel a distance if you offer something that appeals to them. There should be enough for visitors to see and do in your area. In general, you should be able to keep visitors busy four times longer than it took them to get there.

8. Marketing vs. Product Development

Before you market your community, make sure it is appealing to customers. If your product is not of great quality, then your marketing efforts are wasted. Product development should always be a top priority, and it never ends. Having a good mix of product development and marketing is also important.

9. Selling the Experience

Always sell the experience associated with an activity and not the place. If you are using pictures in your marketing campaign, avoid using scenic images. Scenery lasts in the mind for only a few moments. Instead, use images of people laughing and having fun. Viewers are more likely to remember images that include people's emotions.

10. Branding

Even at the community level, branding is critical for success in tourism. Branding is much more than just a logo; it is what sets you apart from your competition, it is your image and your value. Do not try to be "all things to all people."

11. WOW Photography

Nothing sells tourism like great photography.

Photographs used for tourism purposes should have a "wow" appeal in the viewer and should make the viewer want to go to the place depicted. As mentioned earlier, you are trying to sell an experience and your photos should evoke emotion in the viewer. Photography should be the key element in brochures, public relation efforts, and especially on the web.

12. Close the Sale

Most communities and attractions spend a significant amount of money on advertising. The primary "call to action" in advertising is to get the potential customer to call and get a brochure, or for them to visit your web site. If this is the case, the brochure and web site should be good enough to close the sale. Otherwise, your advertising effort is largely wasted.

Pay attention to certain small details while advertising. For example, for brochures, the best colours to use are red and yellow as these colours get the viewers attention. In addition, most brochures end up in racks along with scores of other brochures and the top three inches is all that is visible to the potential customer. Keep this in mind when designing brochures.

13. Public Relations

Even though you need both, publicity is much more important than advertising. Implementing a professional public relations campaign can have several benefits: it will build brand, improve your image, increase credibility and will provide a greater return on investment than advertising alone. Public relation is how you build your brand and advertising is how you maintain your position. Studies show that for every $1 invested into a public relations campaign, you get a $3 return.

14. Effective Web Sites

According to a Nielsen/Netratings study, nearly 75% of the U.S. population has access to the Internet from home. In addition, 94% of Internet users make travel arrangements using the Web. The Internet is by far the number one resource for planning travel and vacations. If you have a tourism related web site, can your potential customers find you easily on the Web? How does your web site compare with the competition? Make the online experience interactive for the customer and remember to promote attractions, not just the place or your organization. Several thousands of dollars spent on web site development and maintenance is not a waste of money. You can even make sure your web site is displayed at the top of a Web search by paying a fee.

15. Frequency in Advertising

Frequency is more important than variety in placing advertising. People viewing your advertisement should develop Top of Mind Awareness (TOMA). For example, when the words "fast food" are mentioned, most people think of McDonalds because they make a good use of frequency in advertising.

Supply Chain Management in Marketing

As intermediaries between tourists and tourism service providers, tour operators bring together a variety of tourism-related services to form a complete holiday package, which is then marketed to customers either directly or through travel agents. Each package generally consists of accommodation, transport both to and from the destination, ground transport within the destination, and events or activities such as excursions and social activities . Because most of the goods and services included in a holiday package are provided by a supply chain of subcontracted companies, organizations and agents, tour operators are not always in direct control of the environmental and social impacts of those products.

Yet, consumers increasingly expect the companies they buy from to ensure that their products provide not just quality and value-for-money, but also safeguard environmental and social sustainability. Companies must take responsibility for ensuring the sustainability of all the inputs that go into their products. For tour operators, who offer products comprised almost entirely of contracted goods and services, this means that effectively implementing sustainability policies requires working closely with suppliers to improve sustainability performance in all the components of a holiday - throughout the life cycle of a holiday package.

Benefits of Sustainable Supply Chain

Working with suppliers to integrate sustainability into the supply chain can benefit tour operators, suppliers, customers and destinations. From a financial standpoint, improved sustainability can lower costs through greater operating efficiency, reduced waste generation, and reduced consumption of energy and water. Sustainability practices can also lead to increased revenue and shareholder value by generating more repeat business and attracting new business from customers that value good environmental and social performance. A strong positive reputation as a company that cares about sustainability issues, coupled with improvements to the quality of the tourism experience provided to clients, can result in increased customer satisfaction and loyalty, strengthened brand value, enhanced publicity and marketing opportunities, and better acceptance by local communities in destinations.

Good performance and a high-quality, sustainable product can also help a touir operator reduce the risk of conflict or problems with suppliers, governments, staff and local communities, and improve its status as a respected partner in destinations. This may mean enhanced access to key business resources such as capital, the ability to develop products to meet growing market demand, improved relationships with governments, and a motivated and loyal staff. The costs and benefits of integrating sustainability criteria into the supply chain will vary for each company, depending on:

- Purchasing and contracting arrangements with suppliers;
- Availability of alternate suppliers in key destinations;
- Suppliers' current levels of sustainability performance and potential for change;
- Barriers to sustainability, such as external factors ;
- A company's main sustainability and operational concerns; and
- Resources available to implement and promote sustainability throughout the supply chain.

In some cases, external factors that are outside the control of either a tour operator or its suppliers may affect the sustainability of the contracted company's services. For example, a destination's wastewater treatment system, waste management scheme, policies on the protection of cultural and natural heritage or social conditions may all influence the sustainability performance of suppliers. Where such external factors limit improvements in sustainability performance, it may be necessary to work in partnership with local and national government authorities.

It is important to recognise that the circumstances and priorities of some destinations, particularly in developing countries, may be very different from those of industrialised countries, and to avoid approaches that would impose undue burdens on a destination. At the same time, however, working more actively with suppliers based in the visited destination can generate action from local authorities by sending a clear message about visitors' and companies' priorities for action. As more suppliers begin to adopt sustainable practices, the public sector also needs to respond by supporting adoption of sustainable practices for public utilities and infrastructure, such as solid waste treatment facilities, recycling opportunities, wastewater treatment plants and public transport.

The following is a sampling of issues that tour operators may want to consider when creating a sustainable supply chain management system. When determining which issues to highlight in a sustainable supply chain policy, it is important to consider what a company stands for and what type of products it sells. A multi-stakeholder process that includes participants from each of a company's various groups of suppliers can help ensure that all relevant issues are considered.

— *Economic Performance Issues*

  — Employee wages and benefits

  - Local purchasing
  - Revenue leakage
  - Linkages with local suppliers and subcontractors
  - Corporate responsibility-related payments
- *Environmental Performance Issues*
  - Energy use
  - Water use
  - Waste management
  - Wastewater management
  - Contributionsto biodiversity and nature conservation
  - Chemical use
  - Emissions (CO_2, ozone depleting substances)
  - Land conversion
  - Air, water and land pollution
  - Toxicity of materials and products used
  - Indoor air quality
  - Noise
  - Purchasing guidelines
  - Built environment (including protection of architectural, historical and archaeological heritage)
  - Environmental management systems
- *Social and Cultural Performance Issues*

General

  - Equal opportunities and non-discrimination

— Human rights (including implementation of the ECPAT Code against the commercial sexual exploitation of children)

Workplace

— Workplace conditions

— Labour relations (including fair treatment, fair wages, security of employment, working hours and employees' rights, such as freedom of association and collective bargaining)

— Health and safety

— Training and education

— Children in the workplace

Suppliers and subcontractors

— Labour relations and human rights practices

— Contracting with small and micro-enterprises, including those operated by indigenous, ethnic or minority groups

— Respect for rights of indigenous, ethnic and minority groups, and of local communities

Community

— Land and indigenous rights

— Consultation and participatory decision-making with the local population and affected stakeholders

— Contribution to community development

— Economic linkages with local communities

Steps for Sustainable Supply Chain

1. Establish a Sustainable Supply Chain Policy and Management System

For a tour operator, effectively integrating sustainability into its supply chain will require the establishment of a coherent company policy and accompanying management system that set out clear targets and actions on economic, environmental and social performance. Building this system on already existing internal processes will help keep down the costs of implementation and promote integration within a company's overall operations.

To establish this policy, a company needs to conduct a baseline assessment of its tourism service suppliers' current performance on sustainability, to determine priority targets and actions. The management system should include procedures for monitoring, reviewing and reporting on progress made in integrating sustainability principles into the company's supply chain. This helps to ensure transparency and allow tour operators to adapt any policies or actions that are not achieving their stated goals. Progress can be measured against the initial baseline assessment.

Develop a coherent policy for improving the economic, environmental and social sustainability performance of suppliers, and for integrating it into existing company management systems. Following are the actions:

— *Building a team to develop and implement the policy*

  — Bring together representatives of each area or department in the company that may have a role in implementing the overall policy, or which may be affected by it .

— Create a management team to develop and implement the policy at each stage, drawing on expertise from all departments.

— Consider inviting one or more of your company's suppliers to participate in the policy and planning process.

— *Assessing the company's strengths and opportunities*

— Assess the company's current position and policies and how they relate to sustainability

— Consider trends and potential developments, including product quality, supplier performance, and markets, as well as the way the company interacts with its suppliers.

— Identify opportunities to improve the sustainability performance of suppliers.

—*Developing a policy*

— Elaborate a common vision that can be shared by all departments in the company, based on the results of the strengths and opportunities assessment.

— Discuss the common vision with key staff, and invite their suggestions for policies and actions to implement this vision.

— Based on these discussions and the common vision, develop and agree on a policy and strategic goals for improved supply chain sustainability, and on the types of methods that could be used to meet these goals.

Table 1: Key Departments to Involve in a Sustainable Supply Chain Policy and Action Plan

Main staff and departmental competencies	How they can be involved
Company Board	Provide resources and top-level support for the programme.
Contracting Director and Managers	Use sustainability performance as a factor in selecting suppliers.
	Incorporate sustainability clauses into contracts with suppliers (a company's buyers are the most important point of contact for suppliers and in some cases may be their only company contact).
Country and Destination Managers and Representatives	Discuss sustainability issues and the company programme as part of regular contacts with suppliers.
	Provide feedback and continuous follow-up with hotels and other suppliers.
	Facilitate dissemination of policy and training and awareness materials.
	Identify new local suppliers entering the tourism sector.
Human Resources Director and Department	Incorporate sustainable action plans into job descriptions and staff appraisals.
Legal Advisers	Provide legal advice on wording, inclusion and enforcement of sustainability clauses in suppliers' contracts.
Marketing Director and Department	Develop marketing plan to reflect company's sustainable supply chain strategy.
	Provide incentives to suppliers by offering additional

	promotion to those with good sustainability performance.
Production Department	Examine the cost implications of the sustainability-induced changes required in the supply chain and their impact on prices.
Quality/Health and Safety Department	Monitor quality and health and safety standards of suppliers. Incorporate sustainability performance issues into monitoring of suppliers.
Sustainability Unit	Provide day-to-day management and co-ordination of the programme. Offer advice on sustainability issues, technical support, etc.
Internal Communications or Training Unit	Provide assistance in development of training programmes for staff and suppliers on sustainability issues.

A baseline assessment of suppliers

Assess suppliers' current sustainability performance and their strengths and weaknesses, to generate data for designing a sustainability action plan, and to provide a baseline against which to measure progress over time and review and modify the sustainable supply chain policy and actions.

Actions

— *Preparing an approach for assessment*

— Develop assessment tools for measuring the sustainability performance of suppliers.

— Select a sample of suppliers to involve in the assessment.

  - Consider prioritising certain supplier groups, based on ability to influence them and the ease of addressing any identified impacts. Trying to tackle every type of service and every supplier or contractor at the same time can be very resource intensive.

- *Assessing suppliers' current performance*
  - Use questionnaires, personal meetings and/or workshops to assess suppliers' current sustainability performance, strengths and weaknesses, their main concerns and the key areas requiring improvement.
  - Determine suppliers' general levels of awareness, technical capacity and desire to be involved in a sustainability programme. In particular, it is important to understand their motives and values, and to identify any potential challenges or barriers to sustainability.
  - Identify any opportunities for additional cooperation with external stakeholders, in particular local authorities or NGOs.
  - Ask suppliers for information on how they select their own suppliers. They may already implement a range of good practices, such as buying food from local producers and organic and/or fair trade suppliers.

Implement an action plan

Prepare an action plan for implementation of policies for improving the economic, environmental and social sustainability performance of suppliers, taking into account suppliers' strengths and weaknesses and existing company management systems.

Actions

— *Defining actions and setting targets*

  — Define and agree on actions and targets to be achieved, based on the company's sustainable supply chain policy.

  — Ensure that targets are SMART (Specific, Measurable, Achievable, Realistic and Time-specific).

  — Set standards by which to measure suppliers' performance .

  — Ensure that standards are achievable. It is better to set standards that are achievable and can provide real satisfaction for suppliers and staff, rather than set over-ambitious standards that are unlikely to be achieved.

  — Develop an action plan to implement the strategy and meet set targets

  — Agree on specific responsibilities for each department and the resources they will need to implement them, such as training or technical information. Incorporate departmental action plans in regular company procedures for reviewing progress and staff appraisal.

  — Prepare a timetable for implementation of the overall plan and for each individual action.

— *Getting the word out*

  — Inform suppliers about the sustainability policy and action plan, and the benefits of improved environmental, social and economic performance, through normal company communication channels, dedicated workshops and personal meetings between suppliers and company representatives.

— Inform staff about the sustainability policy and action plan through training workshops, briefings and feedback materials, and internal capacity-building on how to raise awareness of the policy and provide support to suppliers .

— Establish a system to keep staff informed of progress, for example through staff newsletters and the intranet.

— *Putting the plan into action*

— Consider prioritising suppliers for involvement in the first stages of the programme, based on economic and managerial considerations. It may be more practical to begin with just a few destinations and/or selected suppliers, rather than trying to introduce it everywhere at once.

— Recognise that suppliers may have different priorities for improvements and are likely to make progress at different rates.

— Understand that change takes time. It is important to focus on achieving continuous improvements, rather than trying to achieve everything all at once. The key is to initiate programmes with all suppliers to improve their performance and see measurable improvement over time.

— Consider working with other partners, including public authorities, NGOs and other tour operators operating in the same destination, to help encourage sustainability performance improvements amongst all suppliers, for example by developing a common approach in certain geographic or supplier areas.

Setting standards for specific aspects of sustainability performance is a central part of any system of preferred contracting based on sustainability criteria. A company's standards should reflect the key sustainability issues that form the basis of its sustainability policy. The standards will provide criteria that a company can use in selecting suppliers and in offering additional promotional opportunities and incentives to its suppliers . They can also be included in any contracts signed with suppliers .

Standards may be either performance-based (based on specific levels of performance), process-based (based on mandated procedures and practices), or both. Standards should be set sufficiently high so that they represent a real improvement by suppliers, but also at a level that is realistically achievable. They should also be flexible enough to accommodate different local socio-economic and environmental conditions and the varying sizes and technical capacity levels of suppliers.

It is useful to involve staff and suppliers in defining sustainability performance standards. A company's suppliers can provide valuable insight into local issues and conditions that may affect the potential to improve their sustainability performance. In some cases, tour operators own and run accommodations or other facilities, and thus have direct control over the implementation of any sustainability measures. Such facilities should comply with, and preferably exceed, standards that tour operators require of other external suppliers with whom they contract.

Establishing a programme for working with suppliers will also require internal actions by tour operators themselves. In particular, tour operators will need to consider how to promote the programme within their companies and how to build staff capacity both to support suppliers in improving their sustainability performance and to monitor their progress. New staff training modules and awareness-raising exercises can be developed or incorporated into existing training programmes.

Implementation of a sustainable supply chain strategy may also require changes to individual staff roles and responsibilities. For example, staff involved in health and safety monitoring of hotels may also become involved in monitoring some aspects of sustainability. Such changes will need to be agreed with relevant departments, which should be given appropriate resources and support, such as training, written guidance, technical information and advice. Keeping staff members informed of progress - for example by posting progress reports on staff notice boards and intranet sites or including information in staff newsletters - can also help encourage employees to promote and implement a new sustainability policy.

2. *Support Suppliers in Reaching Sustainability Goals*

Tour operators are well-placed to support suppliers in improving their economic, environmental and social performance. As tour operators interact directly with potential customers, they understand their clients' growing demands for high quality and sustainability. They also often have access to technology and information that smaller suppliers may have difficulty obtaining on their own.

Because tour operators deal with a wide range of different suppliers, they can more easily gather information on a variety of best practices and facilitate the sharing of experiences amongst suppliers. There are a number of ways that tour operators can enable their suppliers to improve their sustainability performance and meet set sustainability criteria and targets. Three of these measures - awareness raising, technical support and the provision of incentives - are discussed in this section. The appropriate mix of support measures for each company and supplier will depend on the results of the baseline assessment and the approach that the company has chosen to adopt for implementing its sustainable supply chain strategy.

Awareness on sustainability issues

Raise awareness amongst suppliers on relevant sustainability issues and demonstrate why sustainability performance is important.

Actions

— *Developing awareness-raising messages on sustainability*

- — Take into account feedback from suppliers, existing relationships with targeted supplier groups, the level of interest amongst suppliers in participating in the programme, and suppliers' current capacity and priorities for performance improvement.
- — Design messages based on the dissemination channels that will be used to raise awareness, such as mailings, personal visits, workshops, etc.
- — Identify potential partners and support. Local partners, such as business associations or training institutes, can help open communication channels with local suppliers, especially amongst smaller enterprises, and may be influential in reinforcing awareness-raising efforts.
- — Keep messages simple. Focus on key issues that are important to the company's situation and its suppliers.

- Provide information in the awareness-raising materials on the overall strategy and time frame for the company's sustainability programme.

- *Communicating sustainability messages to suppliers*
  - Identify the characteristics of each group of suppliers, including their values and concerns, and select appropriate tools, media and styles to best reach these target groups. Tools might include workshops, bilateral meetings or dialogues, briefing materials and feedback forms for staff, checklists and questionnaires, or printed materials, such as leaflets, posters and manuals.
  - If questionnaires or checklists are used, indicate clearly what the information gathered would be used for. Consider preparing a summary report on the results, for example, highlighting sustainability issues identified as priorities by suppliers and illustrating the general level of performance for each of the issues addressed.
  - Use personal communication wherever possible. Staff in contact with suppliers can provide up-to-date information on sustainability issues and the company's progress. Trained staff should be available to inform suppliers about environmental and social issues, provide contact phone numbers, make personal visits, etc.
  - Ensure that sustainability issues are followed up and discussed regularly with suppliers.
  - Encourage feedback from suppliers to help evaluate the effectiveness of awareness-raising activities and provide important information on the attitudes of

target groups to sustainability issues. This feedback can be used to refine awareness-raising activities and plan future developments.

— Monitor the response to the awareness-raising actions. Check how suppliers and staff respond to the project, recognise and appreciate results, and support continuous improvement.

Support suppliers in improving their sustainability performance, particularly in areas that have been identified as priorities. Following are the Actions:

— *Assessing where support is needed*

— Determine where technical support is needed amongst suppliers and establish targets for improvement.

— Identify the most appropriate technical support and capacity-building actions to match the suppliers' and company's targets.

— *Developing and delivering support*

— Identify, develop and deliver the most appropriate and effective technical support tools for suppliers, including printed material, workshops, bilateral meetings or dialogues, briefing materials and feedback forms for staff, training sessions, checklists and questionnaires, and telephone and on-line information and support services.

— Provide training and practical education opportunities to suppliers' staff at all levels, including managers, engineers, hotel maids, catering staff, guides, etc., on reducing resource use and procedures for waste separation and recycling.

— Offer links to networks of local, national and international advisers on sustainability and business issues who can provide on-line and on-site assistance to suppliers - for example local experts on environmental and socio-economic issues, possibly in collaboration with local trade associations and non-governmental organisations.

— Consider promoting the use of eco-labelling schemes to support improvement and provide information on technical issues tailored to a specific destination

— Identify external sources of information and support. Numerous technical materials on environmental management and solutions are already available through international and national hotel associations, international organisations and NGOs. Arranging for suppliers to contact these sources directly can help such organisations disseminate their resources more widely and avoid overwhelming an internal team with requests for information and support, which might be difficult to meet with limited internal resources.

Impact of Global Marketing Strategies

The impact of global markets, communications and telecommunication have changed market conditions and orientations for traditional products. The rise of environmentalism has led to increasing control by "outsiders" over land use and resource development. Although some rural areas still experience depopulation, others are experiencing an inflow of people to retire or to develop new 'non-traditional' businesses. The once clear distinction between urban and rural is now blurred by suburbanisation, long distance commuting and second home development. Rural tourism is a complex multi-faceted activity: it is not just farm-based tourism. It includes farm-based holidays but also comprises special interest nature holidays and ecotourism, walking, climbing and riding holidays, adventure, sport and health tourism, hunting and angling, educational travel, arts and heritage tourism, and, in some areas, ethnic tourism.

There is also a large general interest market for less specialised forms of rural tourism. This area is highlighted by studies of the important German tourism market, where a major requirement of the main holiday is the ability to provide peace, quiet and relaxation in rural surroundings. Because rural tourism is multi-faceted, because rural areas themselves are multi-faceted and rarely either static entities or self-contained, and free from urban influence, a working and reasonably universal definition of the subject is difficult to find. However, in almost every case rurality is the central and unique selling point in the rural tourism package.

The search for a definition must, therefore, begin with an understanding of the concept of rurality itself. Typically rural areas have low population densities: this is a result of small settlements, widely spaced apart. The natural and/or the farmed/forested environment dominates the built environment. Average rural population densities vary enormously between and within the OECD countries: an exact analysis would be valueless because of the varying sizes of the administrative units used for statistical purposes. The OECD Rural Development Programme uses a pragmatically based series of indicators: while at local level a population density of 150 persons per square kilometre is the preferred criterion, "at the regional level geographic units are grouped by the share of their population which is rural, into the following three types: predominantly rural, significantly rural (15-50 per cent) and predominantly urbanized regions". From this array of varying definitions, two clear points stand out.

Many commentators define rural areas as those with less than 10-20 per cent of their land areas covered by the built environment. There are three important implications here. These areas will be dominated by agrarian and forest-based economic activities. They will be, to a large extent, repositories of the natural world and wild-life. For the visitor, they will give an impression of space, and a traditional non-urban, non-industrial economy. Their economies will be strongly influenced by the market for farm and forest products. Although the labour force required for farming and forestry has declined rapidly in recent years, rural areas still show a strong bias towards jobs in the farm/forest sector. Additionally, they usually exhibit low female activity rates outside the home because of the shortage of job opportunities for women in many rural areas. The rapid urbanisation of the nineteenth and twentieth centuries produced new social structures different from the 'traditional' societies of the countryside.

The retention of older ways of life and thinking is important in retaining rural 'character'. It is this residual character which, combined with the scenic values and recreational opportunities of the countryside, attracts tourists from urban areas. It is difficult to define the exact characteristics of rural society. There are great variations between countries and continents, and even within countries. Rural communities can be assessed on a sliding scale with sparsely populated remote wilderness as one end of a polar typology. The other end of the scale can be represented by the so-called "world city", the ultimate expression of urbanisation. Between these extremes lie a variety of situations, largely rural or largely urban, with a mid-point represented by the outermost edge of suburbia, a cross-over point between poles, exhibiting characteristics of both rural and urban typology.

The OECD's Rural Development Programme has developed a useful typology for assessing the economic geography of rural areas. This divides the rural world into peripheral or remote regions, 'intermediate' regions, which make up the majority of the rural land mass, and economically integrated rural regions, often close to large urban complexes. The peripheral regions are characterised by sparse populations, small scale often traditional enterprises, high servicing costs and economic poverty. The economically integrated regions tend to have large farm units, a diversified economy, good services and relative affluence.

The intermediate areas lie midway between these extremes. This typology can also fit the continuum concept: the three types of region are not sharply defined but blend into each other. The typology has important implications for both rural development and rural tourism which will be explained later. The continuum concept copes not only with a variety of landscapes, life styles and demographic inheritance-but also with change. Settlements can move along the continuum, exhibiting change through time. Typically-but not always—the change tends to move districts and settlements towards the urban pole. In the OECD's economic typology, change is also common-and can also occur in either direction.

Thus, rural settlements may remain locationally rural while becoming functionally urban. Settlement size and population density may remain "rural", but economies may become non-agricultural, and society may display increasing numbers of urban characteristics. Different parts of rural society may display more or less urban characteristics. The practical expression of the pro-rural sentiments quoted above has been two-fold. Government policies financially support both primary rural products and rural service provision in every OECD Member country. These financial policies are frequently backed by strong conservation policies, aimed at the retention of existing landscape areas, whole settlements, buildings and the natural world.

Many types of holiday can be developed in both urban and rural locations. Holiday-makers may be involved in both urban and rural activities on the same day. A tentative classification of holiday types is given below: it should be used with care. The listing follows the continuum concept, moving from specifically rural to specifically urban with a broad intermediate category. Traditionally agriculture and forestry were central to rural life. They were the major employers of labour, the main sources of income within the rural economy, and indirectly had a powerful influence on traditions, power structures and life styles. Together, the decisions of farmers and foresters determined rural land use and landscapes. In the late twentieth century, the central role of farming and forestry has been diminished. Both activities have shed much of their labour force. Only five OECD countries now employ more than 15 per cent of their labour force in farming, forestry and fishing: in eight OECD countries, that figure is less than 5 per cent.

The economic power of farming and forestry has declined, not least because those activities are extremely dependent on state subsidies for their profitability.

Traditions are waning before the combined attack of television, power farming techniques and tree processors. Even the role of agri-and arboriculturalists as "landscape gardeners" has diminished: power has begun to move to planners and conservationists. In this evolving situation, two myths have grown up about the role of rural tourism. One is that rural tourism is farm-based tourism.

Farm-based rural tourism has been successful through many (but not all) parts of German-speaking Europe because of a powerful combination of small farm size, interesting scenery, closeness to markets, traditional town/country links caused by late migration from the countryside to city regions, the owner-occupation of farmsteads and the tradition of effective and interventionary local government and co-operative movements. Furthermore, the role of farm-based tourism has been exaggerated because it has received great attention from both agriculture ministries and academics.

Diversification into rural tourism is frequently held up as a potential panacea for agriculture's ills. There is no doubt that in some areas, and for some businesses, tourism can be valuable. Successful farm tourism development seems to require effective co-operative marketing and development efforts. Many areas have no tradition of co-operation between farmers, or between farmers and · governmental agencies. The key relationship in rural tourism is between tourism development and comprehensive rural development, embracing rural services, new enterprise attraction, conservation, a wider role for women and inward investment.

Agriculture has an important role to play in rural tourism, but it is but one facet amongst many: it may be of greater or lesser importance depending on local, regional and national circumstances. Rural tourism is not an accidental or temporary growth phenomenon. Although the travel trade is in some senses a 'fashion' industry, subject to short term trends, the forces behind the growth of rural tourism are more long term in nature. These forces are partly connected to long term changes in the travel market, partly to improvements in transport and communications and partly to the efforts of public agencies charged with assisting rural change. In total, 14 key factors can be isolated which have been responsible for rural tourism growth in the past and which will continue that growth into the future.

The post-war period has seen universal increase in free or assisted education available to the populations of the developed world. This has included longer periods of school-based education, more higher education, the spread of adult and continuing education and the growth of non-formalised education, via radio, television and other media. Research shows that increasing levels of education correlate with increased interest in outdoor recreation, eco-tourism, and special interest holidays. A growing interest in heritage. Over the last 20 years there has been a boom in the level of interest in heritage both man-made and natural. This reflects many factors: a fear of the future, a fear of rootlessness, better education, time to explore, and, not least, better heritage presentation. Increases in leisure time, coupled with higher levels of disposable income, are important factors in developing tourism generally. One specific aspect of this equation is important for rural tourism. This is the growth of the short break, and the second or third holiday market.

The European Community's 1985, Europeans on Holiday indicated that, of those taking holidays, over one-third now take two or more holiday trips involving overnight stays away from home each year. This is important because while a "traditional" resort-based holiday may still account for main holidays, rural special interest holidays can be tried for the second, often shorter, holiday without too much risk. Transport and communications have improved so rapidly and universally in the post-war period that remoteness-in time and cost-is now no longer a major problem for rural areas. This ease of movement owes itself in part to technological changes-jet aircraft, high speed trains, motorways, and roll-on roll-off ferries, automatic telephone systems and fax machines. It has been influenced by better and more widespread money handling facilities, chief of which has been the internationally acceptable credit card.

There have also been key attitudinal changes on behalf of both the travel trade and their clients. Distance and remoteness have become selling points, rather than barriers. Health consciousness has grown and is growing steadily and in the concept of healthy living, active recreation plays an important part. Exercise and sport play central roles in healthy living strategies. Rural areas are well placed to provide outdoor recreation of all kinds from walking to cycling, orienteering, skiing and climbing. The countryside is assumed to be healthy, with overtones of fresh air and bucolic well-being. In contrast, resort holidays based on the sun/sea/sand formula have been found to offer serious health risks.

Medical researchers in Australasia, America and Scandinavia have pinpointed sunbathing as being responsible for higher levels of skin disease, ranging from premature wrinkling to deadly skin cancers. While this problem is still only fully appreciated in the southern hemisphere, it seems very likely that knowledge of the risks posed by sun-belt holidays will grow. Better outdoor clothing has helped rural holidays in both a practical and a fashion sense. High performance fabrics enable wearers to stay warm and dry in adverse weather, allowing tourists to enjoy wet weather and out-of-season conditions. Contemporary outdoor clothing is now extremely fashionable, and available in a wide range of colours and styles. Outdoor recreation equipment has also been much improved and many items, such as the mountain bike, the wind surfer and the 4-wheel drive utility vehicle, have achieved cult fashion status.

A growing interest in speciality food is widely evident, be it wild rice from North America, non-pasturized cheeses from France, cholesterol-free, non-farmed salmon and deer from Scandinavia, or organic produce from the Alps. Considerable space in the press is devoted to speciality foods and food preparation. Rural holidays have been able to capitalise on this trend because the countryside is the source of quality non-processed foods. Green issues have risen high on most political agendas over the last ten years. This interest has been seized upon by the marketeers of many consumer products, including holiday tour operators.

Rural holidays, although not necessarily environmentally friendly, can capitalise on the wholesomeness which the countryside is felt to exude. Authenticity is a quality which is increasingly prized. In a world of video and television entertainment, factory produced goods, and suburban anonymity, the authenticity of the countryside, and the personal touch provided by small scale communities and accommodation units is extremely valuable. An English Tourist Board, motives for taking rural holidays, conducted in 1987, placed this point second only to scenery as a reason for staying in the countryside. This is hardly surprising given the high levels of mental stress experienced by many workers. A 1986 survey of the German holiday market found that 'to switch off, relax' was the number one aim of those taking holidays: this aim was given by 66 per cent of respondents. 47 per cent wished to experience nature, and 32 per cent sought cleaner air and an unpolluted environment. Ageing but active populations are becoming the norm across the OECD countries.

Early retirement is now commonplace, as are active 70-year-olds. In 1971 83 per cent of British males aged 60-64 were still working in full time jobs. By 1995 it is expected that only 55 per cent of men in that age group will remain in full time work. Effective occupational pensions allow this active but ageing population to travel widely: many choose rural holidays for health reasons and to discover new non-urban experiences. The many facets of rural tourism are specially placed to fulfil the needs of this growth market. Individualism is also a growth market, rejecting the mass activities of the past. The growth of individualism has been noted and acted upon by the car manufacturers, by clothing manufacturers, and by many other purveyors of consumer goods. Rural tourism, because of the fragmented and small scale nature of the enterprises involved, is especially capable of exploiting this market trend, although high quality selling and hospitality skills are needed.

The rural agencies, numerous in most countries, have been quick to express an interest in rural tourism and to offer aid and advice. These agencies include those connected with agriculture, with nature conservation, with community welfare, with the arts and crafts, with National Parks, with economic development, transport—the list is almost endless. Although the agencies rarely co-ordinate their activities, and are rarely organisations with any experience of tourism, they have assisted many collective individual enterprises.

The World Tourism Organization estimated the special interest market to be about 3 per cent of the total domestic and international market in 1985. In 1989, the U.S. travel 22 agents revealed that special interest holidays comprised 15 per cent of all bookings. Repeat bookings accounted for one-third of the clients surveyed. German statistics claim that 20 per cent of main holidays are now in the special interest category. Therefore, if levels of income and educational attainment continue to rise across the OECD countries, the market for rural tourism should also grow.

Aside from the bird-watching and hunting/fishing markets, which have a wider appeal across the whole socio-economic spectrum in many countries, rural tourism is generally supported by an up-market clientele. The American state of Wyoming estimates that wildlife tourism is worth over $ 1 billion annually within its borders. Britain's Countryside Commission estimated that visitors to the countryside spent £ 3 000 million in 1986: of this figure £ 1 100 million came from those spending at least one night in the countryside, and the remainder came from day trips. These are gross figures; the net figures after deduction of goods bought in to service tourism, when tax has been paid, etc., would be much lower, but, equally, they make no allowance for the multiplier effect of tourism spending.

Clearly, rural tourism, while still only a minority tourism market, is already making a valuable contribution to rural economies. Its contribution can be expressed not only in financial terms, but also in terms of jobs, contributions towards funding conservation, encouragement to the adoption of new working practices, and the injection of a new vitality into sometimes weakened economies. In total, tourism promises potential benefits to rural development. Pluriactivity can be a further useful by-product of tourism in the countryside. Pluriactivity is the term used when an individual or family carries out more than one type of job to maintain their income. A part-time farmer could also offer accommodation, assist the local administration in service tasks and act as a ski-instructor.

Sea fishermen may take tourist parties on angling trips, on whale watching expeditions off the coast of Canada and the United States, or on bird-watching excursions off the coast of Ireland or Scotland. Pluriactivity guards against recession in any one sector. It is especially important in the rural context because of the cultural importance of the family as a unit in many traditional societies. Visitor information services can be provided by existing outlets, such as shops, thus increasing income flows if payment is made for acting as information outlets. Services can also benefit by the additional customers which visitors provide. The high levels of public transport in rural Austria and Switzerland are in part due to the support they receive from holiday-makers.

Many studies have shown that farm incomes can be bolstered by rural tourism, through accommodation enterprises of all kinds, by developing open farms and other attractions, by increased sales of farm produce, and by increasing female activity rates through additional off-farm employment. There are widespread variations in the levels of farmer participation in rural tourism throughout the OECD countries, varying by region, farm size, age of farmer and other factors. Forestry is an important activity in many upland and climatically marginal regions. Forest regions have suffered serious socio-economic problems in recent years, partly because of the mechanisation of tree felling and processing, and partly because of falling prices following reduced timber demand.

Rural tourism can assist forestry by diversifying income sources for forest communities if the special qualities of the forest environment for recreational use are realised and developed. Landscape conservation has become an increasingly important form of heritage protection. Although this dates back to the designation of America's Yellowstone National Park in 1872, the national park movement is still progressing and most countries now have a wide range of lesser designations covering many types of landscape. Landscape is of crucial importance to rural tourism but, equally, visitor use is vital to the landscape conservation industry.

Rural tourism can assist these smaller settlements to survive, because smaller places have a special attraction for visitors. Careful management of this process is, however, required. Rural arts and crafts have a special place in the cultural heritage of regions and nations. Many commentators have noted that tourism can assist arts and crafts, both by recognising their importance, and by purchasing craft products. Income flows from these activities are well documented. Support between the arts and tourism can be a two-way process. Many communities now use arts and crafts festivals as a marketing mechanism to encourage visitors to come to their areas.

Cultural provision has always been restricted in rural areas. The lack of major facilities such as theatre, opera, music and galleries has been one of the many factors encouraging rural depopulation. Nature conservation, like landscape conservation, is a stated goal of most modern governments. It is, however, an expensive process. Rural tourism can valorise nature conservation in a monetary sense. Many historic properties now charge for admission in order to maintain their fabrics and surrounding gardens and parklands. Secondly, there are important buildings from the past which have become redundant. Churches have lost their congregations, castles have lost their wars, farm buildings have become too small for modern equipment, railway stations have lost their trains, and canal warehouses no longer have barge traffic.

The tourist industry can usually use these redundant buildings profitably and imaginatively: they can become attractions in their own right. Environmental improvements such as village paving and traffic regulation schemes, sewage and litter disposal can be assisted by tourism revenues and political pressures from tourism authorities. These help develop pride of place, important in retaining existing population and businesses, and in attracting new enterprises and families. Small fishing communities are suffering badly from dwindling fish stocks, quota restrictions and international bans on some activities. A number of these communities can successfully diversify into sports fishing, bird and seal watching, and coastal sightseeing.

Some environmental groups claim that potential revenue from whale and dolphin watching could exceed revenue from catching whales for meat. The role of women within the rural community was, in the past, a restricted one. Farming, forestry and mining were very much male occupations. Alternative jobs for women were few. Women were rarely involved in local politics. The widespread emancipation of women, coupled with the possibilities which rural tourism offers, have together done much in many areas to release the under-utilised talents and energies of the female half of the population.

Many studies have highlighted the threats which tourism has already brought to the environment. Intensive skiing has destroyed vegetation and encouraged land-slips; climbing erodes rock faces, and, with modern equipment, destroys their natural condition; walking and riding wears out paths in heavily used areas; noise and litter drive out and injure wild creatures; existing farming practices are upset by fire, dogs and competition for labour. The peace, quiet and authentic nature of the countryside can be seriously compromised. All these issues can be tackled to some extent by the skilled management of the countryside; management of the order required is as yet rarely available. Many local farmers and businesses do not decide to enter the tourism market when opportunities present themselves.

In some respects incomers can provide a valuable transfusion of contacts, capital and skill. But they can also present problems. They may be insensitive to local tradition, cultures, working practices and architectural styles. They may use non-local suppliers for goods and services. They may repatriate their profits and capital gains out of the area. They have little loyalty to their new base of operations and often leave when trading conditions deteriorate. Less tangibly, but equally important, they set up tensions between locals and incomers, and do little to change the dependency culture common to many rural places.

Traffic congestion-usually road traffic, but in some cases sea and air traffic-can be a major problem if an area is successful in attracting tourists. Narrow roads can easily be choked by traffic both inside and outside settlements, parking becomes an issue, non-tourism business can suffer and, in extreme cases, emergency services cannot make urgent calls. The attractiveness of the area as a destination can decline, taking it down-market. There can be side effects on landscape and nature conservation. Traffic management techniques and better use of public transport can help, but the funds and skills necessary are not usually available. The issues of planning, local control, public participation and partnership bring together many of the points covered so far in this part.

In an ideal world, local people and businesses would control tourism development in such a way that the problems discussed earlier would be minimised and benefits maximised. Planning controls would ensure a carefully worked out balance of development between tourism-related and other land uses. Different types of tourism activity would be zoned into the regions best suited for those types of development. Employers and employees would undertake regular training courses to learn the skills of marketing, hospitality, interpretation and tourism planning.

The community would feel that it had "ownership" of its industry in a broad sense. As a result the visitor would feel a genuine sense of welcome from the host population. But real world is rarely ideal. The financial power of the incoming entrepreneur, and the power of skilled outsiders including tour operators and tourist board officials, means that local control is seldom achieved. When locals do have power, they often do not have the foresight, experience or skills necessary.

In some areas local politicians resent and resist development. In others, the promise of new jobs and income can be too great a temptation, leading to the acceptance of damaging schemes. In most cases tourism management is not practised because of cost and political implications. There have, however, been many experiments in introducing local participation into rural tourism development programmes. Most are so recent that evaluation is not yet complete. Canada has pioneered the most widespread attempts at community participation in rural tourism planning.

The OECD Rural Development Programme's typology for rural areas differentiates between remote areas, intermediate areas and economically integrated areas. The typology forms a useful additional set of criteria to consider when assessing conditions for the growth of tourism activities. The economically integrated areas are usually close to large cities, offering considerable leisure market potential. Closeness to cities may, however, result in a higher level of day-visit recreational use, which is less valuable in financial terms than overnight stays.

Remote areas are, by definition, more likely to attract guests who stay overnight, leading to greater net revenue potential per visitor. If teamed with mountain or lake scenery, remoteness-if not too daunting—can be a considerable attraction. But remoteness without fine scenery generally means that there will be little likelihood of rural tourism development. The OECD Rural Development Programme typology can also be a valuable indicator when considering the likelihood of local people taking up new initiatives such as tourism. Peripheral areas may try new enterprises because of a high 'desperation factor', brought about by poverty and decline.

Economically integrated areas may, paradoxically, also be keen to try new enterprises-not because of desperation, but because of spare capital and the large potential markets nearby. It is in the intermediate areas that it can be most difficult to change attitudes and develop new tourism businesses. Farmers are critical in maintaining both the basic rural economy and the scenery on which rural tourism depends. Yet farmers have responded unevenly and often only slowly to the opportunities available through tourism. Some farmers are strongly anti-tourist, resenting visitors on their territory, especially where footpaths or riding trails cross their land. Many would prefer better prices for farm produce rather than incentives to move into the visitor industry. When farmers do diversify into tourism, they often do so together with other farmers, rather than with local communities, and thus potential co-operative benefits are lost.

At the root of many of the problems encountered in involving farmers in tourism is a basic question of knowledge and training. A hotelier would be incapable of working in the farming industry without a lengthy period of training, yet farmers (or their wives) are expected to diversify into providing visitor services of all kinds with little or no training. Training deficiences are not confined to agriculturalists. Many business people and employees working in rural tourism have little or no training in the many skills required for this complex and competitive industry.

Lack of training is one of the reasons why some studies have noted a high incidence of business failures in the rural tourism field. Failure to group and to set up co-operative ventures is a common but not universal problem. Because rural tourism enterprises are small, co-operation with other businesses can bring major savings in marketing and training and in the purchase of supplies. Co-operative groupings can also negotiate with government bodies to fund infrastructural improvements, and can work with the major players in the international tourism market, the tour operators. Interest and success in co-operative ventures owes much to the history and experience of the regions concerned. Where there is a tradition of co-operation, usually in farming, tourism co-operatives seem to work.

The aim of any tourism strategy should be to assist the balanced development of an area, not to convert it into a resort complex dependent solely on the travel trade. The expansion of modern tourism has not been the product of planning but of a largely free market. Tourism is a consumer industry: central planning in this area has had an uneven record. Many small businesses and numerous public sector organisations are involved in rural tourism. The successful promotion of development and management planning requires more than usually informed, skilled and dedicated leadership. This is an intangible factor, but one of great importance. It can help persuade business interests to be kinder to the environment; it can steer difficult government institutions to more pragmatic interpretations of their roles; it can influence the doubting farmer; it can bring new ideas to communities of no hope.

Leadership can be provided by enlightened individuals from the private sector, by politicians, by public sector agencies, by local/regional administrations and administrators, by tourist boards, and by powerful land owners; what is important is that there be leadership, that it be carefully fostered not feared, and that it be fostered in depth, so that when one individual or agency fails, the whole momentum of development is not lost. A number of North American educational institutions provide short courses in leadership for rural politicians and administrators.

In almost all business sectors research and development involves a partnership between the public and private sectors. The need for partnership is very important if rural tourism and its development are to succeed. Rural areas and enterprises have a history of public sector intervention. Rural tourism is growing in a fragmented and ad hoc way:

public sector partnerships can co-ordinate activities. Since many of rural tourism's activities take place in the public domain, careful research into environmental and visitor management is necessary to maintain established community goals such as landscape, nature and heritage protection during the re-structuring of the rural economy away from primary production towards a greater reliance on the service sector.

Market information studies for rural tourism are few, and this is a major problem in determining the size, characteristics and requirements of the market. Without this information, it is difficult to plan infrastructure investment, to provide effective business training, to encourage suitable numbers and types of new entrants into rural tourism provision and, of course, to develop marketing campaigns. Market information studies need to cover market groups already taking rural holidays, and those who do not. For both groups, basic positioning information should include age/family size/occupational characteristics/area of origin/holiday patterns during current year and previous years/ perceived requirements of holidays/likely accommodation type/likely method of travel/method of choosing holidays/knowledge and perception of specified "control" areas.

For those not taking rural holidays, additional questions should cover reasons why alternatives were taken, perception of specific types of rural holiday, perception of specific rural areas, and likely future trends in holiday choice. For those taking rural holidays, additional questions should review propensity to take holidays in various types of rural area, repeat visit likelihood, major strengths and weaknesses of previous rural holidays, the importance of various types of infrastructure, and likely future trends in holiday choice. The development of a standard way of obtaining and analysing this market information would assist rural groups with limited skills and resources, and also enable inter-regional and international comparisons to be made.

3

Joint Marketing Opportunities

Co-operation and partnerships are increasingly being used in the tourism sector to achieve impressive business and community goals. What is surprising is that these partnerships are forming in a sector that has traditionally been viewed as fragmented. More surprising is that the tourism sector has begun venturing beyond its own sector to form partnerships.

Sharing the experience of partnership is important to the further development of the sector and of the communities that support, or are looking to support, a vibrant, dynamic tourism sector. The underlying impetus to partner, or the key motivator to co-operate, is that all partners, whether from the private or the public sector, will benefit from the alignment of resources and objectives.

Partnerships in fact form for a variety of reasons. Partnerships can be formed to create new products or services, to achieve higher levels of efficiency or economies of scale, to open markets that were previously inaccessible or to simply pool resources—financial and/or human. Following are typical partnership objectives:

— *Products*

- — Enhance and preserve resources
- — Set quality standards
- — Develop attractions, theme parks and accommodation
- — Provide technical support for innovative product development programs
- — Contribute to the economic wealth of the community
- — Create sustainable development of tourism sector
- — Overcome trade and investment barriers
- — Protect consumers
- — Deal with competition

— *Research and Technology*

- — Provide research and measurement methodologies
- — Implement Tourism Satellite Accounts
- — Enhance technological innovation and application

— *Human Resources*

- — Set service and quality standards
- — Provide training and education programs
- — Improve productivity and innovation

— *Marketing and Sales*

- — Improve destination image
- — Improve marketing efficiency
- — Improve market coverage and reach

— Provide support for electronic marketing and distribution, including Internet

— Provide support for participation at trade shows

— Harness power of co-opmarketing programmes

— Access new markets

— *Infrastructure*

— Improve roads, transport infrastructure and basic services

— Provide impetus for intermodal transportation

— Improve public health and sanitation

— Improve safety and security

— Enhance telecommunications system

— *Financing*

— Obtain investment and funding

— Leverage public investment

— Obtain start-up financing

— Improve yield

As well, partnerships can go by various names and structures and be formed with the private sector, with the public sector or between the private and the public sectors. The following definitions of the types of partnerships that can be formed were adapted from the *Developing Business Opportunities Through Partnering* completed by the Canadian Tourism Commission in 1995.

— *Consortium* - a pooling of resources to gain a benefit that they could not afford on their own .

— *Joint venture* - a co-operative project (typically bringing different skills/resources) pursue an opportunity. The initiative is often given a corporate entity' of its own.

— *Strategic alliance* - generally a longer-term agreement to achieve common objectives. May involve both smaller and larger organizations with complementary resources or expertise. Termed 'strategic' because the objectives are of critical importance to the overall business/market development strategy of the partners.

— *Co-operative marketing* - an agreement to market partners' products or services through joint promotion. Often relates to maximizing the potential of distribution networks of various partners and gaining familiarity with target markets through an 'in-market' partner.

— *Value-chain relationship* - where organizations in different industries with unique but complementary skills link their capabilities to create value. The relationship is very tightly knit, with joint or overlapping activities occurring in many areas.

— *Organization network* - a multi-organization alliance in which member businesses collaborate to meet common objectives.

— *Outsourcing* - contracting of non-core services to third-party providers.

The key to any successful partnership, however, is the recognition that the partnership is a business relationship wherein the partners share the risks, rewards and responsibility for the success or failure of the initiative.

This is not to say that the partners want or seek the same benefits. For the public sector, a partnership with the private sector can bring:

- Access to new sources of capital;
- Accelerated development of infrastructure assets;
- Risk sharing opportunities;
- Maintenance or improvement of service levels;
- Access to skills in planning, management and service delivery;
- Realization of the value of under-utilized assets; and
- Greater value from economic development opportunities.

On the other hand, for the private sector, partnerships can bring:

- Access to new markets that they would be unable to develop on their own;
- Ability to improve skill levels and performance;
- Expansion of products or services beyond current capability;
- Enhancement of credibility through association; and
- The opportunity to earn a return commensurate with the risks and merits of the venture.

The increasing interest in the importance of partnerships in the tourism sector prompted the World Tourism Organization Business Council (WTOBC) to consider building upon an already extensive study, *Public-Private Sector Co-operation*, published in 2000. The WTOBC contacted the Canadian Tourism Commission, which, since the mid-1990s, has developed strong competence in partnership operations by partnering with both the public and private sectors in all its program undertakings. In 1995, the CTC published *Developing Business Opportunities Through*

Partnering, prepared by KPMG, which has become a benchmark publication within the Canadian tourism sector. As a result of this past experience, KPMG was engaged by the WTOBC and CTC to undertake the implementation of the study.

Creating and Maintaining Partnerships

As the WTO recognized in the 2000 report, two key forces, globalization and technology, are transforming the tourism sector into a dynamic economic force that has never been possible before. The industry is in transition. Sector customers, both business and leisure travellers, have become more sophisticated and are looking for customized experiences.

In response, distribution networks are creating flexible bundles of travel experiences, and destinations are forming wider networks of alliances to deliver a credible, exciting guest experience. Where previously segments of the tourism sector had clear-cut boundaries, now key players - airlines, hotels, attractions and tour operators for example - have discovered that they must get together to market, book and sell the destination in order to get their fair share of a growing market segment. Key challenges are still facing the sector. Much work still needs to be accomplished in order for the sector to capitalize on technology to create sustainable relationships with selected customer segments. In order to do this we need to manage the integrity of the value chain, generate innovative and sustainable business practices, and convince the financial markets to invest.

The tourism sector, perhaps because it encompasses so many sectors of the economy, is susceptible to fragmentation. Travellers are becoming more sophisticated and wanting customized experiences, creating tendencies for the sector to develop micro-segments, niche brands and customized products - all valid strategies. Unfortunately, these same strategies can also build barriers to protect narrow regional identity or business interests that in a globalized world may not allow sufficient leverage of resources. But building partnerships is about trying to find where the commonalities lie, breaking down the barriers in order to leverage what each can bring to the table.

The tourism sector presents any number of opportunities to partner. It is characterized by a burgeoning set of small and medium sized businesses that have the entrepreneurship and flexibility to take advantage of new opportunities. On a global scale, the public sector is looking for new ways to partner with the private sector to strategically develop and market tourism and to leverage available assets for growth.

The destination represents a bundle of experiences that all together create a competitive cluster. The greater number and range of things to see and do, the better the destination is able to sustain visitation in fragile times. But it's individual businesses that make up the 'destination', and it's not just those that provide the attractions and activities, the things to see and do, that are important. The value chain in the tourism sector begins outside the destination, where the idea to travel is first presented and converted into the decision to travel. The opportunity to partner resides in the myriad of links in the value chain.

It's also important to note that the opportunity to partner is not just with organizations that are traditionally viewed as being within the tourism sector. Organizations are beginning to think creatively about opportunities to partner with non-traditional sectors.

Partnerships can then take a variety of forms and involve any number of partners - indeed, and as the WTOBC 2000 study noted, no 'correct' formula or model is available to follow. The formation of partnerships depends on the circumstances, economic, organizational, cultural, and structural capability of the private or the public sector to participate, and the willingness of the potential partners to assume the additional responsibility that the partnership entails.

Each partner brings unique assets and capabilities to the partnership. For its part, the public sector may be able to offer assets that are under utilized or 'soft assets,' such as reputation or an existing customer base. Given the capacity of the public sector to be able to borrow at an effective rate, the public sector can also bring a lower cost for financing capability. On the other hand, the private sector can often bring a business focus and may also be able to bring international operational and marketing experience. In some instances the private sector can also bring capital. However, whether they are from the private or the public sector, the key motivator to co-operate is that all partners will benefit from the alignment of resources and objectives.

Public-private partnerships have become popular vehicles for creating investment in tourism development. But when does it make sense for the public and the private sectors to partner? The public sector will likely have a higher propensity to invest when the dispersion of benefits to the public is high and the return on investment is stretched over a long period of time. In other words, the public sector is more likely to solely own and operate assets such as such as convention centres, museums and large destination at tractors. These assets require intensive and ongoing capital investment, but the payback to the public is substantial in terms of quality of life and the economic impact of the incremental inflow of high-value visitors to the city.

If the public sector is looking to partner, generally it will be in those areas where the dispersion of benefits to the public is high, but the payback to the private sector is within a reasonable amount of time. As the WTOBC 2000 report indicated, the main area for public-private sector co-operation in the tourism sector has been in marketing and promotion. Marketing, particularly in international markets, is inherently expensive and partnerships offer the opportunity to pool limited resources. Other common areas for public-private co-operation are product and infrastructure development; education and training, and; financing and investment.

Public-private partnerships are becoming very popular, but they should not be viewed as a cure-all for public and private sector challenges, such as limited development capital, limited operating funds and inefficient cost structures. Public private partnerships can bring about significant benefits, but they are difficult to achieve and may not be achievable in all circumstances. As demonstrated by the private sector experience in Cape Town's townships, the private sector may need to take the lead at least initially in the development initiative. And, of course, sometimes it just makes more sense for the private sector to create partnerships with each other to ensure competitiveness.

The tourism sector is under great pressure. The financial sector tends to see parts of the tourism sector as being relatively traditional, slow to change and prey to shocks. That the tourism sector consists mainly of small and medium sized enterprises—even micro-enterprises—is part of the tourism reality. Small though many of its members may be, the tourism sector has proven that it can be resilient and creative in response to changing environments. Now, more than ever, if they are to be successful, tourism operations must master partnering to sustain and grow this important sector.

A partnership begins with a lot of preparation, and much of the preparation involves establishing the relationship. It is here that a degree of leadership needs to be present. In other words, the 'soft skills' of communication, negotiation and relationship building prove time and again to be paramount. As the partnership matures and the partners begin to trust one another, initiatives such as sharing databases can take place. If the Ontario Tourism Marketing Partnership Corporation had originally put this requirement on the table the partners would have likely walked away from the process.

The process also requires vision and energy. The creation of a partnership is easier when the idea is compelling, and the benefits are easily seen. But this may not always be the case. Not surprisingly then, many partnerships in the formative stages benefit from the presence of a champion that provides vision, energy and enthusiasm. For example, the Canadian Academy of Travel and Tourism offers a substantial hospitality program through the secondary school system in Canada. But while the benefits are easily seen and acted upon by the school system, the private sector has been slow to contribute resources. The initiative has relied extensively on the project champion to spend the time communicating with and getting buy-in from the tourism sector.

On the same theme, the Canadian Sport Tourism Alliance has been challenged to bridge the gap between two non-traditional partners: sport and tourism. Sport tourism is a relatively new market segment and, as such, the benefits and rewards are not always obvious to potential partners. The initiative has relied on the project champion to spend the extra time, energy and effort to educate prospective partners about the benefits of the partnership.

And finally, in Istanbul, one entrepreneur took a dilapidated and neglected, but historically important, district and turned it into a vibrant and alive tourism district. His energy, passion and vision were needed to overcome the initial resistance of the financial community and the municipal government. But whether there is a project partner or a core team, to be successful the project requires all of the key stakeholders to be at the table and committed to the achievement of the stated objectives.

The project must be financially sound. The private sector will always want to earn a return commensurate with the risk undertaken. In the case of public-private partnerships, the public sector must constantly view the economics of the project from the private sector's perspective. The public sector must ask whether the risk the private sector is expected to shoulder is commensurate with the reward.

For example, in contracting out the concession services of Yosemite National Park to Delaware North Company, the Government of the United Sates has downloaded operating and financial risk onto the private sector. Under the agreement, the private sector had assumed significant risk in terms of environmental cleanup and asset regeneration, which was accounted for in the feasibility assessment. Unfortunately the company was also exposed to unforeseen forces of nature that resulted in the closure of revenue earning assets for a period of time. These incidences have forced the partners to sit down together, to re-evaluate and work towards a mutually beneficial solution.

In forming new partnerships, whether it be for a product or a marketing alliance, organizations are requiring partners to invest capital and commit to staying in the partnership for a stated length of time. In other words, they are requiring partners to recognize the risk upfront so that they remain committed to achieving the rewards further down the road. Without this upfront commitment, the partnership would not be viewed as a business relationship where each partner is responsible for the success or failure of the initiative. The upfront commitment may not necessarily be money. In the case of the Kapawi Eco-lodge in Ecuador, the private sector put up the capital, but the Achuar indigenous community put up the land and other benefits. Both parties, however, committed to remain in the partnership for 15 years. The key success factors to managing a partnership are given below:

Clearly articulated, transparent goals and objectives

Once defined, the vision of the partnership typically stays constant but the activities that surround meeting the objectives of the partnership can and often do change to meet new market conditions. As a result, the responsibilities and activities of each of the partners need to be well defined upfront in the partnership agreement. The agreement can then function as the mechanism that places decisions and disputes squarely in the business arena and eliminates political or other extraneous issues.

The agreement can also be one of the mechanisms that provide assurance to the partners that they are doing the right things, especially in situations where the partnership is relatively new and both partners need time to work out the logistics of the partnerships. For example, the partnership between the Delaware North Company and the

U.S. National Parks Service has been tightly structured and characterized by legal documents and operating agreements. This has proved useful for both partners as they search for new and better ways to improve the services at Yosemite National Park. The contract provides a solid base of understanding from which both partners can move forward.

The types of contracts such as the one signed by Delaware North often take a long time to negotiate and are hard to modify once implemented. This is fine as long as the partnership continues as first envisaged. As the partnership matures, however, the scope of services may change or unforeseen circumstances may arise. Provisions should be in the agreement that allow for organizational flexibility and change.

The Canadian Sport Tourism Alliance found that the agreement with the Canadian Tourism Commission was flexible enough to allow adjustment and this has enabled the Alliance to adapt and be successful in a changing environment. This flexibility became important in the development process of one of its tools, which took far more time, energy and resources than had been originally envisioned.

And yet it was also the lack of a formal agreement with another one of the major partners that created some concern for the Canadian Sport Tourism Alliance. While the issue was subsequently resolved, the situation could have been avoided with the establishment of an agreement that clearly articulated the objectives of the partnership and the responsibility and commitments of each of the partners.

Open and frequent communication

To capitalize on the synergies created during the formation

of the partnership, the operation and organizational structure of the partnership must build and maintain a close, cohesive cooperative culture. Involving individuals in a meaningful way by asking them for input and allowing dissent builds trust and candour, but it also communicates respect for individuals, the work they have done, and the initiatives they have put in place.

Frequent communication was essential because it allowed ideas to be floated or concerns to be heard before they become a major issue. Membership-based organizations, such as Spa Canada and MeetingPlace Wonderful Copenhagen, felt they needed to maintain close dialogue with all their members so that the partnership remained relevant. Both formal and informal meetings needed to be held regularly, reminding us that one-on- one, private conversations are also extremely important. The timing and efficiency of the communication is also imperative to sustain commitment to the overall vision and goals of the partnership over time, particularly if the partnership is focused on a specific goal with a finite end.

The Tourism Olympic Forum in Sydney was a partnership formed to ensure that key stakeholders were able to leverage the once-in-a-lifetime opportunity of holding the Olympic and Paralympic games to its fullest extent. Well-run meetings were held regularly and frequently as the Forum spoke to community groups, the tourism sector and their associations and other government departments to give updates on the Olympic initiatives and give advice on how to leverage the opportunity. Participants were able to come, get the key points, leave and report to their members.

The partnership needs to be realistic about the amount of information that people can absorb - as well as prepared to share - and that the partnership needs to communicate through a variety of media to suit the needs of the partners. Timing of communication to gain realistic outcomes is key. And finally, try to capture everything on paper. By capturing key decisions and the reasons surrounding the final outcome allows for historical understanding of why final decisions are made.

Build capability through continuous learning

Partnerships can provide insight into the strengths and weaknesses of the individual partners. They can be powerful platforms for continuous improvement as the partnership moves to address any performance gaps. Often the exclusive domain of large businesses, partnerships can offer the small and medium size enterprises in-house training and a cohesive brand delivery mechanism. This certainly is one of the key success factors for the Arts in the Wild Product Alliance formed by the Ontario Tourism Marketing Partnership Corporation in Canada. It is also a key factor in the success of the Sustainable Tourism Enterprise Program in the Caribbean spearheaded by Organization of American States (OAS) and the United States Agency for International Development (USAID). The result of an extensive set of partnerships, the program provided the small tourism sector with:

— A comprehensive set of management and operational toolk its easily accessible on line or at walk-in resource centres;

— Basic computer training delivered through one-on-one training sessions;

— One-on-one coaching and training to international standards in the management and operation of hotel properties; and

— A brand system under the umbrella brand 'Caribbean Experiences' supported by associated standards and a rating system.

Without the partnerships formed, the small Caribbean tourism enterprises would have been hard pressed to participate in such programs.

Indicators and measurement

Key performance measures must be built into the review process in order to allow partners to determine if the value received was worth the effort. The process by which the performance of the partnership is monitored can be both formal and informal and measure quantitative and qualitative aspects of the initiative. Whatever the measures are, the measurements serve to remind the partners of the original vision of the partnership, why the partners joined and what the benefits are. If the key performance measures do not align with partner needs, then an imbalance can arise over the perception of risk and reward. For example, MeetingPlace Wonderful Copenhagen, a destination marketing initiative formed to market Copenhagen to the meeting and incentive travel market, is currently undergoing a re-examination of its key performance measures to more accurately reflect the concerns of its largest stakeholders.

Another benefit of keeping and recording data is that it allows the small and medium sized enterprises to intelligently respond to new investors whether they be from the public or the private sector. For example the Geographic Information System (GIS) that forms the basis of the Open Africa marketing database allows for detailed data collection. Once compiled, the route stakeholders can report on who is offering what product, where and how many are employed. With this information, the route stakeholders can better leverage their efforts by, for example, providing interested investors with detailed and accurate statistics and data.

Adequate resourcing

Failure to identify and empower a champion all too frequently contributes to unsuccessful partnerships because this role requires substantial time, effort and skill. But in the tourism sector, where human and financial resources are often stretched, we can rely too heavily on the project champion. If the organization could have someone to deal with the operation of the partnership and another to create marketing and fundraising campaigns, the organization would be further along. By not staffing and financing the operations of the partnership adequately, in effect relying too heavily on one person, the risk is that the partnership will be unable to meet some or all of its goals.

To meet this risk, the Ontario Tourism Marketing Partnership Corporation provided a consultant/facilitator to support the partnership in the early years. They found that when the partners of the alliance get together, they bond and develop trust; but as they go back to their businesses, they get caught up in the day-to-day, time goes by and the commitment gets fainter. The job of the facilitator is to ensure that the partners maintain the original vision by staying in constant contact and trouble shooting when necessary.

Planning and risk management

The tourism sector is subject to economic, social and political upheavals - a situation unlikely to change. The onus is on the sector to think about and plan for times of crisis. For its part, the Nepal Tourism Board, a newly formed public-private partnership, is currently in the process of formulating a crisis plan to deal with external shocks, just as large companies have a risk management plan in place to deal with large, negative events. But how can the tourism sector remain agile? Partnerships must be proactive instead of reactive by being brutally honest about capabilities and by assessing risk continuously. Those companies that can withstand the pressure are those that assess the risks and opportunities and create alternative action plans.

For example, the Nepal Tourism Board's original mandate was extensive, but in the time of crisis that followed its initiation, many of the strategies and actions that were planned could not be implemented. Therefore, Nepal turned to the potential of collaborative marketing and found that where one country could not do it alone, a consortium of countries could potentially leverage their marketing budgets and product experiences to attract more visitors to the region.

Funds for marketing initiatives.

The following issues should be considered when inviting new partners into the partnership. The partnership requires:

— A mechanism to evaluate the quality of the new product, or new marketing initiative, especially if the older partners have gained substantial market share;

— A mechanism to raise the quality of the product through product development initiatives and education before new product is allowed to enter the partnership; varying degrees of export readiness can increase the risk of the partnership losing its credibility in the marketplace;

— Assurance that once the partnership expands, all partners will still be aligned to the original goals and not diluting the efforts of the original partners;

— A communications plan so that the customer understands the linkages to the new product and accepts the relevance of the new packages; and

— A strategic review that assesses the relevancy of the partnership to ensure that the partnership does not exist simply for the sake of continuing.

The requirements for increasing the level and frequency of communications in order to ensure all stakeholders are aligned and working towards the same goals often places great strain on the partnership's resources. New ideas and objectives add volatility. Working with a large number of partners of varying marketing readiness and financial capability requires extraordinary skill and capabilities.

With this, has come other benefits such as the requirement to preserve the region's cultural and heritage resources in order to develop the new product. Indeed, the community benefits in the following ways from a healthy partnership:

— Image and destination enhancement;

— Widened market reach and coverage;

— Preservation of cultural and heritage resources;

— Education, training and development of work-place skill sets (such as, sales, service, quality, leadership);

— Introduction of quality standards;

— Improvement of roads, transport infrastructure and basic services;

— Improvement of public health, sanitation, safety and security;

— Reduction of trade and investment barriers and leveraged public investment; and

— Greater competitiveness.

Whether involved formally in the partnership or not, to leverage the benefits, the community has a responsibility to implement consistent policies and co-ordination in the field to ensure that the 'occasional ambassadors,' such as the police, taxi drivers, retailers, public transport drivers, and municipal workers are aware of the initiative and playing a co-ordinated, positive role.

A smart partnership will nurture the community to garner the needed support, communicating the spin-off benefits and the mutually beneficial policies and activities that could help all parties. For example, the partnership that has formed to extend the tourism product in Crete has just begun to address the fact that much of Crete's tourist product closes in the winter, a rhythm of life that the local population may be unwilling to break. But if other operators see that product remains open in the winter and more visitors are coming, operators may stay open, giving Crete a competitive critical mass of available product in the' off season.'

By involving the broader community, the tourism sector remains dynamic, and consolidates the destination's brand. If unable to create a compelling vision in the community, the partnership risks creating competing social interests resulting in interest groups with conflicting motives and goals.

Hungary has had a long history in spa and wellness tourism. The use of Hungary's thermal baths and medicinal waters dates back to ancient times and has cycled through the ages, peaking during the Roman, Turkish and the Austro-Hungarian eras. In more recent times, the 1920s through the 1930s saw a massive revival and interest in Hungary's spas, particularly in Budapest, the '*City of Spas*.' But during the 1940s and 1950s, the spa culture declined and the bath and spa assets began to be neglected.

In 2001, Hungary embarked on a massive revitalization strategy that would stimulate economic development through targeted public investment. Within the tourism sector, wellness and medicinal spa tourism was identified very quickly as one of Hungary's potential competitive advantages. Hungary had a historical reputation for its medicinal waters and product was available: 800 thermal wells operated in Hungary, the majority of which qualified as medicinal. In addition, 1,200 non-medicinal pools in approximately 350 public baths were available.

Spa and wellness tourism had several strategic advantages. As spa tourists tend to spend more and stay longer, spa and wellness tourism would then also serve to shift Hungary's tourist visitor profile from a high number of visitors with low spend, to higher-value tourists that may be smaller in number but would spend more money. And given the aging population, demand for wellness tourism was expected to grow. In addition, the spas and pools were scattered throughout Hungary and their development would help to achieve the government's aim of spreading economic activity in a number of geographic areas.

Given its strategic nature, under the Szechenyi Plan for tourism, the spa and wellness product was allocated two-thirds of the available funds. Much of the initial investment would be needed to invest in the spas and public baths currently available. These spas and public baths in most cases were owned by the local government and consisted of a large spa/bath complex that generally had a big public pool, a children's pool, thermal waters, and a inspecially amusement pool.

But the large central spa assets were not typically the profit maker of the region - although these public pools were the attractor. The income and profit generators of the economy were the other businesses that surround the spa/bath complex. Fundamentally, the government did not want to own and operate the large spa/bath assets. And yet they understood that any development would require a mix of financing that would involve the municipality, the private sector and the government.

The next level of investment by the Hungarian government in a project was directed at the medicinal or wellness hotels . In these types of projects, the private sector had to invest at least 33 per cent of the total project cost, before qualifying for government support. In 2001 the government would provide 15 per cent of the total project cost. The maximum grant to any one project was US $2-2.5 million. Still, a higher proportion of the overall government investment was concentrated in those towns where a large spa bath complex existed because the government wanted to continue to concentrate investment in those areas that could develop a critical mass of product.

The third level of government investment was targeted at the unexploited hot springs. Most of this funding was directed at feasibility studies and planning initiatives. To support the bricks and mortar initiative, the government also invested in education. The state would provide 50 per cent of the cost of education for individuals taking programs related to spa treatment, massage, sport healthcare, language, marketing, and hospitality and protocol training.

To meet the new demand for tourism and healthcare education, colleges and other educational institutes initiated new programs and schools.

The strategic plan also wrestled with the problem of how to cluster and brand the spa product. Under European Union requirements, Hungary had to form seven regions out of its 19 historical counties. In many cases, the resulting new regions not only lacked the structural and organizational mechanisms to manage the partnerships efficiently, but they also had to learn the art of co-operating. Each region could have up to 15-25 spas and hotels plus any number of restaurants, bus companies, and consulting and educational providers.

Yet in order to leverage the spa asset development, to effectively communicate the unique spa experience, the Szechenyi Plan encouraged the mayors and municipal departments, hotel owners and other private sector entrepreneurs to coalesce around a regional brand based on the unique natural or cultural resources of the region, for example:

— Family holiday based on the spa experience

— Turkish Hamam

— Roman bath

— 19 th century historical monument

— Medicinal spas

— Wellness (massage and spa treatments, food and diet, spiritual connectivity)

— Active wellness (sport, physical activity aimed at the younger market)

As a result, regional committees have formed with representatives from the public and private sectors to define the regional cluster and the brand with varying success across the country. As noted, however, these types of initiatives take time. The Szechenyi Plan brought people together that have not worked together before, requiring a new way of thinking about their spa assets, and necessitating a new way of thinking about how the public and the private sector could work together.

The Szechenyi Plan was undertaken in two major planning phases. In the first phase a spa-tourism sub-committee of 22 tourism professionals was invited by Economic Affairs to develop the overall strategic plan. The sub-committee undertook a situation analysis and identified preferred towns where thermal water was in supply and could be the focus of development.

Over the last two years, the participating partners in the initiative have not changed, but new associations have sprung up. For example the Hungarian Spa Marketing Association has formed to leverage and assist individual spa marketing programs. As well, associations have instituted new activities. For example the Hungarian Hotel Association formed a sub-committee on wellness hotels that is quite active in the Szechenyi initiative.

Because of the central importance of the spa initiative to the government's tourism objectives, the government monitors both the success of the public private sector product development initiatives underway and the resulting demand. The spas themselves are monitored for number of visitors, annual income and annual profit. The hotels are monitored for number of guest nights, annual income and annual profit.

The Szechenyi Plan for the development of spa and wellness tourism faced a number of risks. The stakeholders in the Hungarian spa industry were not used to working together in partnership, there was fundamentally a lack of trust and many in the private and public sectors were afraid of losing market share to competitor regions, competitor hotels, and so on. If the Szechenyi Plan could not in the end mobilize investment, then the government would face a massive loss of credibility and the impetus would be lost.

Many of these upfront risks were managed through a strong public relations, education and communication campaign. Initially the campaign was aimed at the local-area governments because, while the municipalities owned at least 90 per cent of the spas, many were new to marketing and managing these spas as a for-profit venture. Yet these spa assets were the lynchpin to getting the private sector on board because if these spas were generating higher turnover, the risk to entering the market for the private sector would be minimized. The reward for both the local area and government would be a strong, prospering private sector.

In Denmark, MeetingPlace Wonderful Copenhagen is a partnership formed by the private sector in co-operation with the local marketing agency, Wonderful Copenhagen, to make Copenhagen and the Oresund Region the leading destination for international association congresses and corporate meetings in Northern Europe. To this end, the partnership is primarily focused on marketing and image enhancement, although it also undertakes product development to create and continuously update interesting products that would attract international congresses and provide something new and different for repeat visitors.

The partnership undertakes three key activities:

— Marketing Copenhagen as a destination for corporate meetings;

— Product Development with the Meetings, Incentives, Conferences, Exhibitions (MICE) network, involving local members, to create interesting product; and

— Networking opportunities for members.

MeetingPlace Wonderful Copenhagen was formed in 1994 under the initiative of the private sector. In 1994, two of Copenhagen's largest hoteliers, each with 500 rooms and substantial meeting facilities, informally began talking about sales and improving demand. Through these discussions, both came to realize that they were not selling their hotel as such, but selling the destination. If one hotelier was successful in bringing in a large meeting, other hotels would, in fact, benefit - one hotel would get the direct bookings and the other would get the overflow.

In addition, each hotel was aggressively spending in the same markets. By coming together and pooling their funds, the cost of promotion went down and the effectiveness of marketing went up. The network successfully attracted the two big hoteliers onto the board and, instead of talking hotel operation and development, the group now began to talk destination marketing. Prevalent in the discussions was the dissatisfaction with the public-sector-managed convention bureau, which from the private sector point of view was having difficulties in meeting the business needs of hoteliers. The group lobbied to have this institution closed down and, in its stead, the private sector formed the MeetingPlace Wonderful Copenhagen partnership.

Structure and Operation of the Partnership

The activities of the partnership are carried out by the local marketing agency, Wonderful Copenhagen, in close co-operation with the Danish Tourist Board. Wonderful Copenhagen employs approximately 70 people of which 25 are working for MeetingPlace Wonderful Copenhagen as part of their duties. Wonderful Copenhagen in effect supplies the administration of the meeting and social events, distribution of the business leads that develop and oversees the marketing activities and product development for the partnership. The partnership is funded largely by the membership.

Of the 6 million Danish Kroners , 4.4 million Danish Kroners are raised from membership fees, which Wonderful Copenhagen administers; Wonderful Copenhagen also funds the remainder. At least half of the funds go to marketing activities, 40 per cent to salaries and 10 per cent go to other expenses. Wonderful Copenhagen is also allowed one person on the board. The board formally meets four times per year and holds a number of other informal meetings for educational seminars, social events and networking opportunities.

This very informal partnership was created to increase tourism on the Island of Crete in Greece, during the traditionally low winter season, when facilities and equipment are closed or operating at the break-even point. The idea for the partnership was conceived in November 2000 by Spyros Kokotos, founder of Elounda SA, and owner of Porto Elounda De Luxe Resort. The hotel had remained open for the previous five winter seasons and had only broken even. Nevertheless, Kokotos saw the potential for generating a more active tourist season if other partners would become involved. Any additional visitors, even if heavily discounted, would bring in welcome additional revenue.

One of the key deterrents to attracting tour groups to Crete in the winter season is the lack of access. The difficulty of getting to Crete discouraged tour operators from recommending that clientele try an unproved winter holiday destination. Undaunted, Kokotos, met with the owner of Aegean Airlines in 2001, Theodoros Vassilakis, and proposed the scheme of direct flights from Heraklion, Crete, to destinations in continental Europe.

The partnership is very informal, with Aegean Airlines primarily managing the offer. Each hotel has provided Aegean Airlines with its clientele list in Germany for the airline to use in its initial promotion. The hoteliers are at the ready to offer their services to guests referred to them by either the company or associated agents at the discounted rate agreed upon in the original meeting. The partners' performance is not monitored apart from tracking the additional interest in visitation.

The financial risks of the venture are high. Aegean Airlines has opened three new connections to capture a new market segment in a traditional low season. Demand may not pay for the capacity. The hotels are staying open and profit margin is low to non-existent through higher food and employment costs. In addition, the partnership has not been formalized and the partners have made no commitment to the project. Nor has any formal strategy been voiced to date. Clearly, the promotion is in its early stages and still largely ad hoc. The five hotel entrepreneurs know each other very well and have co-operated in numerous other ventures; but the looseness of the partnership increases the risk of it falling apart.

However, the potential benefits are clear. No other airline is taking visitors directly to crete at a price point that is hard to resist. By making an investment now, Aegean Airlines and the hotel partners are hoping that crete will extend its tourist season to the winter, encouraging visitors to stay longer and spend more money. It is still too early to tell the results of the partnership, as the offer is still in its first season. Further, at the time of publication, there was an economic downturn in Germany. To make the partnership truly successful, many more people and organizations need to believe in the project and get involved. Nonetheless, to date, Aegean Airlines has published a brochure and is pleased that two major tour operators have agreed to market the product.

The partnership is still convincing the Greek National Tourism Organization (GNTO) to allocate some of its budget towards promoting the product Crete in the Winter at the airports Aegean flies from. The nature of the tour business requires the tour operators to make a good profit, quickly. The product that Aegean Airlines is offering is new and needs to be communicated properly. In order to sell the new package, Aegean Airlines must break through clutter in the distribution channel because there are many other tour choices. The partnership has to educate the tour operators that direct access is available and that Crete is a high-value destination in the winter. The partners can do this by, for example, reducing the tariffs even lower to promote interest.

The partnership may need to review the product offering, its strengths and weaknesses and the opportunities and threats in order to remain competitive. The partners do not expect to see results in these early days and understand they are investing now for rewards later. Much of the product closes in the winter on Crete and it is a rhythm of life that may be hard to break. But it is the belief of the partners that if other operators see that product remains open in the winter, there will be more available for visitors to stay and enjoy.

In Egypt, the Red Sea Riviera Development was first reported in the WTO Business Council 2000 report and concentrated on the Taba Tourism Development Corporation (TTDC) that was developing an integrated resort destination along the Gulf of Aqaba. This resort development is just one small part of the overall redevelopment of the area. The history of the project dates back to 1991. At that time, the private sector started to lobby the Egyptian government for opportunities to invest in touristic ventures. At the same time, the government of Egypt was looking for means to promote development and turned its eyes to a sparsely populated area that stretches from the Gulf of Suez to the Sudanese border. The region was beautiful, home to migrating birds, white sand beaches and some of the world's most fantastic coral reefs.

The mechanism to jump-start the development was creating the Tourist Development Authority (TDA) under the auspices of the ministry of tourism. The TDA was formed to be an economic body that would specialize in land for tourist development only; the government ceded the land to TDA control in 1991. The TDA took the next two years to plan the development using well known. international engineering and planning firms. After the two-year planning period, the government started to promote the area for tourism investment, which started to flow in 1994. The initiative changed the role of the public sector in Egypt from owner-operator to planner, regulator, promoter and facilitator.

The development plan called for the creation of 51 integrated tourist centres or 120,000 rooms by 2017. The integrated tourist centres would be similar to towns, but their main function would be tourism. An investor could take a huge area and assume responsibility for the entire development including roads, sewage, planning and development. The TDA created a vision for the area. Its role was to help the investors follow the vision. In this capacity, the TDA provided the investors with engineering plans and feasibility studies to help carry out the project. Only a certain number of rooms for each area were allowed, taking care to protect the fragile environment. Major infrastructure, such as roads, water and sewage networks, that are part of the overall national system, would be supplied by the TDA.

However, the private sector investors would be responsible for any internal infrastructure to a resort town, such as flood control dams, water desalinization plants, sewage, electricity, communication and road networks, leisure and cultural facilities, golf courses, shopping centres, hospitals, schools and hotels, marinas, and airports for light cargo. For example, the Orascom Projects and Touristic Development (OPTD) developed a tourism town called El Gouna. Investment to date included five-star hotels, plus a number of other boutique and four-star accommodations. They have also opened an 18-hole par-72 golf course. The infrastructure that the OPTD has invested in includes four electrical power plants, a water treatment plant, roads and communications infrastructure, two marinas, a private airport, an international school and a hospital.

Sustainable Tourism Partnership for Urban Area

Urban tourism is a cluster of economic activities with

significant socioeconomic and environmental consequences on the individual cities. The principal aims of the Sustainable Urabn Tourism (SUT) Governance project were to develop, validate, and deploy a general framework for urban sustainable tourism partnerships between researchers, city officials, tourism stakeholders, and community representatives and to elaborate and promote innovative forms and instruments of local governance involving the principles of sustainability and participatory decision making.

Europe's cities and towns contain a rich cultural heritage. Yet, maintaining this heritage presents many challenges, including dealing with the adverse environmental and social impacts of mass tourism. Demands from urban tourism alike are high and growing, hence the pressures and problems associated with the management of the sector have to be systematically tackled by all parties concerned. In their quest to further foster democracy and community prosperity, local authorities must seek tighter relations with a wide range of actors so the necessary political and operational consensus can be achieved to tackle problems successfully in benefit of all residents.

Developing and operating public-private cooperations between the concerned parties is thus fundamental to effective urban governance of sustainable tourism. Achieving this involves advancing knowledge and practice about the types of partnerships that can be formed to promote urban sustainable tourism; the roles of government and other stakeholders; how local governments can apply such partnerships to long-term local tourism management and development; and the critical issues and challenges to local governments seeking to create such partnerships.

The principal aim of the international research and policy project "Sustainable Urban Tourism: Involving local Agents and Partnerships for New Forms of Governance" (SUT-Governance) was to develop, validate, and deploy a general framework for urban sustainable tourism partnerships that is applicable to a variety of urban municipal contexts by drawing on detailed field work in four European countries: Germany, Austria, Greece and Bulgaria. The broader goal of the project was to elaborate and promote innovative forms and instruments of local governance to improve urban tourism development involving the principles of sustainability and participatory decision-making.

The European dimensions of the "SUT-Governance" initiative are evident with respect to the six fold European concerns for Sustainability, Competitiveness, Governance, Local Agenda 21, Innovation, and Enlargement. Sustainable urban tourism (SUT) is a holistic, equitable, and future-oriented development strategy, part of the wider Urban Sustainable Development Agenda. Operationalisation of SUT requires recognition of two fundamental principles imbedded in the sustainability-induced "integrated development" paradigm: (i) Sustainable tourism implies sustainable ends (outcomes and impacts of tourism products and services) and (ii) Sustainable tourism involves effective delivery means (strategic policymaking and implementation).

Policy for sustainable urban tourism demands working approaches, i.e. SUT must be viewed as a consistent and continuous development strategy ensuring the balance of the present benefits of tourism with the future opportunities of the host community. Therefore SUT must been taken as a (i) policy option with community-centred objectives and

(ii) process of governing which has to be sustained in the life of the community. As such, SUT must (i) affect urban policy and development, considering both, industry and community long-term progress and (ii) account for both tourism product and its sustainability implications.

Implementation of SUT calls for a multi-stakeholder approach to deal with the multi-functional nature of policies and actions, build consensus and share the responsibilities, risks and benefits from urban tourism in context of Urban Governance (taken as relationships and collaborative actions between urban actors to plan and manage the city affairs aiming at fostering democracy and community prosperity and involving government, private sector, and civil society).

Effective facilitation of multi-actor collaboration in SUT requires public-private partnerships. The latter can provide for, among others, enhanced tourism resources and services responsive to human needs; broad based sustainability gains; utilisation of community and business links and capacities; increased effectiveness and efficiency of local organisations; reduced conflicts, boosted trust and actor confidence; improved public policy and greater policy legitimacy; collective responsibility for planning, decision-making, problem solving, and project implementation and evaluation; community dialogue; responsible, engaged and involved locals and tourists; and combating local inequalities and fostering social inclusion. Therefore, partnerships must become a key principle of quality management of public services in city tourism towards urban sustainability and more local democracy.

Success of SUT partnerships depends on the efficacy of the (i) partnership process (ii) tourism activity and its implementation and (iii) activity resolutions for a long term and far reaching community sustainability Both, "development" and "marketing" tourism partnerships can promote sustainable community development, one, by increasing and effectively managing the use and increase of the local tourism "stock", and two, by sustaining and enhancing the partnership process and culture in the locality.

Implementation opportunities for SUT partnerships are multiple and can improve the urban built, natural environment, social fabric, human behaviour, and the overall local capacities. Benchmarking SUT partnerships is key to improving collaborative practices and must become a consistent part of tourism quality management in the cities. By and large, the project's results will assist a wide number of tourism decision-makers and stakeholders in their efforts to improve urban sustainability and governance in the European cities: Urban administrators and authorities, tourism businesses and organizations, academics and researchers, European and international policy-makers, civil society, tourists and consumer groups.

The success of the project has much depended on the close cooperation between the researchers, city officials, tourism stakeholders, and community representatives from the participating countries, cities and the partnership initiatives. The aim was to identify, elaborate, and validate a set of best practices for sustainable urban tourism, with an understanding of the conditions in which those practices were established in order to develop an integrated framework model of SUT Partnerships success.

In tourism, the social, economic and environmental impacts on the local communities are interrelated, overlapping and mutually reinforcing. Partnerships therefore appear essential in order to tackle the problems of local tourism, their causes and the externalities. This view must underpin urban policy for sustainable tourism as it has been done in urban regeneration, employment and social inclusion programs in the 1980s and more recently, in EU policies in support of local and regional development.

City authorities logically have a central role to play in promoting and sustaining collaborative partnerships. In view of the growing complexity of urban development today, it is becoming increasingly necessary to make all active participants in the urban environment, i.e. the urban decision makers, face up to their responsibilities and allow the citizens they represent have a say in the running of cities. Further-more, in the cities, where local governments have usually strong influence and power, tourism industry is less fragmented and disunited, and community groups are more influential, the role of public administrations in uniting the stakeholders for the establishment of a long-term local development framework in which collaboration is a cornerstone to success, appears an ultimate necessity .

To fulfil its Agenda, the "SUT-Governance" project carried out twelve Pilot and eight detailed SUT Partnership case studies in diverse European cities. Central to the research efforts were the eight "Best Practice" Partnerships for Sustainable Urban Tourism, two in each of the four collaborating cites - Graz, Heidelberg, Thessaloniki and Veliko Turnovo. These already established multi-actor collaborations in tourism marketing and management, sustainable tourism, urban renewal and regeneration, integrated local development, healthy communities, and regional integration were nominated based on their accomplishments in tourism, effective partnerships, sustainability, and favourable community impacts.

The partnership cases promoted by "SUT-Governance" demonstrate the practical ways in which communities;

governments and the private sector are working together to improve tourism practices towards a better urban governance and long-term community prosperity. Other cities and communities in Europe and around the globe can learn from these successful solutions for sustainable tourism development of the urbanising world. The database and the analytical summary reports developed by the project can be used for providing analytical and policy framework, assessment of current trends, benchmarking practices, enhancing per formance, capacity building, networking, and technical cooperation in urban tourism activities.

Participatory governance arrangements have emerged as new innovative tools in promoting the objectives of sustainability in many policy areas in Europe and across the world. Their effectiveness in the field of urban tourism, depends upon both national frameworks and local contexts. Urban tourism is a cluster of economic activities with significant socio-economic and environmental consequences on the individual cities. This applies especially in tourism intensive cities generating a substantial part of their employment and income opportunities from tourism.

The need to provide sustainable solutions to tourism related problems triggers the formation of participatory governance arrangements combining efficiency and democracy in innovative ways. The effectiveness of the latter in the area of urban tourism depends upon and varies according to the political culture and the specific socio-economic characteristics of the cities. However, the general trends are embedded in the specific national and local frameworks favouring particular combinations of actors and activities and forming country-specific and city-specific trajectories of sustainable tourism.

As the interrelations at the European, the national and regional and/or local scale are being restructured under the strong pressure of globalisation, individual cities emerge as the most appropriate level for the implementation of the new ideas of participatory governance involving the networking of actors and the participation of a variety of stakeholders in specific types of partnerships, initiatives and policy making processes. Thus, "SUT-Governance" argues, the similarity of scope behind this mosaic of cultural diversity will strengthen the overall prospects of European cohesion.

4

Hospitality and Marketing

Developing countries are particularly challenged in order to compensate for long distance travel, language differences, and less complete infrastructure to receive tourists other than in beach resorts.For most countries, knowledge of the volume of border crossing tourism is largely limited to the numbers of arrivals and the expenditure by international tourists in the host country published with varying delay by governments and presented annually by the World Tourism Organization (WTO). Some more frequent statistical surveys are carried out based on samples covering also domestic tourism and especially hotel performance indicators, but these do not produce figures representative of the total size of the industry.

Only a dozen countries have so far started to develop statistical instruments to measure the whole tourist industry (Tourism Satellite Accounts), and at present results are published only after long delays. In 2001 until September 11 th , travel and tourism had been growing at the annual rate of 3.8 per cent and was expected to maintain that level of growth for the full year. In the event, according to WTTC estimates, travel and tourism demand worldwide in 2001 ended 1.3 per cent down on the previous year.

The real decline for the whole of 2001 as compared to the expected growth was therefore 5.1per cent, of which it has been estimated that as much as 4.4 percentage points can be attributed to September 11 th alone. In 2002, the year-on-year decline of travel and tourism was expected to continue, with WTTC forecasting last spring a slight decrease by 0.4 per cent for the whole of 2002. The forecast was adjusted in fall when WTTC estimated a flat performance as compared to 2001.

On the assumption that last year's pre-September 11th growth of 3.8 per cent would normally have continued throughout 2002, this would mean another real annual decline for tourism of close to 4 percent, of which around 3 percentage points can be attributed to the events of September 11 th alone. Countries most affected by the September 11th events were the United States, with international tourist arrivals having fallen to their lowest point between September and November, on average over 30 per cent below the level of the same period the previous year.

Countries in the immediate neighbourhood of the US also received significantly less tourists than at the same time the previous year, e.g. In general, all countries that would normally have expected a high proportion of their incoming long-haul tourism to originate from the United States experienced steep declines in international tourism in the first three months following September 11. In Europe, those worthy of note include the United Kingdom (-12 %), Germany (-17%), Switzerland (-16%), Italy (-11%) and Austria (-9%) - and elsewhere, the Philippines (-25%) and Australia (-21%). Some other countries amongst those whose tourist industries are important elements in their national economies suffered badly such as Egypt (-55%), Tunisia (-25%) and Morocco (-22%). In addition to security aspects, the general economic downturn in 2001 also contributed to the poorer performance of international tourism in 2001 compared to the previous year. Here, the main causes are to be found in those major sending countries such as the US, Germany, and Japan.

South American markets suffered from economic instability in Argentina. An additional factor for the US as a receiving country, which lost as much as 2.5 per cent on international arrivals in the first nine months of the year, was its strong currency. Among the countries performing worse as a destination for the full year 2001, compared to the year 2000, were the US, Argentina, Brazil, the UK, Mexico, Germany, Italy, the Dominican Republic, Jamaica and the Bahamas. Other countries experienced a significant drop in their 2001 total tourist numbers year-on-year because, rightly or wrongly, they were associated with security risks, and this was for various reasons not necessarily connected to the September 11 th events. These countries included Egypt, Nepal, and Sri Lanka.

By contrast, there were some countries, notably in Europe bordering at the East Mediterranean Sea and in Southern Europe that in 2001 continued to receive higher numbers of foreign tourists than in the previous year, probably because they provide a convenient alternative to long-haul destinations for many European tourists. Thus Turkey, Croatia, Slovenia, Spain, Greece and Cyprus all benefited in 2001. It was also observed that several emerging tourist destinations in Europe showed strong growth in the full year 2001, notably Bulgaria, Slovakia and Estonia.

France (+1.2%) also recorded some growth in 2001 versus their previous year totals, benefiting from their familiarity and proximity with European holidaymakers and even compensating a temporary 20 per cent drop immediately following September 11th which was probably due the sudden lack of Americans visiting Europe. Australia and New Zealand reported a short period of decline in inbound tourism immediately after September 11th, but most of these losses were partly offset by something of a boom in numbers of foreign tourists later in the year. Some countries, such as the UK, Germany, China and Canada continued to send record numbers of tourists to this part of the world throughout 2001. They did not prevent, however, a year-on-year decline of 2.7 per cent in numbers of international arrivals, mainly accounted for by 4 th quarter decreases from Japan and the US.

Notably, the region with the best performance as tourist destination in 2001 was South East Asia and the Pacific, which in spite of a decline after 11 September still ended the year with a growth of 5.5 per cent, mainly due to intra-regional tourism. Performing regions were also Africa and Central America, albeit on a small basis in absolute terms. The United States is the country whose hotel, travel and tourism industry was most seriously affected. According to the US Office of Travel and Tourism Industries, the total number of international arrivals fell by almost 11 per cent over the whole year 2001. This was largely because of a dramatic 30 per cent drop in September, moving to a 34.0 per cent loss in October, with an average 31.8 per cent loss of business over the last four months of the year compared to the same period of the previous year.

October was the worst month. The numbers of international arrivals slowly started to recover in November. Certain countries supplying travellers to the US performed worse than others because they were more seriously affected by economic crises. These included Brazil; Germany and Japan. By the end of the year, however, it was the German market that had performed worse than any other, which is probably due to generally nervous consumer behaviour in the light of the country's poor economic performance. Demand for accommodation in the US is estimated to have suffered a far more modest decline than international arrivals, another indication that domestic tourism was less affected and it was long-haul travel that suffered most.

Accommodation demand had already declined by 6.0 per cent in the third quarter of 2001, as compared to the same period in 2000. However, the decline in the fourth quarter was markedly greater, but still only a fifth of the decline in international arrivals. Early forecasts by the Travel Industry Association of America already suggested that after the 7.6 per cent drop in 2001, the recovery in consumer expenditure levels on travel in the US would be slow in 2002, with an annual growth rate of only 2.2 per cent. Leisure trips in March, April and May 2002, for example, were 4 per cent below the level in the same period a year ago.

Overall, first quarter 2002 international arrivals to the US were down 12 per cent. Four of the top markets - the United Kingdom, Germany, the Netherlands and Switzerland - posted declines for the first quarter of 2002, but the declines are less than those recorded in the pre-September 11th months in 2001. Mexico and Spain are the main markets posting positive growth in numbers of arrivals through the first quarter 2002, at +22 per cent and +6 per cent respectively versus the same period last year. Recovery in the US is not being enjoyed equally by all sub-sectors of the industry.

Leisure tourism services are recovering faster, for example, than the sub-sector catering for business travellers. The number of Japanese travelling abroad was down 9.1 per cent at the end of 2001 versus the previous year, according to a report released in January 2002. Whereas in May 2002 the number of bookings of foreign trips through Japan's top 50 travel agencies was still 6 per cent less than the previous year, July and August, the peak season, have been especially slow, with 10 to 20 per cent fewer bookings than in the previous year. By contrast, the numbers of visitors to domestic destinations were up by 4.6 per cent to 2.07 million.

In the period immediately following September 11th , the largest travel agent (JTB) saw an increase of 19 per cent in their bookings for domestic tours departing during the October-December period. China experienced some impressive growth in both domestic and inbound tourism, with domestic tourism developing particularly strongly. Total annual revenue from tourism has grown on average by 12.7 per cent over recent years, much faster than the gross domestic product (GDP) which grew by an average rate of 7.4 per cent. More than 73.34 million overseas tourists visited China during the first 10 months of 2001, an increase of 5.7 per cent on the same period of 2000, or almost double the world's average growth rate for 2001 before September 11th .

The total amount spent by overseas tourists in that period grew by 9.3 per cent to US$14.8 billion. Over two-thirds of the revenue is still, however, from domestic tourism. Spain's tourist industry, which directly employs more than a million people and accounts for 12 per cent of the economy, is suffering a protracted crisis, recording 10 per cent less visitors for the first six months of 2002 compared to the same period the previous year. The number of German visitors to Spain in July 2002 was 20 per cent lower, pushing down the hotel occupancy rate by 5.5 per cent. Reservations made by German tour operators tumbled by as much as 37 per cent. The crisis is attributed partly to growing unemployment in Germany, but also to price increases in Spain, with German tourists preferring cheaper destinations such as Turkey and Croatia.

In Switzerland, tourist numbers for the six-month winter season 2001-02 were a dramatic 6 per cent down on the previous year's winter season result. Yet this was still 1.4 per cent above the average for the previous five winter seasons. Increased domestic tourism seems to have stepped in to replace international visitors, whose numbers dropped by 10 per cent. The number of tourists visiting from the US was nearly 20 per cent less and from Japan 31 per cent less than in the same period the year before.

Overnight trips to Canada were up by 0.6 per cent for the first five months of 2002 compared to the same period in 2001, boosted by an increase in US travellers entering Canada by car. On the other hand, the number of Canadian tourists to the US or overseas was still down by 7.2 per cent (at 1.5 million) in May 2002, which represented something of a recovery because it was down 11.3 per cent for the five months before, compared to the same period a year ago. The government of Morocco predicts that tourism revenues will have dropped by US$700 million by the end of 2002, down by one-quarter on the total revenue of US$2.7 million reached in 2001. Morocco's tourist industry recorded a 43 per cent revenue drop in January 2002 compared to January 2001. The industry currently employs over half a million people, serving some 2.4 million foreign tourists annually.

Major markets supplying most of Australia's tourists showed dramatic falls in outbound tourism during the 12 months to July 2002, with the number of visitors from neighbouring New Zealand dropping by 25.5 per cent, from the UK by 17.7 per cent and the United States by 8.4 per cent, according to the Australian Bureau of Statistics. Overall, international visitor arrivals have fallen 8.4 per cent to 409,400 from January to July 2002, compared to the 446,900 tourists for the same period last year. These results were attributed September 11 th mainly, but Australian tourism leaders feel under pressure by the lasting downturn, leading them to reconsider their whole marketing strategy. A return to pre-September 11th levels of international arrivals was still seen as being a long way off. After the bomb attack of October 2002, the Australian tourism industry fears negative effects of tourists avoiding Asia.

Singapore and Bangkok are stopovers on the most popular route from Europe to Australia. Any disruption to the flow of tourists to them would have a severe knock-on effect on Australia. Industry reports in late October 2002, however, suggested the tourist numbers from all markets would remain largely unaffected as a result of the 12 October Bali attacks.

Employment numbers in the tourism sector do not react immediately to a decrease in business because the special characteristics of employment relationships in the sector allow for some labour cost reduction to take place before workers finally become unemployed. Flexible working arrangements such as part-time or on-call working are common for at least one quarter of the labour force and help to avoid their complete unemployment in a business crisis, albeit with reduced income. Employees accounting for almost another quarter of the total have full time but temporary employment contracts and are the first victims of formal unemployment when reducing their working time and income becomes insufficient to address the income crisis of the enterprise.

Employers usually hesitate, however, to reduce their core of trained staff. Only if a crisis persists, businesses tend to re-structure and workers are eventually laid off permanently. The WTTC estimates a 7.4 per cent drop in tourism demand over the years 2001 and 2002 combined, instead of the 3.8 per cent growth that had been anticipated previously for each of these two years. The sector is now seen as being in a state of stagnation, which is a dramatic change in fortune considering its previously very high growth rate. The WTTC estimated that over 6 million jobs would have been lost in the tourism industry worldwide in the years 2001 and 2002, which represent 8.6 per cent of employees, or one in every 12 jobs in the industry.

The process of attempting to derive employment estimates from demand estimates has to take into account that normal growth may not result in increased employment because normal growth is achieved largely through gains in labour productivity. WTTC estimated therefore that a growth of demand by 3.8 per cent would have entailed a growth of employment by only 2 per cent. Given this proportion, the dramatic effects on employment forecasted by WTTC can be better appreciated. WTTC foresees a modest recovery of employment in the travel and tourism industry worldwide in 2003. However, with a growth of 1.7, the year 2003 will still end with a 6.4 million jobs lost as a result of the crisis compared to the expected normal annual growth rate of 2 per cent in that year. The Travel Industry Association of America (TIA) estimates that 19 million Americans were employed directly or indirectly by the travel industry, with an annual payroll of $174 billion.

The year 2001 ended with domestic travel volumes and expenditure down 3.5 per cent and 7 per cent respectively, and volumes and expenditure from international travel to the US down 12.6 per cent and 11.2 per cent respectively. Employment in the whole industry in the USA was down 5.8 per cent for the year, with an estimated 1.1 million jobs lost. High volume tourist destinations such as Las Vegas, Orlando and Honolulu are expected to have suffered major losses in 2002 due to cutbacks in travel. Among 315 metro areas examined by the Milken Institute at the end of 2001, many jobs would be lost as a result of the events after 11 September 2001 in New York, Los Angeles and other big cities.

A ranking of industries most affected by job losses after September 11 th shows the hotel and catering sector represented by the top two categories listed. Over two-thirds of the estimated 760,000 total direct jobs expected to be lost in US metropolitan areas were in core sectors related to travel and tourism. The general economic downturn in 2001 had already started to affect all forms of consumption and travel and tourism was probably one of the sectors that suffered most because it is a market in which consumers can easily make savings.

Indeed, future variations in the level of consumer expenditure on tourism will probably be driven mainly by variations in levels of present and expected household income. The Travel Industry Association of America (TIA) undertook three Travel Confidence Surveys in the US, one from 21 to 22 September, another from 12 to 13 October 2001 and the third from 2 to 4 November 2001. In these polls, only 14 per cent of respondents cited safety as their top travel concern. On the other hand, 42 per cent cited economic concerns as reasons for not travelling. Nonetheless, the fear factor continued well into 2002 as a strong deterrent to travel in the US and the health of the industry continued to be affected by federal alerts, air-travel-related accidents and other concerns.

Tourism would recover slowly and regain the levels of before September 11 th by the third or fourth quarter of 2002. This forecast would be in line with experiences from previous security crises affecting tourism, albeit local, whose effects lasted for about one seasonal cycle. The continuing economic slowdown in the western world, as well as more recent terrorist activities targeting tourists in Djerba, Bali and Mombasa, however, are having an added effect on the tourism crisis. The year 2002 has been one of rather little growth or even slight decline of tourism performance indicators, with the possible exceptions of the Asian Pacific region and South Africa which has recorded double digit growth of tourism out of Europe in 2002, or China which does continues to grow rapidly both as a destination and as a market.

According to German tour operators, because of higher price levels, total turnover for the 2000/01 season which ended in October grew by twice as much (+ 6.8%) as the number of bookings, reaching a total of Euro17.4

billion. For 2002, despite bookings being down, German tour operators expected a turnover close to that of 2001, mainly because certain customers are making higher value choices even if they go for shorter stays. In general, tourism demand was in the last 12 months or so subject to important structural changes including a re-distribution of demand between countries and regions.

Leisure destinations located close to important markets have prospered; domestic tourism has made a difference; long-distance international air transport has suffered more than international tourism in general due to increased short distance trips across borders; business tourism and conventions, luxury hotels, and cruises during the winter season were particularly affected, while social tourism, rural tourism, rail and road travel made gains. Among the destinations receiving European tourists, short-haul destinations have generally benefited at the expense of long-haul destinations, with demand for North America showing the greatest fall in 2002 so far.

The main long-haul destination to buck the trend has been China, but a number of other Asian destinations and South Africa have similarly recorded double-digit growth out of Europe this year. International arrivals to countries in the European region will show little change in 2002 over last year which closed with a decrease of -0.6% in international tourist arrivals in Europe. Austria, as a typical short haul destination for European markets saw foreign leisure arrivals grow by a massive 12% in the first half of 2002. This growth, however, is expected to have eased to a rate of only around 2% for the whole year. For France, preliminary data on international arrivals (classified hotel accommodation only) suggest that the lucrative US market remained down by no less than a fifth in the first eight months of 2002 as compared to the same period in 2001, whilst growth in the Canadian market was replaced by decline. All international arrivals together performed at a low 0.5 per cent growth, as the performance of the major generating markets within Europe has been considerable with tourists from the UK increasing by close to 7 per cent, and arrivals from Germany still increasing by 14 per cent.

A slight growth of foreign arrivals to Italy is anticipated for the remainder of 2002 which will close with a growth of 0.9 per cent. Tourist arrivals at Spain's frontiers increased in the first two quarters of 2002 by comfortable 6.9 percent, but only by 0.2 per cent in the second quarter as compared to the same periods in 2001. The summer period may not have been any better. It was, however, in the United Kingdom, where after a weak winter and spring period, July 2002 arrivals exceeded those of the year before by as high as 15 per cent and even those of July 2000. Expenditure increased less, but still by 7 per cent. Canada had continued growing as a destination for foreign tourists during the crisis year 2001, albeit at a slower pace, since most of foreign travelers came from the USA and increasingly used surface transport, in part substituting Canada for a long haul destination elsewhere.

In the first six months of 2002, however, the number of foreign tourists from the USA slightly shrunk (by 0.2 per cent), and the receiving of overseas tourism, which had been down in 2001 by 8.4 per cent (arrivals) and 4 per cent (expenditures) continued declining by 13 per cent (arrivals), reducing anticipated overall growth of foreign arrivals in 2002 to only 0.1per cent. Japan receives one international traveler only for five Japanese outbound tourists. Out of the modest number of less than

5 million that do arrive, it is estimated that over a quarter are in Japan on business and that half of this market originates from Asia. Having suffered in 2001 only a slight 0.3 per cent decrease of the- annual growth rate for all tourism, with a higher growth rate for leisure tourists of 0.9 per cent, Japan is estimated to benefit in 2002 from an impressive growth in foreign arrivals of 16 per cent, to a large extent due to an increase of the number of tourists from China.

Outbound tourism from Japan, important for many destinations in the world, is currently forecast to record modest growth in 2002 of a maximum 1-2% after a 9% decline in 2001. The Pacific Asian countries have been doing well as destinations in spite of the world crisis in 2001 and 2002. High GDP performances in mainland China, India and South Korea suggest the trend of Asian intra-regional tourism will continue. India as a source country appears to record strong double-digit growth in 2002, albeit on a small basis. Inbound tourism in India, however, after dropping in 2001 by a moderated 4.2 per cent (arrivals) and 5.5 percent (expenditures), continues suffering from the conflict with Pakistan and the closeness to Afghanistan. Northeast and Southeast Asia are driving the region's growth - both as destinations and as markets.

During 2001, almost 65% of international visitor arrivals in Northeast Asia came from within Northeast & Southeast Asia. For destinations within Southeast Asia the proportion was over 64%. China has continued to show strong growth in 2002. In the first eight months of 2002 foreign arrivals in mainland China increased by more than 16%. Good increases of inbound tourism have also been registered by Thailand and Vietnam. However, the impact of the Bali tragedy on the region's tourism remains to be seen. Elsewhere in the developing world, only South Africa and Central America and perhaps the Caribbean are expecting slight increases of inbound tourism in 2002 over 2001's level.

The USA has been one of the source markets hardest hit by all crisis factors together: the events of 11 September 2001, the continuing threat of terrorism in 2002 and the economic recession. A strong growth of 4 per cent or more is predicted for 2004. Such forecasts seem to have the unanimous support of the specialist community, but the risks are also clear: they depend on the absence of further terrorist attacks; more selective reactions by consumers who should not stop travelling altogether when security threats in fact are limited to a location; the development of the conflict in the Middle East and its oil price implications; and last not least on the general prospects of disposable income. In any case, forecasts by renowned specialists and organizations seem to be highly insecure.

Due to the continuing weakness of the world economy, travel and tourism demand in 2003 is likely to be substantially slower than projected earlier, with business travel in particular hit hard by the pressures on companies to cut costs and bolster their profitability. International visitor spending is now expected to recover by a modest 1.6% in 2003 after falling 10% over the previous two years, leaving international visitor spending in 2003 more than 20% below what might have been expected if it had grown by a more typical 5% a year since 2001.For foreign tourist arrivals to certain European countries in the years to come, forecasts indicate different growth rates. Austria will remain at a modest 2 per cent growth of foreign leisure trip arrivals in 2003. A modest turnaround, with growth of 2% to 3% is expected for the next 12 months also in Germany.

In France, international arrivals are expected for 2004 to be back to the pre-2001 growth rate of over 4 per cent, albeit under the assumption that long haul tourism to France will recover. Foreign visitors to Italy in 2003 are expected to increase by 2.7%, making a total of 39 million. Likewise, a growth rate between 2 and 5 per cent is assumed for the near future in Spain. In any event, the terrorist attack will bear on the performance of the industry in the region of South East Asia and the Pacific, the only region still experiencing strong growth in its tourism flows after September 11, 2002.

Probably, the whole region will be affected, as experience shows that tourists' and tour operators' decisions and preferences reflect rather superficial perception of geographical locations and of cultural profiles of destinations. Bali and with it the whole of Indonesia will suffer badly from the effects of the attack, whereas the impact on other countries in Asia is more difficult to anticipate, as especially East Asia and the Pacific had been experiencing strong growth in spite of the global tourism crisis of 2001.

In addition, Asia's tourism, more and more relies on growing intra-regional and domestic tourism which, hopefully, will be affected less by the Bali event less than was transatlantic travel after September 11th , 2001. Indonesia's inbound tourism had done well in the years following the economic crisis of 1997-8 which it overcame as early as 1999 in terms of tourist arrivals. Receipts from international tourism, however, remained in 1999 as much as 25 per cent short of what they were in 1996, which indicates cheaper tourist arrangements or shorter stays per arrival.

In 2001, the whole region of East Asia and the Pacific was little affected by the impact on tourism of the events of 11 September: due to a high growth rate in arrivals before September 11, the region still closed the year with a growth of 5.5 per cent. After the attack of 12 October, Bali's tourism industry virtually collapsed: Airlines cancelled and re-routed a number of their scheduled flights; tourists went home or left to other nearby destinations such as Fiji and the Philippines. As a result, hotel occupation rates tumbled from a comfortable 70 per cent to less than ten per cent. In absolute terms, it can be estimated that from an average of 100,000 tourists present in Bali at any time, not more than 15,000 stayed on.

Moreover, it can be assumed that the tourists who stayed on were of Indonesian origin as they represent 15 per cent of all visitors to Bali, and those who left were foreign tourists, leaving behind a devastated tourism economy, especially as far as foreign exchange is concerned. An estimated 5.1 million tourists visited Indonesia in 2001, contributing 5.3 billion dollars to Indonesia's balance of payments (about 9.2 % of total exports). Most of these tourists appear to end up in Bali at one stage or other. Bali's Minister for Culture and Tourism estimates that the island's tourism economy employed a portion of 65 per cent of the total labour force, i.e. 1,1 million out of the 1.71 million people in employment in Bali with a resident population of 3 million.

The hotel and restaurant sector alone produced in 2000 a share of 21 per cent of Real GDP and probably employed an even higher share of the labour force. As Bali is considered a magnet for tourists to come to Indonesia and also visit several other parts of the country, the Minister for Culture and Tourism estimates that as many as 2.7 million people may be out of their jobs across Indonesia soon if tourism does not recover quickly. He said that Tourism employed more than seven million people in the South East Asian archipelago and last year brought in 4.7 billion dollars in revenue, or about 10 percent of Indonesia's gross national product (GNP). Due to slower economic growth and to extra public spending to promote tourism after the Bali bomb attack, Indonesia's public finances will slide deeper into the red, by about 1.5 per cent of gross domestic product next year, up from an earlier projection of 1.3 per cent.

The Indonesian economy is now forecasted to expand by just 3.5 to 4 per cent in 2003, down from an earlier estimate of 5 per cent. Prospects to overcome the crisis are not so bad, though, if the steady high growth of international tourism to countries of the region is taken into account. Asia was the only region in the world that maintained strong, albeit uneven growth in tourism during the difficult period after its economic crisis 1997-98. A great deal is due to the growth of intra-regional tourism in Asia. During 2001, around 65% of international visitor arrivals in both North East Asia and South East Asia came from within the north eastern plus south eastern Asian region. Prospects of intra-regional Asian tourism count in that from China a total of seven million people traveled overseas in the first half of 2002.

The main markets for Indonesian tourism, however, are still Japan and Australia, where Indonesia will make special marketing efforts to counteract the tourism break down after the Bali bombing. Budget tourists from neighboring countries like Singapore and Malaysia, as well as many domestic visitors from Indonesia's main island of Java, are replacing tourists from Japan, Australia, and Western markets. Until the end of 2002, their presence largely prevented major layoffs in Bali's tourism industry to occur. But the changing face of Bali tourism means the average visitor stays for a shorter time and spends much less than before-less than half, according to some estimates. Rooms were available in package tours for as little as 25 US Dollars a night. The discounts mean that the income of workers employed in Bali's tourism industry will get squeezed, even if job losses remain modest. The terrorist attack in Bali will also have a negative impact on the outbound tourism economy of Australia and put a number of Bali travel specialists in Australia out of business. Bali and other islands in the Indonesian archipelago are popular and cheap destinations for Australian families, backpackers and surfers.

According to the Australian Bureau of Statistics, in the seven months to July 2002, 144,400 Australians visited Indonesia, amounting to 7.5 percent of outbound tourists. The Asian region may suffer from indirect effects of the bombing in Bali unnecessarily. This concern was expressed by the Association of South East Asian Nations (ASEAN) when it rejected warnings and advice issued by Western countries including the United States, Britain, Australia and Japan. Such advice had covered all of south east Asia, where tourism accounted for 10.8 percent of GDP and 8.2 percent of employment last year. In US, national tourist authorities and tourist boards, as well as the tourism industry itself - at local and national levels - have reacted in a number of ways. One way, for example, has been to make their destinations more attractive to customers.

In many cases, special committees were set up to deal with the situation after September 11th. Partnerships were established between the private sector and public authorities to tackle problems of financial bottlenecks, e.g. the funding of marketing campaigns or the prevention of bankruptcies in the sector. The measures taken range from price reductions introduced by individual enterprises in the areas of travel, hospitality, tour operating, culture and recreation, to large-scale advertising campaigns by tourist authorities. These have often depended upon substantial injections of finance by both the industry and governments.

Advertising campaigns strongly address the domestic tourism markets. For instance, a campaign run by the Travel Industry Association of America (TIA) features the slogan "See America." A comprehensive plan of action was developed by the Travel Industry Association of America to enable the industry and government to work together to reassure the public that travel is safe while rebuilding consumer confidence in travelling both to and within the United States. The USA Small Business Association (SBA) approved a total of US$21.6 million on disaster loans for small travel agencies. The average loan size was US$50,579. One of the reasons was that SBA recognized the hardships facing travel agencies nationwide in the rapidly changing travel market, especially after September 11 th . The SBA also recognized that travel agencies were dramatically affected by reduced airline commissions and advances in technology, specifically the use of the Internet.

A campaign by the Canadian Tourism Commission (CTC) invited Canadians and near-border Americans to re-discover or discover Canada. In fact, the Canadian Government has been supporting a massive marketing campaign by contributing the equivalent of US$13 million to help the hotel industry recover from a loss of US$3.5 billion incurred in 2001. Austria also ran a major campaign to attract European tourists to their winter sports resorts aimed at replacing missing overseas visitors. One of the most impressive programmes to boost tourism is being developed in the United Kingdom.

To overcome the country's deep crisis in international tourism, the British Government and a number of British tourist industry organizations have announced they will back a new international campaign, boosting marketing support for the British tourist industry to the tune of £ 40 million. The government will provide up to £20 million for this new initiative addressed to seven main market countries and aiming to recover at least half of the estimated £2 billion.- 35 - lost by the tourism industry last year. The campaign features over 1,000 special offers put together by both big and small companies throughout the industry, giving discounts of sometimes as much as 50 per cent.

The New Zealand government announced that it is to make US$2.5 million available for the expansion of New Zealand's official tourism classification and quality-grading company, Qualmark, in order to help attract more tourists through improved quality of services. Another example of government support is that of India where, among other relief measures implemented, a 10 per cent expenditure tax on all food and beverages served by hotels was lifted in federal budget announcements in the spring if this year.

In Japan, the government is providing financial support to the troubled travel industry, of which 99 per cent consists of small and medium-sized enterprises. The government's credit association is doubling the maximum loan guarantee for tourism enterprises and government-affiliated financial institutions are doubling the ceiling for unsecured loans. In general, the tourism sector has been given increased attention by public authorities as a result of the 2001-2002 crisis.

Even in southern Europe, which did comparatively well immediately after the September 11 th , both State authorities and the public were sensitized by the crisis and initiatives for private-public partnership increased. One example is a special Euro-Mediterranean group that has been set up on the initiative of Spain and Tunisia to encourage tourism cooperation between the countries of the European Union and Northern Africa. Ranking of most frequent cost reduction measures in the U.S. lodging industry after the events of September 11th In a number of countries, some measures as described above have already been taken. Others will need more time to develop.

The ILO has monitored the developments in the industry with particular emphasis on human resources development, because it was recognized that information on the employment effect of the crisis is still scarce. There is also a need to find more examples of positive action taken by enterprises, social partners and governments aimed at mitigating the impact of the crisis on employment and working conditions. Furthermore, improved methods of measuring the impact on employment of developments in tourism, as well as a series of case studies on good practices, will help to strengthen the capacity of the tourism sector to handle human resources challenges both in normal times and in times of crisis. In cooperation with different partners, the ILO is prepared to assist developing countries in the modernization of their training systems in the tourism sector in order to help reduce their vulnerability to increased international competition. Raising the quality of services is one possible way of helping to rebuild tourists' confidence after a crisis and it might also have a chance of increasing customer loyalty to a particular destination. These reactions can have a significant effect on a country's revenue from tourism in a very short period of time.

Trends in Lodging Industry

Tourism is the world's largest industry (hotel being major), generating around 10% of the global GDP. It is India's third-largest industry in terms of forex generation. India ranks 34 th in the world in terms of tourism receipts, accounting for only 0.7% of global receipts.

The Indian hotel industry is very highly taxed, compared to global standards. Taxes include sales tax, entertainment tax, expenditure tax and luxury tax, apart from income tax and taxes on food & beverages. Taxes (central and state) can account for as much as 30% of the total bill value in India, as against only around 10% in other Asian countries.

Hotel industry revenues follow seasonal patterns in India, with the peak season, which extends from October to March, registering significantly higher revenues than the off-season. Hotels offer steep discounts during the off-season in an attempt to maintain occupancy levels.

The major hotel chains in India are :-

1. Indian Hotels Company Limited (the Taj group).
2. EIH Limited (the Oberoi group).

3. ITC Hotels Limited (Welcomgroup).
4. Asian Hotels (operating under Hyatt brand).
5. Hotel Leelaventure.

There has been a negative demand-supply gap in the hotel industry in India. The situation is exacerbated with a number of new hotel projects planned by major groups. Besides off-season discounts, hotels are increasingly resorting to steep discounts. The situation was aggravated by the terrorist attack in the USA in September 2001, the riots in Gujarat in February 2002 and the general economic slowdown - all resulted in very low room occupancy levels. The number of foreign tourist arrivals, which can be used as an estimate for room occupancy, increased at a CARG of around 5% over the last decade, but declined by around 10% in FY'02 from FY'01. Arrivals in the first four months of the current year (M4'03) also was lower by 21.9% than in M4'02.

The hotel industry is capital intensive, with a high gestation period. The inclusion of long-term funds lent to the hotel industry by financial institutions under the purview of Section 10(23G) of the Income Tax Act, 1969, will encourage the flow of funds towards this sector, at lower costs, and thus, give a fillip to new construction/expansion/modernisation projects in the hotel industry.

Bringing the hotel industry under the purview of Section 72(A) will allow amalgamation of hotel companies to reap the benefits of carry forward of losses and unabsorbed depreciation. The development of infrastructure, as envisaged in the Budget, will increase both domestic and international traffic (and therefore occupancy levels), for both tourist and business categories.

The lodging industry in the United States as a whole achieved a room occupancy rate of 59.2-percent in the year 2002 compared to 60-percent in 2001 and 63.5-percent in 2000. These falling occupancy levels reflect the most significant decline in the industry in over 50 years. A low occupancy rate, combined with a drop in room rates have resulted in lower room revenues and profits. Smith Travel Research (STR), a lodging industry consulting firm, projects the 2003 occupancy rate in the U.S. to be 59.4-percent and the 2004 rate to be 60.6-percent.

The lodging industry is heavily dependent on consumer confidence or how people feel about the current economic environment. Business travel, the largest segment in the industry, fluctuates directly to overall economic conditions. Leisure travel is usually avoided or postponed in times of economic uncertainty. The demand for lodging will not pick up until people are more confident about the state of the economy.

The Midwest (Wisconsin, Michigan, Minnesota, Indiana, Iowa and Illinois) experienced a decline in room occupancy rate in the year 2002 and again in 2003. Wisconsin's decline of 0.6-percent for 2003 was the smallest in the region. Wisconsin was the only state in the Midwest to experience a rise in ADR (average daily rate) for both the year 2003 and 2002, with a 0.9-percent increase in 2003.

The following are some of the major trends facing the lodging industry:

Consolidation: The joining or merger of two firms is referred to as consolidation. There is a long-term trend toward consolidation in the lodging industry due to the benefits of size and market penetration. Marriot Lodging, for example, now operates 11 brands ranging from Fairfield Inns to Ritz Carlton hotels.

Larger consolidated companies can offer economies of scale that provides effective cost controls, frequent traveler programs, reservation systems, sales and marketing programs. Acquisition activity has been slow in the last three years after significant activity in the late 1990's.

Third party reservation: Companies like Travelocity, Expedia, Priceline.com and Hotels.com are used increasingly by travellers for reserving their hotel and motel rooms. By the year 2005, an estimated 1 in 5 hotel bookings will be made online, up from 1 in 12 bookings in 2002. According to Jupiter Research, online hotel reservations will grow from $5 billion in 2002 to $14.8 billion in 2007.

According to Cendant Corporation, customers shopping for a room online want a friendly and efficient booking experience, great prices, and a well-known and trusted brand.

New technologies: Technology is being used to attract potential customers and to keep operating costs lower at hotels and motels. High-speed internet, wireless internet access and teleconferencing capabilities are some examples of technologies that are attractive to business travellers. Some hotels are using automated guest check-in to keep their costs down.

Operations: During times of declining occupancy and economic uncertainty, lodging operators are continuing to explore new and effective cost controls. The challenge is to maximize cash flow without hurting customer service. Outstanding customer service and guest rooms are critical factors in maintaining and improving market share.

Customer market segments: Some companies are paying special attention to certain customer segments that may not be very sensitive to economic conditions. These can include seniors, fraternal and religious groups and wedding parties.

Development: Extended stay hotels have emerged with a unique, apartment-style format (with kitchen, dining and work areas) for longer-term stays. The growth of condominium hotels represent an alternative to traditional lender financing and, at the same time, provides a "built in" customer base. Boutique hotels that offer a "home away from home" feeling are becoming more popular as these hotels offer unique personalities achieved through their designs and surroundings. In a bid for additional sources of profit, hotels are adding new services and amenities such as spas.

There is a slowdown in new hotel construction as lenders are more interested in deals such as refinancing, consolidation, renovation and repositioning of existing properties. Lenders are also becoming stricter about their terms. Local and regional banks, the biggest funding source for limited-service hotels, are requiring developers to have strong existing relationships with the banks and solid project characteristics like location, brand and management.

Successful existing properties are continuously renovating their properties. Furniture, fixtures, equipment and building materials need constant update regardless of economic conditions.

Excess supply is a significant problem faced by the lodging industry. Occupancy levels have fallen in the last few years due to room supply increasing faster than room demand. Hotel companies are solving this problem by reassessing their capital plans so that they can decide whether to undertake certain projects. Some companies are also eliminating certain properties or parts of their properties that they feel do not have a strategic value. The cutting back of room supply may be a blessing for the lodging industry in the long run as it allows demand catch up with supply.

5

Economic Development and Tourism

Tourism is a significant industry in many of the world's poorest countries. It can have important impacts on the livelihoods of the world's poor, but these impacts are rarely well understood and may often be negative. Strategies for enhancing impacts of tourism on the poor need to be developed. This requires starting with understanding how different tourism approaches affect local people, how the wide range of costs and benefits are distributed among stakeholders and what factors affect benefits to the poor. However, there is a general lack of information on which to base such an understanding, despite a growing interest in promoting local benefits from tourism, particularly around nature conservation areas.

Having grown faster than the world GDP since the 1950s, international tourism is today one of the most important tradable sectors, with expenditure on tourist goods and services representing some 8% of total world export receipts and 5% of world GDP. In spite of this, the importance of this sector for a country's overall growth performance has been often neglected in the economic literature. For instance, in the recent impressive survey on the economic analysis of tourism, only very few papers out of the hundreds reviewed deal explicitly with the long-run growth consequences of specialisation in tourism.

Consequently, not much work can be found on theoretical models aimed at explaining some interesting empirical findings characterising the relationship between economic growth and tourism specialisation in cross-country data. Consider, for instance, the following experiment in which two separate lists of countries from the World Bank data set are used. The first list includes the top fifteen fastest growing countries in per capita income, from 1985 to 1995 . The second includes the fifteen countries with the highest degree of specialisation in tourism, defined as share of international tourism receipt with respect to the value added.

There are two empirical regularities which might characterise the tourism sector when viewed from a macroeconomic perspective: (i) tourism specialisation can make a country grow fast; (ii) countries specialised in tourism are generally small ones.

Point (i) above indicates that tourism specialisation might not be detrimental to economic growth. While obviously no sector is "detrimental" to growth in an exogenous growth setting, things may be very different when the growth rate is endogenously determined. Much of the recent literature in this field points to the key positive role the more innovative sectors play in such determination. Considering countries in isolation, a larger innovative sector may spur faster growth in the long run.

If trade induces different countries to specialise in sectors with different dynamic potentials, and technological spillovers across sectors and countries are not strong enough, then uneven growth is normally obtained. While these preliminary remarks may not sound too promising for countries specialising in tourism, the endogenous growth setting is nevertheless the one we need to consider in order addressing fact (i).

International trade will force all countries to specialise completely according to the comparative advantage they have when trade opens up. The growth rate of a country therefore depends on such complete specialisation. Therefore, productivity grows faster in countries specialised in M (measured in terms of this good) than in the other countries. However, with preferences assumed to be homothetic and identical everywhere, the terms of trade move in favour of the slow-growing good, tourism, at a constant rate.

In words, tourism is not harmful for growth if the international terms of trade move in its fast enough to more than offset the difference in sectoral productivity growth. For this to happen, the two goods must not be close substitute. The empirical value on the elasticity of substitution between manufactured goods and the tourism is therefore an important piece of the evidence when it comes to evaluating the long-run consequences for an economy that specialised in tourism.

Recently, Candela and Cellini have provided an explanation based on the idea that countries with different absolute (population) sizes face different opportunity costs associated with tourism specialisation.More precisely, they note that, within Lucas's framework, "the smaller is a small-economy, the easier the pattern of the term of trade offsets the technology gap disadvantage", so that "the opportunity cost of specialisation in tourism is smaller, the smaller is the country".

Countries specialised in tourism are small and they grow fast-faster than the others, on average. Countries specialised in tourism have experienced a per capita income growth of about 5% per year during the period 1985-1994. During the same period the average growth rate at the World level was equal to 0.8%, and for the subset of developing countries it was equal to 3.6%. In other words, extending Lucas's approach by introducing heterogeneity in absolute size across countries does generate an explanatory hypothesis of point (ii). However, the same modification makes the model incapable of jointly explain point (i). Analytically, it is not difficult to single out the source of the problem. To address point (ii), CC rely on a strong and generally regarded counterfactual scale effect based on the size of the labour force. As a consequence, the smaller countries' growth path is the slower one .

In the following, we propose an alternative explanation in which a resource-based comparative advantage is what characterises the heterogeneity across the existing countries. Most of the small fast growing countries specialised in tourism ground their supply of tourism services on their natural resources. This suggests a second hypothesis - alternative to the one based on absolute size- to address point (ii).

Some indirect evidence available in the empirical literature, as well as casual inspection of the data, suggest that small countries are likely to be characterised by higher than average per-capita amounts of the natural resource which attracts tourists. In the dynamic setting, comparative advantage in tourism depends on the size of the natural resource suitable for tourism development relative to some measure of the country's size, such as its overall population. In a rather traditional fashion, heterogeneity in relative endowments of natural resources explains the pattern of specialisation obtained in the international marketplace. Clearly, this analysis can be regarded as an explanation of point (ii) only insofar as the relative endowment of natural resources is shown to be significantly higher in small tourism countries than in the non-tourism countries, especially the larger ones.

Tourism has become a major industry in Indonesia within the last three decades. Clientele and investments from Japan, Australia and other countries of Southeast Asia have also helped in fuelling the growth. To quote Cochrane, 'Visitor arrivals to Indonesia increased by more than 400% in the decade 1985-1994, and reached over 5 million by the end of 1996. The industry is the country's third largest foreign exchange earner, generating $5,172 million in 1995'.

Two studies, *'Perspectives on tourism in selected Balinese villages'* by Geoffrey Wall and *'Tourism and cultural minorities'* by Jean-Luc Maurer and Arlette Zeigler, are useful in understanding the impact of tourism in Bali. Bali, with a population of about three million, is the most popular resort in Indonesia and received 1.9 million tourists in 1990. Tourism and the handicrafts industry contribute significantly to the island's economy, estimates varying between 20-40% of GDP.

The strongest impacts from tourism are felt in the southern part of the island - largely in the 'tourism triangle' of Kuta-Denpasar-Sanur, where resort tourism is dominant. In this 'triangle' major resorts, such as the 2,500 room complex at Nusa Dua are built with large investment inputs, generally require imported technology, materials and foreign-trained staff, occupy acres of valuable farmland and consume vast amounts of water. Gains to the local community from employment generated by the industry are limited, particularly when compared with losses - displacement can arise as a major issue when access to farmland and irrigation water is reduced, and the ability to earn a livelihood from a shrinking natural resource base is limited.

Deliberate policies and plans to spread the positive economic impacts of tourism without encouraging adverse socio-cultural impacts, have ensured that many traditions have been retained. For example, planning has concentrated on providing tourist facilities in Kuta, Sanur and Nusa Dua in the south of the island, but has also designated excursion roads to facilitate the movement of tourists from the three major accommodation nodes to various attractions in the interior of the island. Geoffrey Wall's study allays fears that, with millions of visitors to the island, tourism dominates the economy and social development of Bali.

Although tourism and tourists have a significant influence on the economy, social norms and aspirations in some areas, tourism remains a peripheral or non-existent activity in large parts of the island. Traditional institutions and occupations still govern a large number of the island's villages and in some, these cultural traditions have even been used to manage tourism-related activities. Lodges are designed along similar lines to traditional houses, with rooms often built as an annexe of the central courtyard and are generally family owned and run. Similarly, most restaurants are managed either by families or by voluntary associations or sekaha with clear principles for division of work and revenues. Voluntary associations are also used for car and bicycle rentals and running minibus services.

Many cultural activities have developed within the framework of mutual aid groups, known as banjar, which usually function around feasts. These activities require little capital and use mainly local technological resources, and are therefore well suited to the Balinese way of life. While most of Bali has retained its cultural roots, the resilience of the Balinese society is put to the test at large resorts, as the five star culture begins to take its toll. A subculture dominated by the unrestrained pursuit of money, drugs and sex is developing, especially amongst a minority of Balinese youth residing near the complexes.

In Philippines, Marinduque Island in Luzon has a highly seasonal tourist trade which is important to the local economy but does not dominate it. Most impacts have tended to be positive. Tourism is based on a blend of indigenous traditions and Christian rites at Easter and Christmas, which attracts non-resident family members and friends, expatriates in the Philippines and foreign tourists. Informal accommodation continues to be important, and formal accommodation is confined to a relatively small part of the island. For the majority of the population, tourism is an additional, rather than principal source of income. Although, the study does not compare economic gains from tourism to other sectors, it appears to be relatively minor.

Guided by a National Tourism Master Plan drawn up in 1991, the tourism industry in Vietnam has witnessed phenomenal growth in the 1990s, with the number of foreign tourists increasing from about 250,000 in 1990 to about 1.6 million in 1996. Growth has been dominated by large-scale investments in joint ventures between foreign corporations and local state enterprises.

International tourism in Nepal has grown from a trickle in the early 1960s to about 300,000 visitors per year in the early 1990s, growing at about 6% each year between 1976 and 1992. An ambitious Tourism Master Plan was drawn up and a Ministry of Tourism was established in 1977.

Tourism is now a major foreign exchange earner for Nepal, and the average contribution of tourism earnings to GDP increased from 1% in 1974 to nearly 4% in 1992. The share of tourism in the total value of merchandise exports more than trebled from 19% in 1973-74 to about 60% in 1989, decreasing again to 36% in 1992. Asians and Western Europeans constitute more than two-thirds of the incoming tourists. Since the 1980s, the Asian market has grown more quickly than the West European market.

Nepal is known for mountain tourism - mountaineering, trekking and rafting - though less than a third of visitors partake in these activities. The majority of Indians spend time in recreational and religious activities in the Kathmandu Valley, and on relatively short drives to Pokhra and the Chitwan National Park or other protected areas in the terai region.

The Centre for Resource and Environment Studies (CREST) of the International Centre for Integrated Mountain Development (ICIMOD) synthesises existing literature to provide an overview of mountain tourism, and includes an analysis of community related issues as well as national level economics. It also examines the relationship between government departments and ministries, especially those dealing with tourism, forests and nature conservation.

Wells analyses the economics of nature tourism and focuses on the concept of consumer surplus: 'the difference between what an individual pays and what they would have been prepared to pay', and on how this could be reduced to pay for nature conservation activities. Zurich attempts to build models to describe the movement of adventure tourism to remote frontiers, and the impact this has on 'destinations located among isolated, subsistence populations', using Nepal as an example.

Dibya Gurung examines gender issues in the context of tourism, with case studies in the Annapurna region providing useful insights. The Jefferies report describes the beginnings of nature conservation efforts in the region around Mount Everest, especially in the context of tourism impacts and the efforts by the park management to address community related issues. CREST looks at the Annapurna and Gorkha regions. Banskota and Sharma also examine the initiative to link conservation and mountain tourism around the Laltang National Park and the impact of tourism on the Pehwal Lake, near the fast-growing town of Pokhra at the gateway to Annapurna.

Tourism is the dominant source of income in areas that have become popular for trekking, mountaineering or wildlife, but impacts have also been felt in other regions through backward and forward linkages. With the introduction of fees for trekking and mountaineering, tourism has become an import source of revenuc for the government.

Development of tourism activities in Sagarmatha National Park took place in the context of a society that was undergoing rapid transformation. With the closure of the border between Tibet and Nepal in 1959, trading activities which were the most important source of income for the Sherpas were suspended. The loss of income was soon compensated for by economic gains from tourism according to Wells. By 1986 two thirds of the families living in the park were participating in the tourism industry.

Locally owned and operated lodges were established. By 1991 the number of lodges had increased to 82. Wells also gives a graphic description of Namche Bazaar to illustrate the pace of economic growth, 'Namche Bazaar, the tourist centre in the park, includes new tourist lodges, grocery stores, tea shops, a bank and a telegraph office, a scene of apparently unbounded small-scale capitalism. A remote and somewhat poor rural society has rapidly become affluent and cosmopolitan with considerable economic aspirations, although the resilient Sherpa society and culture has remarkably cohesive'.

The impact of mountain tourism appears to have been more beneficial for host communities than cultural and recreational tourism. A large number of women tend to get involved in the tourism industry in mountain tourism areas, often in a position of control. A survey conducted by the Nepal Rashtriya Bank in 1990 showed that less than a sixth of those employed in Nepal's tourism were women. However, female employment was greater than male employment in Sagarmatha, Annapurna and Latang, the three main destinations for mountain tourism, which account for over three quarters of mountain tourism. Lodges owned and managed by families from local communities dominate the accommodation and catering sectors in these regions. In contrast, larger hotels, where self-employment becomes less important, dominate the accommodation and catering sectors serving cultural and recreational tourism.

Tourism is confined to small regions. Large areas, especially in northern Nepal, have a high tourism potential but have not been able to realise it due to the lack of proper development. In most conservation areas, there has been little consultation with people residing in and using the conservation areas, and there are conflicting interests that have not been resolved, resulting in the army having been deployed to protect these areas. The Annapurna Conservation Area, whose management plans were designed after extensive consultation, is the exception. Managed by the King Mahendra Nature Conservation Trust

(KMNTC), the Annapurna Conservation Area Project (ACAP) has succeeded in integrating tourism with local community development.

There is a strong link in Nepal between conservation and mountain tourism. The areas visited by tourists outside Kathmandu are largely protected areas. Jefferies, who was the project leader of the New Zealand Sagarmatha National Park Project provides valuable insights into how various initiatives to control the impact of tourism on the environment were first conceived and implemented. One example of efforts to reduce the impact on the environment focused on finding alternatives to wood as the main source of fuel at trekking lodges along the Sagarmatha route. It seems to have had a significant demonstrative effect.

The idea of opening visitors centres to introduce visitors to the natural and cultural heritage was first tested at Sagarmatha. Traditional land use practices were given due consideration while planning and implementing park management activities. This was a relatively new concept at the time and had still not been fully adopted in many protected areas, even in protected areas where people's participation was an important objective. This has now become a standard recommendation for effective park management.

In recent years, further progress has been made in minimising environmental impacts through regulations and environmental education. However, despite the successful demonstrations and efforts to enhance people's participation, environmental issues in the popular trekking and mountaineering areas remain problematic, particularly deforestation induced by trekking and an unchecked spread of litter. The level of integration between tourism departments, industry, and the conservation agency responsible for the management of protected areas, is very poor. There is a need for further institutional strengthening and development. Efforts are being made to learn and build on successes such as Sagarmatha and Annapurna, and to institutionalise participatory methods within the Department of National Parks and Wildlife Conservation (DNPWC).

Upper Mustang, on the other hand, illustrates a case where the vested interests of its organised tourism industry, especially tour operators based in Khatmandu, have prevented local communities making significant gains from tourism. Strict regulations, made in the name of protecting local communities and cultural and natural heritage, have minimised participation of the local community in the industry. The local people have gained little from the growth of the industry. This remote and underdeveloped region, which was closed to western visitors until March 1992, is significant because it is one of the last remains of untouched Tibetan art, architecture, religion and culture. Living conditions are harsh. Most of Mustang remains under snow for four to five months a year and basic necessities such as drinking water, health services, schools and alternative sources of energy are virtually non-existent.

There are strict regulations that control the flow of tourists to the area. Initially, only 200 visitors were to be allowed entry into the region, but under pressure from travel and trekking agencies the number of visitors rapidly increased and over 500 visitors were allowed into the area in the first eight months. Within less than a year of opening the area, the number of tourists allowed to visit the area was increased to 1,000 a year, and there are fears that the number of tourists is already too high for an area with only 1,000 or so households scattered in 32 hamlets.

High tourism fees are imposed: US$700 for up to ten days of trekking and US$100 per day for each day thereafter. However, direct economic gains to the region have been limited by the regulations governing tours, which leave little room for local entrepreneurs to thrive. TANA, a tour agency association with considerable clout in Nepal, played a significant role in drawing up guidelines for trekking. Travellers are not allowed to visit the area independently, but must visit with a tour operator, who generally provides accommodation in tents as well as food.

The regulations also require that the agencies must recruit their full complement of porters before reaching Upper Mustang, thus denying another income earning opportunity to the local population. An innovative initiative to bring in substantial revenue by building up the existing tradition of inn keeping was reported by Myra Shackley. However, Gurung's article and Banskota and Sharma's study, both written almost four years later, do not mention the existence of such a programme.

Tourism in India has grown significantly since the 1970's, through both international and domestic tourism. The two destination areas analysed here, Himachal Pradesh and the hill areas of Uttar Pradesh, are both in the Western Himalayas and so focus on mountain, recreational and religious tourism. They provide interesting comparisons with developments in Nepal. Unlike Nepal, tourism is not a major sector of the economy of these destination areas.

Domestic tourism provides up to 95% of the market in these regions, with 60-70% coming from the northern region of India. Pilgrimages form an important market segment, especially in the UP Hills, where 70% of domestic tourists are pilgrims. Large crowds, often concentrated in small towns, are common in both areas during the peak season.

Himachal Pradesh, east of Kashmir, has become a major tourist destination in the Indian Himalayas. Recent political instability in Kashmir and the UP Hills has contributed to the increasing number of tourists visiting this area. Other factors attracting tourists to Himachal Pradesh include the international popularity of His Holiness the Dalai Lama and the growing interest in trekking in the Himalayas.

Kullu Valley, especially the town of Manali, is perhaps the most important tourist destination in Himachal Pradesh after the capital city of Shimla. The Kullu Valley has historically formed a part of important trade routes, though unlike many other areas of the Himalayas, it has experienced a relatively long period of social and political stability. The growth of tourism in the valley, particularly in Manali, has been phenomenal since the 1970s. Improved transportation networks, construction of accommodation facilities and vigorous marketing by the state government facilitated this growth. The number of visitors grew from 38,000 per year in 1975 to 130,000 in 1985 and visitations were projected to be 250,000 by 1990. Domestic tourists now dominate the tourism market by a ratio of 20:1 and total tourism revenues were estimated at Rs2-2.5 billion, about a fifth of the state's domestic product.

The rapid growth in tourism has had significant impacts on society and the environment in and around Manali. A small cluster of villages has rapidly become a semi-urban area, with large in-migration from elsewhere in the state, the country and even from other countries. While the social structure continues to be relatively unaffected, there is a visible change in individual behaviour. Environmental impacts as a result of population and infrastructure growth have been more dramatic and are likely to increase as options for construction in areas not prone to floods and erosion become fewer. In one of the studies for Kullu Valley, local residents expressed a strong dislike for agency tourism as it brought little benefit to them.

The Himachal Pradesh government has tried to control the development of Manali as a tourist resort, through the development of Master Plans. Berkes and Gardner study shows that Manali has continued to grow rapidly since Singh conducted his research, though is not clear to what extent this is a result of master plans. Two of the positive features of more recent policies of the State Government, noted by AME are the dispersal of tourism to areas that have a potential, but are yet to be developed as tourist destinations, and constant appraisals of tourism activities. The State Government's policies also emphasise private sector provision of accommodation, catering and transport facilities, so that it can concentrate on building up infrastructure.

Kinnaur is a relatively prosperous district as a result of horticulture, and is known for its cultural diversity and the better status that women here enjoy than in most other parts of the state. The district was only opened to tourism in 1992, and attracts mostly middle and upper-middle class Indians, who tend to stay for a relatively long time, and return several times. The Himachal Pradesh Tourism Development Corporation has a five year Master Plan to develop tourism in the district, which includes plans to set up a complex with accommodation facilities, improve infrastructure and provide civic amenities in important towns. The plan also proposes the introduction of paying guest accommodation, providing roadside facilities for catering and vending, and for promoting local handicrafts.

The paying guest scheme, which was developed by the state, is identified as a positive aspect of tourism in the area by AME, but recommendations are made to improve it further. The existing paying guest accommodation is close to the tourist centre itself, and is approached when government accommodation is not available or at the suggestion of earlier visitors. The study recommends that, if the paying guest scheme expands, the government will provide a centralised system for disseminating information on the availability of accommodation, and prioritises the provision of telephones to houses within the scheme. With a large number of repeat visits, a guesthouse with accommodation for about eight to ten persons could develop a regular clientele and ensure viability. The risks would be low as most guesthouses are being run as an adjunct to orchards.

At present, tour agencies operating in Kinnaur prefer to accommodate their groups in camps, which raises the question of whether there is scope for an alliance between the tour operators and guesthouse owners, or whether they are best left to develop as different forms of tourism in the area. In most orchard areas in the state, labourers demand a good wage for a significant part of the year and activities such as vending would have a high opportunity cost.

The hill districts of Uttar Pradesh (UP) are best known as pilgrim centres, revered and visited for centuries by people from the rest of India. Prior to road access, pilgrims trekked up, staying in local rest houses called Chattis and significantly supporting the local economy. Estimates made in the late nineteenth century show that about half of the total income of the region was earned from tourism. The number of pilgrims has increased hugely with increasing access to road transport.

The hill resorts, established by the British, have become popular with the middle class residing in the north Indian plains. Two nature reserves in the foothills, the Jim Corbett National Park, the first park to be gazetted in the country, and the Rajaji Park, are also popular destinations. The number of foreign tourists is increasing, attracted by the yoga and meditation centres. The overview of AME for Himachal Pradesh and the hill districts of UP is complemented by a case study on Badrinath, the major pilgrimage centre of the UP hills. Now that road transport predominates over walking, pilgrims contribute much less to the local economy in the smaller villages between major towns or pilgrim centres.

Tourism continues to generate about half of the domestic product of the region, but now a large proportion of this goes to entrepreneurs who have recently moved into the area. Many pilgrim centres have now become starting points for trekking tours, which are often controlled by people from outside the region. Most accommodation is now provided by the state and private sectors, and is frequently managed by recent migrants.

The Badrinath Tourist Zone covers the Alknanada Basin, catchments in the Greater Himalayas and a small part of the Zanskar Range. The tourism season is short, determined by the open and closing dates for the main temple at Badrinath. Other important pilgrim centres include Kedarnatth, and Char Dahm for Hindus and Hem Kund for Sikhs, with other attractions of trekking to the Valley of Flowers, and skiing at the resort developed at Auli. The study on Badrinath Tourist Zone states that the local population is fairly small and therefore almost all could benefit. Hindu religious bodies used to manage all of the pilgrim centres, but the fact that management is now in the hands of bodies appointed by the government has meant that the interests of local communities are disregarded. As a result, traditional systems have come to a halt and the government is left to cope.

The development of infrastructure connected with modern tourism has not extended to smaller settlements en route to the pilgrim centres, and they have therefore lost some of the income they earned before road transport changed the nature of pilgrimages in the area. There is a paying guest scheme supported by the government, though it is a poor attempt to replicate the chattis managed by village communities where the pilgrims were accommodated before the advent of roads. The AME study reports that individuals often misuse the scheme to increase their physical assets.

Garhwal Mandal Vikas Nigam (GMVN), a state government enterprise plays a major role in providing accommodation facilities and transport. The study also warns against the government's proposal 'to acquire land and distribute it at very low prices to outside business interests...as it will deprive the local people of benefits'. The study also warns against further road construction, as this would lead to environmental degradation. Improvement of foot routes to the interior villages in the Zanskar Range is recommended instead, together with the organisation of outlets to facilitate marketing of woollen carpets and other woollen goods from this region, and the training of youth from these villages as guides.

Growth in tourism activities has also been accompanied by a number of negative environmental impacts. Sanitation facilities at Badrinath and Joshimath, another important pilgrimage centre further downstream, have failed to keep pace with the ever-increasing pilgrim traffic despite constant efforts and seasonal preparations. The problems have been further accentuated in Badrinath by the lack of a regular source of finance for the municipality.

A road network providing easy access to these centres, has led to phenomenal growth in the number of tourists. This has resulted in a depletion of forest cover mainly as a result of trampling that has occurred along the Lakshman Ganga leading to Ghangaria, from where one visits Hem Kund, and at the Valley of Flowers, an important biosphere reserve of the country. Fortunately, as night camping is not allowed in the Valley of Flowers, this has helped in limiting the damage, confining it to the entrance and fringes of the Reserve.

ECONOMIC IMPACTS

The way in which local people are economically affected by tourism depends critically on whether and how they participate in the industry. While definitions may blur, it is useful to distinguish between participation in the formal sector (such as hotels), the informal sector (such as vending, boating) and in the secondary enterprises which have linkages with tourism (such as food supply). As indicated below, the case studies suggest local participation in the formal sector is highly variable, participation in the informal sector is often considerable and very important, while linkages are often critical in handicraft production but variable or limited in other sectors.

Formal sector: The better-off segments of local communities tend to dominate accommodation provision, but do not always monopolise it. As tourism is introduced, the relatively better-off households can begin by offering hospitality through home-stays, in many places only charging for food. Home-stays also become an important source of income in more developed destinations during peak seasons when accommodation in guest houses, lodges and hotels is not easily available. In Cemoro Lawang/ Ngadisari some accommodation is provided by poorer people, especially in households beside the road leading up to the caldera rim. Similar evidence was found in other case study areas. Backpackers and domestic tourists often provide a market for poorer households.

As tourism grows, lodges and hotels begin to replace home-stays. In some cases, this marks an increasing involvement of outside investors, as in the Boracay case study reported earlier. In other cases, local entrepreneurs maintain a key role - such as the local apple orchard owners in Kinnaur and locals who have expanded their premises in Marinduque. Once luxury resorts develop, as in Bali, the scenario becomes more complex with international investors beginning to play an increasing role. Transport tends to fall into a grey area between the formal sector and informal sectors.

Most destinations have a fleet of taxis, jeeps or other motorised transport, often driven by the owners. In Kinnaur, the number of taxi drivers increased dramatically within two years of travel restrictions to the area being relaxed. In 1992, there was only one taxi in Reng Peo, an important town in the region, but this increased to 50 by 1994. Remote villages now also have taxi operators. Owners' associations, operating on rota systems are becoming a common phenomenon. This is well documented for taxis and horse rides in the Bromo Tennger study in Indonesia where horse and jeep owners' associations provide a contact point for tour operators and hotel owners, as well as standardised prices and practices. Unfortunately, the jeep owners suffered a setback when a road was constructed, allowing tour buses to reach a car park just below the caldera ring, the main tourist attraction. In other places, taxi drivers have lost custom as organised tours have begun to replace independent travel.

Information on employment in formal sector tourism is scattered and not very systematic. There is mention of high placed jobs in resorts going to non-locals, expatriate staff, or foreign trained nationals who are unlikely to integrate into the local community. However, there is almost no mention about who gets the middle and lower ranking jobs. Cleaning and driving may be dull and grim, but they can be significant sources of employment and livelihood improvement locally. Given the potentially large scale employment in mass tourism, this area needs more attention.

It seems that middle-ranking jobs often go to urban migrants, many of whom are likely to gradually integrate into the local society, or form a separate community with the possibility of boundaries merging between the two. But the longer the resorts have been established, the more likely it is that local populations will pick up the skills to fill these positions. The potential for employment of local staff also seems to improve as one moves away from the luxury resorts to less upmarket tourism. This potential is highlighted in the study on livelihood security in two villages near Manali in India where unprecedented growth of tourism and subsequent urban expansion has led to increased employment opportunities.

Informal sector: Several case studies indicate the importance of the informal sector for enhancing local benefits. The informal sector includes tourism-related activities such as collection and sale of fuel wood for the tourism industry, vending, and running tea stalls. The income generated by the informal sector can be quite staggering. 1979 estimates for Pagboche, a small village in the Khumbu region of Nepal, showed an income of NR120,000 from the sale of fuelwood alone. Comparisons with income from formal employment have not been made, but it appears likely that the contribution to total income would have been very significant for 1979.

In some instances, the poor can gain significantly from the informal sector related to tourism, - in Pangandaran, for instance, 'informal sector activities are particularly attractive to lower class people for a number of reasons: they do not usually require special skills or education; they need little capital investment; they can be undertaken as a secondary occupation in addition to routine occupations; and they do not require government permits or follow government regulations'. In particular, vending provides a relatively easy entry into tourism-related trades for the poor, particularly women. It is often a seasonal activity, providing a substantial boost to the income of poor.

However, the informal sector tends to get the least attention when interventions are planned, and interventions are frequently detrimental to this sector - particularly to vendors whose access to tourists can be restricted. The market has traditionally been outside, but the authorities have built on the space once occupied by the ethnic minorities. It is rarely recognised that vendors are sometimes the only point of contact between the local community and tourists, and are hence crucial to a tourist's impression of a place, as well as to the expansion of economic opportunities for the poor.

One documented exception is the initiatives in Yogyakarta in Indonesia, where a flexible licensing system, cooperative and an association have been established, though the authors also note that 'during the same time period and for the same reasons, similar associations were established in other developing countries'. Casual labour and self-employment provide major avenues for local communities to enhance livelihood opportunities from tourism. Unlike formal employment, self-employment tends to highlight the entrepreneurial spirit of village communities. Villagers are used to stringing together a livelihood from a variety of sources, often giving them a natural knack for enterprise, and the range of case studies highlight a wide variety of ways in which local people have exploited their opportunities.

Casual labour or self-employment linked to formal sector tourism emerges as important. For example, there is evidence that agencies organising trekking and mountaineering activities in Nepal depend on a well-organised labour market to employ porters, cooks and guides on a seasonal basis, often with labour contractors acting as intermediaries. An estimate made in 1989 showed that trekking alone generated 0.5-1 million man-days of employment in a year. The seasonal nature of tourism in most destinations can be a disadvantage, especially if the dependency on tourism is significant. However, seasonal opportunities can also be beneficial. They could be an additional source of income, providing a cushion in time of need.

In Marinduque Island there is a large influx of tourists during Easter, many of whom stay in private homes, providing an extra income for the owners . Or, as it happens sometimes, the tourist season coincides with the lean season, when the availability of other income earning opportunities is low.

In most regions near the sea, fishing boats divert their activities to tourism in peak seasons, ferrying people or providing pleasure rides. In Pangadaran, 'many canoe owners switch their boats from fishing to conveying tourists to the game park, a much more remunerative activity than fishing. For the longest trip the price was Rp40,000 in 1992'. The lodges of Nepal, the losman of Bali and the hotels and restaurants in Boracay and Sa Pa and the vending stalls of Yogyakarta also create jobs, either seasonal or more continuous. Much of the literature lacks specific focus and quantification, making analysis difficult.

Role of Agriculture

Significant gains may accrue from economic linkages between tourism and other economic sectors such as horticulture, dairy and handicrafts. Agricultural economic linkages are not well explored in the literature, although the impact can be quite dramatic. In Nepal, income from tourism combined with horticulture, poultry and dairy has often helped to reverse the trend of out-migration. A study found that profits from fruit cultivation in the Rasuva district, have been much higher than those from grain crops. Per hectare yields from a fruit orchard was worth ten times that from a paddy field and more than thirty times than that from a maize crop. Tourists provide the main market for fruit harvests, both in Kathmandu and the local area.

In the Kullu Valley in India, the local government made special arrangements for the semi-nomadic Gujjars to use the forests for grazing and milk production, as the tourism industry was facing milk shortages. As it became more lucrative over time, local villagers used it as an important supplementary activity, and many are now keen for the grazing rights given to the Gujjars to be withdrawn. The Bromo Tennger Semeru National Park in Indonesia shows how expansion of the informal sector can lead to further linkages in surrounding areas. There are 450-500 horses in Ngadisari/Cemoro Lawang, with around one-third owned by people in neighbouring villages. Grass is brought in from other villages to fulfil their fodder demands, creating further employment.

The environmental impacts of agricultural change vary. In parts of Nepal, tourism has provided the impetus for a change in land use on highland slopes from unsustainable dryland agriculture to horticulture, reversing the trend of gradual degradation. In Bromo Tengger, the cropping pattern has also changed to vegetable growing, but accompanied by increased fertiliser and pesticide use. This change has been facilitated by an injection of money from the tourism industry. In Vietnam in Sa Pa, tourism has increased the demand for non-timber forest products so ethnic minorities have experienced an increase in their income, but at the expense of the environment.

The growth of the handicraft industry around tourism has been better documented, and it clearly can be a very significant source of economic benefits. The 1990 Nepal Rashtriya Bank report showed that 14.7% of tourist expenditure was spent on shopping, mostly on handicrafts, curios, jewellery, carpets, garments and books. A survey in the Kullu Valley showed that on average a visitor spent Rs420 on gifts, compared with Rs600 spent on food and accommodation. In Yogyakarta, the handicrafts market supports a web of communities in and around the city with complex systems that have evolved for production, distribution and sale of handicrafts.

In Kullu, the craft industry, which initially received a boost from tourism, now provides significant income in its own right. Shawls and caps constitute the valley's souvenir industry and are also an important export item. Native costumes such as pattoos, patti, namda, gudma and pullans are popular with residents and domestic tourists, and basketry and wooden toys are also popular cottage industries. The government has set up training and technical centres to build on this success.

The Sa Pa case study points to possible dangers when local crafts become a tourist attraction. Initially, ethnic minority women earned attractive income from selling traditional embroidery. With the growth of the industry, competition from imitators has made the market more competitive and has undermined the cultural value of the crafts. The embroidery is done intermittently between other tasks, at home and in the market. Crafts are often sold at very low prices, undervalued in relation to the time and skills involved, because the women need cash. They are exploited as primary producers, and the value added is reaped by others, further along the market chain.

Interventions may be necessary to prevent the emergence of such negative impacts. An innovative intervention in Irian Jaya, with the craftsmen being paid adequately for their highly skilled labour, has helped to preserve traditional skills and helped traditions evolve in a modern context. The Asmat Art Auction, organised in October every year for the past fifteen years, generates high profits to traditional wood carvers on the island. Wood carvers from more than sixty villages crafted around 200 artefacts each, all of which were auctioned in 1995 and 1996, fetching an average of US$ 10 per piece. In addition there were competitions that gave away valuable cash prizes.

In India, handicraft markets in major cities and tourist centres are being organised by government agencies and NGOs, though the impacts are not documented in the studies analysed here. The Indonesian case of Bali is unique in that their handicrafts are not only very popular but the Balinese also hold classes for tourists to learn them. In Vietnam, 'craftlink' has been established by a consortium of NGOs who work with ethnic minority women. The goal of craftlink is to provide a means to link the women to markets and to develop and improve their skills.

Impacts of natural resources

Apart from the cash-earning opportunities offered by tourism, there are many other ways in which the sector affects local livelihoods positively and negatively. One of the main issues to emerge in the case studies is the impact on natural resources and local access to them. The other is socio-cultural impacts. However, impacts on natural resources are often considered as an 'environmental' issue from a conservation perspective, so it is not always easy to assess exactly how environmental change is experienced by local residents. Poorer sections of the community whose dependence on natural resources is significant are especially vulnerable to loss of access. Communities may also be affected indirectly, through increased environmental vulnerability caused by longer-term degradation.

Water availability in local communities

A number of studies report that water availability for local communities is reduced by diversion to the tourism industry, especially for luxury resorts. This has now become an important environmental issue in Southeast Asia. In Serangan, near Bali, the development plans include a luxury cruise terminal, a marina, golf resort and numerous other tourist facilities and environmentalists predict water shortages on the island: 'It may be hard to imagine liquid shortages on the lush island rippling with rice terraces, but hotels and golf courses are mighty thirsty beasts.

Although the developers promise to recycle waste water to maintain the golf course and other grounds, the project will still require 5,000-7,000 cubic metres of water daily'. In Ubud also in Bali, water shortages occurred in the cities when water was diverted to the hotels, leading to water resource 'grabbing' by the ruling clique. Similarly, building golf courses in Indonesia is one of the most blatant transfers of land and water resources from the poor to the rich.

Forests Resources

In mountain areas, forest degradation is a major issue, although different studies emphasise the issues differently. Problems are greater where the influx of tourists is concentrated in small areas. A study of the Ghorepani in the Annapurna region of Nepal found the fuelwood requirement of a subsistence household averaged only 22kg/day, while the demand of a tourist lodge was as much as 220kg/day. Forest cover was being depleted at the rate of one hectare a year. On the other hand, other studies emphasise that tourism demand needs to be put in perspective and can be a minor contributor to wood use. For example, a study in Nepal by a UK based consultancy firm, Environment Resources Limited (ERL), estimated that fuelwood demand from natural resource tourism was only a fraction of 1% of the total highland fuelwood demand.

However, the demand for fuelwood for tourism is localised and can have a high impact on the tourism resource. Tourism can have greater affects on forest use through indirect effects of rising prosperity. Again these can be positive or negative. In Khumbu, 'increased wealth from tourism has been used to build larger houses and hotels, both of which rely on increased use of wood for heating and cooking, accelerating the exploitation of forest resources'.

Conversely, in the Bromo Tengger National Park, fuelwood consumption in the two major tourist villages seems to have decreased as other fuels such as paraffin, kerosene and electricity replaced its use. The forest bordering the fields was in good condition, and in many cases the trees encroached upon the farmers land.

If tourism does exacerbate deforestation, this in turn affects many other livelihood concerns, such as time spent on fuelwood and water collection, quality of grazing areas, fodder availability, nutrient replenishments of the soil through mulching, soil erosion, water retention capacity of soils and availability of forest foods and herbs for consumption and sale. Many of these changes affect the poor, who have a greater dependence on common property resources, and especially poor women who rely heavily on fuel, fodder and food from the forests.

In Himachal Pradesh, this has led to women playing a major role in checking the deforestation; women's groups in villages near Manali have been the most vocal and effective in taking action against forest use for collection and sale of fuel wood, and harvesting of trees to cater to the demand of the tourism industry. The men of the village, who make the most money from these activities, have now joined forces with the women as the levels of deforestation have become alarming, and have gone further than localised action. Regulations for timber harvesting for local use were changed through political action.

The active role being played by such groups in checking deforestation has been an important factor in the success of the Joint Forest Management (JFM) programme in the area - a programme, enabling local communities to play a more active role in the management of forest resources. Measures to limit deforestation have also been attempted in Nepal.

'Forest depletion caused by tourism in heavily trekked areas has been recognised, and regulations for carrying kerosene or gas for organised trek groups and mountaineering to avoid the use of fuel wood has been introduced. This regulation does not cover individual trekkers who constitute over 60% of the total trekkers, and stay in lodges and private houses that use mostly firewood.

Even in the case of organised groups, the enforcement of the rule is hampered by the lack of a system of monitoring, particularly in the areas outside parks and reserves'. Several other measures have also helped to limit damage, and move towards rehabilitating the lost forest cover. These include the revival of traditional community based systems for forest protection and management, large-scale tree planting activities and introducing energy efficiency and alternative sources of energy. The creation of national parks has also made a significant impact on the status of the forest cover.

Problem of garbage disposal

The problem of litter and garbage disposal in tourism areas in Nepal, especially at popular destinations such as the Khumbu and Annapurana regions, seemed at one point to defy solution. Regulations make tour organisers responsible for garbage and litter disposal, with the involvement of local communities. A local NGO, the Sagarmatha Pollution Control Committee (SPCC) has been formed with support from the Nepal Government and the World Wild Life Fund. SPC has taken a lead in solving this issue in a way that now enhances local livelihoods.

Local communities, with women's groups often taking the lead, are gradually becoming experts in the art of sorting and recycling garbage and finding solutions for nonbiodegradable garbage. 'Women's groups in Langtang-Helam regularly clean the trails and village area, separating garbage into burnable and non-burnables, and burying and/or recycling. In some areas, the tourism management committee have started collecting deposits on bottles as an incentive to return bottles to Kathmandu for re-use by the beer producers'. Although the Khumbu region is still not litter and garbage free, a practical way forward is being pursued.

Coastal Tourism

In most areas of coastal tourism, fishermen seem to benefit from the opportunities tourism brings. But coastal tourism can reduce local people's access to the beach or to common property resources near the coast. This emerges as a problem in Pangandaran and Bali. Coastal eco-systems serve many functions, supporting both local livelihoods and industries, so ecological disruption can have many ramifications.

Serangan and other resorts around Bali illustrate the potential threat of tourism to the environment and to the livelihoods of local communities, particularly the poor, who are most vulnerable. The beach of Candidasa disappeared following the bombing of coral reefs and overzealous construction. Ambitious plans to salvage Serangan island, which was being threatened by shoreline erosion, have led to protests from residents of nearby beaches when fishermen and small hotel owners in Buntun opposed plans to blow up a mountain and extract rocks to build a sea wall around Serangan Island. In the *Far East Economic Review*, Cohen reports that 'they fear that the excavation may jeopardise tourism developments along their own quiet shoreline, particularly if landslides damaged precious coral reefs. Saving one beach only to wreck another is not their idea of good environmental policy.

Environmental disputes threaten to disrupt development across the archipelago'. Environmental impacts of tourism on coastal systems were noted in several of the case studies analysed, indicating the coastal areas in the Philippines and Vietnam studied by Trish Nicholson, but did not emerge as the most dominant issue. In Marinduque Island, there was apprehension that a proposed large tourist, residential and yacht-basin project for corporate investment might destabilise the local ecosystem and impact on fish spawning grounds. On the other hand, a village association managing picnic pavilions was planning an integrated marine resource management plan that included a fish sanctuary, designed to improve fish stock and to be used for recreation.

In Boracay (also in the Philippines) coliform pollution was found in the water supply and in inshore waters in 1996/7 as well as algae on coral, but it was not clear whether this was an indirect impact of tourism. Also 'the need for both water systems and adequate sewerage disposal for the island was signalled by planners in 1986 as an urgent need'. At the time of the research, 'neither has been installed despite a 300% increase in residents and 600% increase in tourists in the intervening period'. A piped water scheme was initiated in 1997 and a bilateral project funded by the Canadian government has now been started to retrieve the situation.

In Bali, some heavily built up areas led to severe erosion. There are several groups which have taken up the case of golf courses and the beaches of Bali, drawing attention to the impact of golf courses.on the environment and the availability of land and water resources for the local population, and campaigning against the further proliferation of golf courses.

Environmental threats

In urban areas, the problem is not necessarily loss of access to natural resources, but increased vulnerability to natural disasters such as landslides. An increase in environmental vulnerability due to tourism-related construction activities and inadequate attention to urban planning issues has been well documented for Manali. The combination of a relatively high probability of seismic activity in the region, multi-storey construction and the concentration of large numbers of people in peak tourist seasons increases risks associated with earthquakes, and attendant hazards such as landslides and snow avalanches.

Rules and regulations to minimise these risks have been made, and mechanisms to guard against violations have been put in place, though inappropriate construction seems to have gone on at a discomforting pace. Numerous examples of improper siting of structures exist throughout the area, despite the preparation and approval of Master Plans. A major new hotel development has taken place in flood-and erosion-prone areas. Extensive areas of ribbon development are located along the only main road upstream from Manali, where the channel morphology indicates high energy flooding. The need for construction material for rapid development of tourism has also put pressure on timber resources and gravel in stream beds. As building continues in the area, more people, structures, livestock and agricultural land will be exposed to flash-flooding and debris torrent hazards.

Cultural and Social Impacts

Preservation and maintenance of Buddhist monasteries and Hindu temples in the Nepal and the Indian Himalayas have been improved by income from tourism, both directly through fees and contributions paid by tourists, and indirectly as the incomes of local communities improve and they are willing to spend more on the preservation of their heritage. According to Zurich, 'the Khumbu Sherpa ceremonies, such as the Mani Rimdu festival at Thyangboche Monastery, have attracted international recognition, which in turn has financed the construction of local religious sanctuaries'. However, with the monetised tourist economy, 'religious life in Khumbu appears less attractive than in former times. In effect, tourism may safeguard the artifacts of culture but destroy the spirit that initially created them'.

Cultural heritage is an important attraction in other destinations such as Yogyakarta and Badrinath (India). However, the case studies analysed did not conduct research on the impact of tourism on cultural heritage. Some places are completely transformed with the advent of tourism. Boracay Island, for instance, saw a two-fold increase in the resident population from 3,000 to 9,000 within a decade, and several small hamlets in the Himalayas have been transformed into buzzing small towns, especially during peak tourist seasons. However, the case studies indicate that fears of tourism threatening local cultures are often misplaced.

The cultural changes that accompany tourism are part of the general changes that take place as communities adapt to new economic realities, similar to those taking place as societies shift to more intensive agriculture and animal husbandry or industry. However, some communities are more able to resist the pressures for cultural change. The Tenggerese in Indonesia are an example of a host community whose cultural identity remains strong despite the high tourist flow through their communities. Bali and Marinduque are further examples of regions where cultural identity is not severely weakened by the tourism industry.

However, there is sometimes a threat to cultural norms, especially when culture itself is treated as a commodity. In Vietnam, for instance, the 'love market' of Sa Pa is one of the major tourist attractions. This market is the social event of the week for the ethnic minorities, where they sell, buy, socialise, meet friends and look over potential partners during an evening of song. The local community now plays music only for a fee and the original style and functions of the 'love market' have disappeared after only five years. This is largely due to the of the actions of 'hounding tourists' keen to get a photograph and attracted by the sensationalisation of the tradition.

Nature tourism can also lead to changes in the relationship between local communities and nature. The research and conservation needs of the international community often play a major role in how the wilderness is now defined. The Tharus of Nepal residing in the Royal Chitwan National Park viewed the wilderness as a 'jungle', to be used for daily needs and enjoyed as central part of their life, a 'jungle' that they knew intimately. This 'jungle' no longer exists as the park, with its exclusions and authoritarian structure has replaced it .

Sex and drugs

The many aspects of cultural change also include drug abuse and sexual exploitation. Some of the studies report the incidence of prostitution in tourist areas, with tourism providing a ready market for prostitutes. In Pangandaran, prostitutes from neighbouring regions join local prostitutes during peak tourist seasons. Dibya Gurung, in her study on Nepal indicates that there may be a co-relationship between tourism in urban areas, poverty and sexual exploitation. In Davao City, Mindanao (Philippines), 'The conflation of rapid localised commercial development, entrenched widespread poverty, and a tourist "boom" represent a potential new source of commercial sexual exploiters of children'. The case study records that a large number of women and even children come to the city for the sex industry, or are pushed into it involuntarily.

In several cases, such as Sauraha in Nepal and the 'tourist triangle' of Bali, there are descriptions of how young men from host countries have been lured by the sexual mores of visiting western tourists. This, however, seems to be limited to a fringe of the society although one that forms a highly visible part of the tourism industry.

Health and Education

Growth in tourism can also lead to better educational and health facilities in tourist destinations. Sometimes this is a result of direct interventions as in the case of the Mt. Everest region and the Himalayan Trust founded by Sir Edmund Hillary which is supported by several tour and travel agencies and maintains more than twenty schools, runs a hospital and a trekker's aid post. The impact on education and health is often more indirect, an outcome of increased incomes or the creation of a demand for educated personnel by the tourism industry. Local communities also benefit from the infrastructure created for the tourism industry. Unfortunately the information on these aspects is scanty in the literature reviewed. None of the studies analysed elaborated on any negative impact on health due to increased workloads and commercial sexual activities resulting from tourism.

Natural Resources for Poor People

Pressure on natural resources can particularly impact the poor. Where tourism grows rapidly it can reach thresholds where impact becomes significant. This was evident in Pangandaran, for instance, where the landless were displaced from their homestead lands as they were taken over for building tourist facilities and in the Manali area as deforestation linked to fuel for tourism made it harder for the village women to collect fuel, fodder and leaves for mulching and manure.

Status of women

The status of women begins to change with the growth of tourism. With an independent source of income, women begin to have an increased say in decision making within the household. However, this also means an increased workload for them, which is a common refrain that emerges in case studies that have analysed gender issues.

In Sa Pa, women are the major earners of revenue from tourism. This is predominantly evident concerning handicrafts where the women make and sell them directly in the market. Men make tourism-related income from guiding up Mount Fansipan, collecting wood and non-timber forest products for sale to tourists, hotels and restaurants. Women in destinations characterised by smaller hotels and lower levels of investment have proved themselves to be adept at managing small guesthouses and restaurants and running other small enterprises. In the three important destinations for mountain tourism in Nepal - Sagarmatha, Laltang and Annapurna - more women than men are engaged in the accommodation sector.

The proportion comes down drastically, to about one eighth, if statistics for the accommodation sector for the country as a whole are considered. Employment of women is least important in the safari resorts of Chitwan National Park, where according to a survey carried out in 1991, only 2.8% of those employed were women. The case studies analysed here do not have an adequate analysis of the factors that may be at work here, such as comparison with the employment of women in other organised sectors, the availability of trained personnel, cultural traditions or sexual discrimination.

Women find most opportunities in the informal sector, with activities ranging from collection and sale of firewood and carrying loads from road-heads, to shops and teashops and managing guesthouses in their own right. In Manali, where outsiders have dominated the industry, only one woman in thirty households surveyed was formally employed. It appears where outsiders rule the industry, most jobs are for males, and where local communities dominate, significant employment opportunities are generated for women.

The Annapurna Conservation Area Project in Nepal has a positive programme for the involvement of potential women entrepreneurs in tourism, Developing Women's Entrepreneurship in Tourism (DWET). One of the prominent features of DWET is the provision, in flexible terms, of loans to women to carry out income-generating activities. The selection for DWET trainees is participatory and based on intensive consultations. The most visible shortcoming of the programme is its failure in establishing adequate linkages between training and follow-up activities. Among the poor, women are often most affected by negative impacts. In Himachal Pradesh, this has led women to play a major role in checking deforestation. Both women and men suffer from sexual exploitation associated with the tourism industry.

Migrants and locals

The balance between long-term residents and migrants within the tourism industry varies widely. Migrants are often entrepreneurs with better access to skills and capital than locals, but they may also be poor and unskilled seekers of employment and self-employment opportunities. Therefore they may be important from a poverty perspective, as well as being an important stakeholder driving tourism development in a destination.

In many areas, local entrepreneurs have used the opportunity to build up a thriving business, while in other areas, migrants have filled the niche. The scenario becomes more complex as luxury resorts move in, with several stakeholders playing a role. The history of social and economic processes prior to the development of tourism, and government and international policies play an important role in determining who gains from tourism growth. Land ownership, access to financial capital and entrepreneurial spirit are particularly important.

In Nepal, modern tourism came into vogue at a time when the traditional trading livelihoods of the Sherpas and Gurungs were disrupted by conflict between India and China. These ethnic groups, with enterprise and capital to spare, were well-placed to seize the initiative at the very outset. There are several other instances where local communities have been able to retain a dominant position.

However, the initiative is not always taken and retained by local entrepreneurs. Outsiders may also seize the initiative first or take over later. In Sauraha, Nepal near the Chitwan Royal National Park, the original inhabitants, the Tharus, were not involved in trade when tourism became popular in the region, but were dependent on forests and shifting agriculture for their livelihoods. Migrants from further north had already started to move in to farm when the forests were cleared, only a few years before the advent of tourism. These migrants and their relatives had entrepreneurial skills, capital and political influence enabling them to take the lead role in industry development.

In Boracay Island, though the initiative was first taken by the locals, it is the outsiders who now dominate the industry. In Manali, the enterprising Lahauli neighbours, with a strong trading background combined with financial backing from the Tibetan refugee community, dominated the provision of large but basic accommodation in 1989 when Singh conducted the study. The establishment of medium or large hotels by the Lahauli's and other non-locals may have handicapped the development of guesthouses scattered through the region. The study did not explain why the local elite did not take the lead.

However, Singh speculated that the Lahauli entrepreneurs, who migrated from a neighbouring region and are relatively well integrated into the local economy and society, may go on to lose their dominant position to entrepreneurs from Chandigarh and Delhi, and multi-national corporations . Pangadaran, Indonesia, is another example where recent migrants have dominated the accommodation and catering sector.

New migrants, including hotel and restaurant owners, tour operators and their employees and those involved in the informal sector form an important class of stakeholders, often facilitating tourism and associated employment. Their interests sometimes conflict with those of the older residents, though they can, and do tend to compromise over time.

Dynamics of Tourism Industry

The extent of local entrepreneurial involvement in tourism not only varies between places, but also changes over time within destination. The pace, scale and type of development are some of the factors affecting local involvement. As the number of tourists increases, home-stays often begin to be replaced by lodges and hotels, which implies fewer opportunities for the less well off. A gradual shift from home-stays to lodges and hotels is well documented in Ngadisari, Indonesia, near the Bromo Tengger Semeru National Park. In 1977, there was only one hotel in the area and 56 households provided board and lodging, so the majority of tourists stayed with villagers. By 1997, a network of hotels had developed in the area and only six households offered home-stay facilities.

Tourists now generally stay with the villagers only when hotels are full . A contrasting example is found in Bali, where tourism started and was sustained for a long period by accommodation in losmen, around the family compounds. The losmen tradition continues to play a role even after the advent of the mass market resorts. Some interesting examples of the expansion of locally-owned accommodation facilities emerge from areas where upmarket hotels were not dominant.

In Boracay, existing resources were used to start accommodating visitors, ranging from using part of the house for visitors, building extra rooms, expanding as tourism generates additional income to selling some land to outsiders and using the proceeds to build their accommodation facilities. Slow development of tourism and the pre-existence of some local capital and entrepreneurial skills play an important role in facilitating such trends.

The Marinduque and Boracay cases, illustrate the differing dynamics as tourism activities take root in an area, particularly in the accommodation and catering sectors. In Marinduque Island, new migrants are not an important stakeholder group and the economic gains for the local population are clear. Tourism has had impacts on the local culture such as the politicisation of festival activities, with the festivals loosing their participatory nature. On the whole, however, the local economy is strong enough to have integrated tourism well with the life and culture of the island's economy.

By contrast, tourism has transformed the landscape of Boracay Island by 1995. The population of the island doubled in a decade. Farming and fishing were no longer the main sources of livelihood for the original inhabitants. Tourism and tourist related activities had replaced these as the principal sources for earning a livelihood. The growing number of residents and tourists contributed to pollution, especially since proper water and sanitation systems had not been installed. New migrants dominated the tourist trade. Increasing competition, low wages and rising prices were beginning to make their impact felt on the original inhabitants, especially on the poorer sections. Boracaynon entrepreneurs providing accommodation facilities in cottages were struggling to survive, and many, especially women, who went under ended up joining the non-formal sector of tourism.

Mass tourism

The mass tourism, especially that associated with luxury hotels and resorts, does not always bring the best returns and has significant negative social impacts on local communities. For example, the government of the Mindanao Islands invited bids for hotels and tourist resorts in Samal Island and Davao, which were largely taken up by foreign conglomerates. Nicholson found that this type of intervention does not tend to alleviate poverty, but is likely to be exploitative and leave the poor worse off in economic terms. Wall,who surveyed and analysed the attitude of villagers towards tourism in different regions of Bali demonstrates that villages located near luxury and mass tourism complexes were less enthusiastic about the advantages of tourism than those who had been less exposed to the impacts of mass tourism.

In Pangadaran and in Boracay Island the researchers feared that some of the gains to the local community were reversed as luxury and mass tourism became more dominant. However, while several case studies suggest that mass tourism is less beneficial relative to other types of tourism, they do not assess how important it is for expanding the tourism economy, or speculate on the counter-factual - whether smaller scale tourism would have flourished more without mass tourism.

Domestic tourism: Many of the case studies indicate that domestic tourists contribute more to the informal sector (which is important to the poor) than international tourists. In several domestic tourism destinations it is noticeable that formal sector enterprises are also provided by local entrepreneurs - such as the local orchard owners in Kinnaur in the Indian Himalayas. Similarly Marinduque also caters to the domestic, middle and upper class market, and small businesses who have diversified and expanded their premises seem to be the main accommodation providers. Other players, including the local 'elite' families and absentee investors, seem to play only a marginal role.

Domestic tourism can also help to minimise seasonal variations and provide long term sustainability for investments in tourism. Domestic tourism sometimes provides the market for the industry in the off-peak season when prices are lower. Hoteliers in India operate a dual pricing system with a dollar rate for international tourists and a rupee rate for Indian nationals. The latter is much lower and ensures high occupancy rates . This suggests that it is important for tourism planning to embrace domestic tourism and not only international tourism. However, it is imperative that the different needs and demands of these two groups are recognised.

Domestic tourism is already important in almost all the countries studied except Nepal where regional tourists from India make up the largest segment of the market. For example, domestic tourists constitute up to 95% of total tourist numbers in the UP Hills and Himachal Pradesh. The Indian government's scheme for subsidising holidays for its employees, known as Leave Travel Concession, has done wonders for domestic tourism in India. A whole infrastructure, consisting of moderately priced accommodation, catering services and tour packages have thrived around this scheme. The scheme provided a critical mass for domestic tourism in specific destinations.

Land ownership laws and traditions

In Kinnaur, state laws which make it difficult for outsiders to purchase land in the region, have made it difficult for non-locals to build hotels here . The Tenggerese in the Bromo-Semeru area in Indonesia were also, until recently, able to monopolise accommodation facilities, because of their distinct ethnic identity and norms which do not allow the sale of land to outsiders. However, outsiders have been able to build hotels on designated forest lands, through using their political and bureaucratic clout. This trend, plus more recent competition from hotels in the nearby city of Surabaya, have threatened the Tenggerese monopoly on accommodation.

The same laws for land transactions apply in India in the Kullu Valley as in Kinnaur. Over the years, as land prices have soared, local land owners and prospective purchasers have tried to circumvent.them by making transactions with third parties from the local areas acting as buyers, or through mutual understandings about use rights. This tends to depress land prices. The government has succumbed to pressures by leasing out government lands. This has had an impact on the local communities who used to use the common lands for livelihood purposes, particularly the poor, whose dependence on commons for livelihood tends to be greater have been particularly severely affected. In Boracay, tourism has assisted in the process of concentration of land ownership among a few families. Land prices have soared, and the smaller guesthouses find it difficult to expand due to lack of capital.

Role of private sector

External companies, such as tour and travel agencies at the national and international levels, can strongly influence development at a destination, and the nature of benefits and costs to local people. They can facilitate tourism growth in an area, but also tend to act as 'gatekeepers,' retaining a large portion of the revenues collected from tourists. Marketing capacity, the ability to invest, and 'concentration of industry support (airlines, cruise lines, car rentals, hotel chains) in the developed countries' are key to this. Several case studies illustrate how a greater role for external tour agents means a small role for local entrepreneurs and the informal sector - though, as with mass tourism, it is impossible to access whether a smaller share of a larger cake is better or worse for locals than what would have happened without inputs from outsiders.

Tour packages that provide all facilities and services, and resorts with their own shopping complexes tend to marginalise the informal sector. In Bromo Tengger Semeru, guided tours usually stay only a very short time in the area, sometimes as little as two hours. Even in Yogyakarta, many tourists are taken to the temples and then straight back to the airport, despite the fact that many handicrafts made in Yogyakarta are unique. In response, the informal sector has organised itself, and received legal recognition. Independent transport owners have also often responded by forming associations and standardising prices and services in Bromo Tengger and Himachal Pradesh.

Group treks in Nepal organised by trekking agencies tend to hire porters, cooks, guides and other support staff in urban or semi-urban centres, probably contributing to the trend towards urbanisation. In contrast, independent travellers making their own arrangements tend to recruit from local areas. Moreover, the quality of the employment tends to be much better than that of trekking organisations, with the independent traveller often treating the employee on more equal terms and where necessary, taking care of the personal needs of the employee.

Upper Mustang provides an extreme example where regulations ensure that outside agencies dominate the market to the exclusion of local entrepreneurs. According to estimates based on 1,000 trekkers visiting Lo every year, the cash paid by groups for porters and ponies could contribute nearly NR2 million a year directly into the Mustang economy. However, as a result of the guidelines, the poor of Lo-Mahtang are denied the opportunity to earn an income as porters, from hiring out their yaks for transport, or from offering home-stays.

Even the most important national NGO working in the field of nature conservation - KMTNC - is unable to do little to counter this impact. In some of the other Nepal case studies, such as the overview by AME, there are discussions on the relative merits of independent travellers and guided tours, mostly indicating that local communities gain more with the former. Strong local feelings against guided tours also come through in one of the Manali studies in India. In Serangan, where there has been active opposition to the development plans for tourism, the record on compensation and other social issues seemed to be positive.

Land compensation, usually a matter of heated dispute, proceeded smoothly, with less than 25 families relocated. Developers contributed generously to the upkeep of the Pura Sakenan temple and the other lesser temples on the island. More than 250 fishermen were put to work on a reclamation site, with promises of future training in the tourism trade. Best of all, developers established weekly meetings with community leaders to process complaints. Plans to build a supermarket facing the temple were withdrawn when villagers objected. Things changed when it came to actual implementation.

The tender for reclamation was awarded to a company with little experience in reclamation. They were making a mess of it. Another environmental study was made and a plan to blow up a mountain to build a sea wall had been put forward at the time of the report. A result was awaited. Seven Balinese families who owned the mountain had agreed to lease their land. The local fishermen, however, did not approve. They were afraid that the excavation would expose them to landslides during rainy seasons, having an impact on their fish catch and on the coral, an important asset for tourism in the area.

Role of Governments

Most tourism departments have their genesis in efforts to build up tourism as foreign exchange earners in the seventies and the eighties. Building up an infrastructure and marketing internationally are normally the main concerns. The *Vietnam National Administration of Tourism* (VNAT) for instance, is concerned with the lack of infrastructure and with the need to improve accommodation, transportation and access, including in remote natural areas. VNAT is both an administrative and policy-making body with a strong commercial interest, being owner of several large tourism companies and hotels.

There is a direct conflict of interest that permeates down to the local level where provincial and district government departments have their own tourism companies. The government is the most influential partner even in private sector tourism, since it owns most land and their former or present employees have easy access to land on which they can invest to build facilities for tourism.

Government decisions can strongly influence the degree to which tourism is concentrated or dispersed geographically. The Bali Tourism Study, completed in 1971, has guided the growth of mass tourism. The Plan was undertaken by SECTO, a consortium of French consultants, and was sponsored by the United Nations Development Programme and the International Bank for Reconstruction and Development. The plan envisaged concentrations of tourists in Kuta, Sanur and Nusa Dua and 'excursion roads to facilitate the movement of tourists from the three major accommodation nodes to various attractions in the interior of the island'.

In Vietnam, the VNAT focus on opening up mountain areas and promoting ecotourism. Tourism Master Plans have played an important role in accelerating the pace of growth of tourism in Boracay Island and in Pangadaran. The policy of the tourism department in Himachal Pradesh in India, in contrast, emphasises development of accommodation and catering facilities and provision of transport facilities by the private sector, while the state government concentrates on building up infrastructure to facilitate the industry. The policy also promotes dispersal of tourism to areas that have potential but are yet to be developed as tourist destinations.

There is an emphasis on adoption of villages by trading organisations, banks and other agencies for community development activities and a scheme for encouraging communities in popular destination areas to establish accommodation facilities with at least 50 beds. The policy also recommends the constant appraisal of tourism activities with local people and with visiting tourists. Unfortunately, the literature available does not document the efforts to implement the policy.

Tourism departments have also often played the role of providing finances, subsidies and access to land and other natural resources to the private sector for building up tourism facilities. In many Southeast Asian destinations, tourism is focused around conservation areas or has actually led to the declaration of natural conservation areas. Conservation agencies therefore often play an important role. But in many cases they find their role difficult, which can hamper tourism development or constructive relations between key stakeholders. There can be tensions between the conservation agency and other governmental authorities responsible for local or tourism development.

Tourism development in conservation areas can exacerbate tensions with local people - or help create momentum for addressing the problems. For example, in Nepal, despite very positive trends, tensions still persist. The employment of the army for protection of the park areas from use by the local communities remains a contentious issue in Sagarmatha and Chitwan National Parks, and the cost for retaining the army presence in the park areas is also very high. However, over the years, especially in the past couple of decades, valuable experience has been gained in improving the linkages between tourism, nature conservation and local communities.

The Annapurna Conservation Area Project (ACAP) recognised that human use could not be excluded from protected areas. Building on lessons learnt at SNP, planning and implementation was entrusted to an NGO, giving the programme flexibility and the capability to respond to community needs more effectively than a government department. The promise of spending the revenue from trekking and mountaineering fees in the Annapurna area itself was a major incentive for facilitating participation by local communities.

World tourism grew by 260% between 1970 and 1990. The World Travel and Tourism Council (WTTC) highlights the following global condition of the broadly defined travel and tourism industry, which includes both leisure travel and business travel :

— GDP output was $3.5 trillion in 1999;

— Accounts for 11 percent of all international consumer expenditures, 11.3% of all capital investment, 6.7% of all government spending;

— Is the world's largest tax contributor with an estimated $800 billion contribution in personal and corporate taxes for 1999;

— Accounts for over 25% of the world's trade in services;

— Is the world's fastest growing industry, expected to become the largest industry (outside of agriculture) by 2010; and

— Is the world's largest employer next to agriculture, providing direct or indirect employment for 200 million people or one out of every 12 workers .

The WTTC includes in travel and tourism:

1. Personal consumption of transportation, accommodations, catering/retail, recreation/cultural services;
2. Capital investment made by travel and tourism companies;
3. Government operating and capital expenditures that make travel and tourism possible; and
4. Business travel expenditures by companies and governments.

The recreation, travel, and tourism sector is a diverse group of industries comprising an essential component of the US economy supplying goods and services purchased by leisure, business, and other travelers. These industries include the lodging industry, the airline industry, travel agents, tour operators, tour guides, car rental companies, meeting and convention planners, restaurants, resorts, amusement parks, camping and recreation areas, natural attractions found in parks and forests, and other suppliers of all these businesses.

The structure of the recreation and tourism industry is very fragmented, and there are fewer frames of reference than exist in other industries; consequently, the core unit of information required is generally the 'size' of the market. There are so many large and small players in the accommodation and hospitality marketplace (for instance) that it is very difficult to esti-mate what the market share of a particular hotel brand is at any one point in time. Conse-quently, it is difficult to ascertain supply and demand in the same way as other industries.

The company and branding structure of the hospitality industry in the U.S. marketplace is quite different from other areas in the world: in the U.S. 75% is branded properties (e.g., Marriott, Sheraton, etc.) whereas outside the U.S. this accounts for only 25%. In other areas of the world hotels are often owned by tour agencies (e.g., Air Tours Ltd.), but in the U.S. tour operators reserve travel arrangements, and the accommodation at the destination will be in one of the large branded properties. However, it is a perceptible trend in Europe that consolidation is occurring.

Tourism is one of the most important economic activities in the Caribbean, contributing to over half of Gross Domestic Product (GDP) in many countries. Tourism represents 31.1 percent of the overall GDP of the Caribbean region and provides nearly 3 million jobs. The share of tourism in GDP ranges from a third to a half for most countries and is 60 percent or more in the Bahamas, the Cayman Islands, the U.S. Virgin Islands, and St. Lucia. Moreover, tourism continues to grow, in most cases at a higher rate than GDP as a whole . Caribbean countries rely directly on their natural environment and climate for economic growth and development and as the main impetus for attracting visitors, both land based and cruise ships.

The essential draw of the Caribbean is the three S's: sun, sea, and sand. The importance tourism plays in the aggregate economies of Caribbean states has resulted in agriculture ranking as third in the economies of most islands, and the manufacturing sector is small. While the U.S. and Europe dominate the list of the 15 most important tourism destinations in terms of total receipts (9 out of 15 destinations), if tourism is considered on a per capita basis, the countries of the Caribbean constitute a significant portion of the market. Tourism is thus an important economic business and the environment, on which much of it depends, an important economic asset. Tourism and the environment are crucial as generators of GNP (both nationally and per capita) and as an export industry. The latter is particularly important in the Caribbean where tourism receipts pay for much of what is imported, both to service the industry itself and also to pay for the imported commodities consumed by the populations of each country.

Threats to the natural environment of the Caribbean arising from the pressure of high tourist numbers have been well documented. Congestion, pollution, and erosion are environmental problems exacerbated by high tourist numbers. In some locations coral reefs are an important part of the resources used by the tourist sector, for uses including snorkeling, fishing, and diving. Reefs are an important factor in ameliorating the impact of storms on the coastline, and overuse can severely damage reefs and reduce these benefits.

A particular problem is ship-generated waste. Difficulties have arisen attempting to get a coordinated response as this problem is not confined to one country in the region. The 'Wider Caribbean Initiative for Ship Generated Solid Wastes Project' is an example of how such a problem can be addressed. Financed by the GEF, it has provided incentives and a framework for the various players and cruise lines to work together. Almost all ship-generated waste is currently discharged at sea, polluting international waters and coastal zones and in some areas threatening the tourist trade.

The high volume of cruise and commercial ship traffic in the Caribbean and the dependence of the region on its coastal areas for income and employment make it particularly vulnerable to this problem. In 1991 the Wider Caribbean Sea was designated a "Special Area", on ship-generated waste, of the MARPOL 73/78 Convention. The Wider Caribbean Initiative for Ship Generated Solid Wastes Project is designed to redress and prevent further pollution of international waterways in the area. To be effective, port reception and waste facilities need to be established throughout the Caribbean region, and a regulatory framework must be in effect throughout the region, otherwise pollution will travel with the currents.

Business forecasting for the industry is usually at macro-level-it is a broad-based industry assessment. There is unlikely to be any general business models that would behelpful to determine the effects of weather, climate, and ocean conditions on the industry .There are a number of business models developed for the industry by academic research organizations and others, but these are not widely used in the industry. This is primarily because few people know about them .

With increases in disposable income and leisure time over the past two to three decades, travel and recreation has become a high profit and high growth industry. While industry research and representative organizations such as the Travel Industries Association of America (TIA) produce a wealth of statistics and trends analyses about the leisure and tourism industry, they do not pay any attention to the weather in a formal sense as a determinant of leisure or travel trends. However, the TIA does produce 'seasonal forecast data'. TIA's travel forecasts include both domestic and international visitation, travel price inflation, and travel expenditures.

The modeling system is a combination of national time series models and regional models, estimated with cross-sectional time series data by major categories of person-trips. Historical time-series data from TIA's TravelScope® consumer travel survey (Travel Price Index and Travel Economic Impact Models) are linked to forecasts of macroeconomic indicators from DRI·WEFA's U.S. Economic Service and Regional Information Service. Person-trip forecasts are benchmarked to the TravelScope® time-series.

The customer base of recreation, travel, and tourism is extending to include both younger and older customers. Additionally, the customer base is becoming more sophisticated and is demanding a wider range of products, many of which are specialized. Developed countries are undergoing major demographic changes that will directly influence the future trends and patterns of recreation and tourism. More employers are extending holiday allocations, and more of this time is being used for travel. Two income households generally have more disposable income but often have difficulties arranging long vacations, which encourages a distinct trend toward shorter, more frequent vacations. The increasing population of physically healthy, mobile, and affluent older people is also having a major impact on the industry. These trends and others are leading to the development of new and specialized products. Additionally, continued deregulation of the airline industry is likely to result in cheaper and more frequent travel on an extended choice of air routes .

As the travel industry expands, users of services are becoming more discerning and sophisticated and are demanding higher quality and increased value. The homogeneous mass-market is being supplanted by a multitude of niche markets where nature, education, cultural interaction, and healthful pursuits are gaining in importance. Mass-markets will continue to cater for the young, budget conscious, and specific sectors, such as: the all-inclusive vacation, gaming, mega-theme parks, and the cruise business . An increasing trend is for 'life-style' vacations, i.e., activity focused, which may attract a smaller specialist clientele. The travel, recreation, and tourism industry is vulnerable to adverse and extreme weather conditions, which result in variable profits and episodic and unpredictable damage costs. Clearly there is scope for ameliorating these problems by applying climate data to facilitate damage preventative measures and reduce the "window of disruption" caused by severe conditions.

The leisure and recreation industry in the United States is also highly vulnerable to security issues.The reluctance of Americans to travel even internally within the U.S. after the events of September 2001 has resulted in a sudden and unforeseen impact on leisure, tourism, business, and conference travel industries. Some of the economic impacts on the industry of the recent terrorist attacks may be temporary, but there may be long lasting effects: it is envisioned that business travel will be reduced with greater use being made of video-conferencing. Such changes may be financially and environmentally beneficial so companies may adopt these changed businesses practices on a more permanent basis. The influence of weather, climate, and ocean conditions must therefore be assessed in the context of other influences and risks to which the industry is vulnerable. Extreme weather conditions have an analogous impact to the events described above, but there are subtler but just as financially important (in the long term) impacts from short-term weather conditions to long-term global warming.

The majority of tourist movements are 'seasonal', and therefore climatically driven to a large extent. However, this is not a clear-cut relationship; for example, the highest tourist movements are in the summer when families are more dominated by school vacation breaks than strictly by the 'weather' per se. Hotels/motels/B&Bs are used for over half (56%) of overnight trips in the US. This translates to 260 million overnight trips per annum, including a hotel/motel or B&B stay. Travel involving hotel/motel/B&B trips is more likely to be taken for business reasons (45% vs. 22%). Such travel is also more likely than average to be taken by air (34% vs. 18%). The average duration of a hotel/motel/B&B stay is 4.0 nights. One in six (17%) hotel/motel/B&B stays includes children .

The Travel Industries Association of America (TIA) has identified specific travel patterns associated with sectors of the population. This is significant for the industry because when planning a resort for recreational activities, generally planners cater to particular market segments. There does not appear to have been any research into whether specific cohorts of the population are more or less sensitive to weather issues or conditions per se. According to TIA research, weekend travel is increasing in popularity, with over half of all U.S. adults, nearly 103 million, taking at least one weekend trip per year. Compared to five years ago, day trips and weekend trips appear to be more popular today than trips lasting about one week or longer. Interest in longer trips lasting more than one week seems to be declining-43% of weekend travelers claim they are taking fewer trips than they did five years ago.

Vacation leave is usually favored for travel. Over one-fourth of employed travelers (28%) use all of their vacation time traveling to points at least 100 miles from their home, and two-thirds of employed travelers (65%) spend at least one-half of their vacation time traveling. On average, employed travelers spent 56% of their 1997 vacation traveling. If weekends are excluded, this translates to travelers spending about 8 days out of 14 vacation days 'on the road'. The TIA also found that business travel volume fell to 212.9 million person-trips in 2000, a 2.4 percent decline from 1999. This represents 34.2 million business travelers, about one in five (17%) of U.S. adults. Overall, business travel comprises 22 percent of total U.S. domestic person-trips. Over half (51%) of all business person-trips are taken for general business purposes (meetings, presentations, consulting, sales, etc.). About one-tenth (13%) of business person-trips are taken for the primary purpose of attending a convention or seminar. More than one-third (36%) of business person-trips are made by those traveling for combined business and pleasure purposes. Thirty-six percent of business person-trips include air transportation. Among overnight business trips, 85 percent include a stay at hotels, motels, or bed and breakfast establishments. About one in five (18%) business trips includes multiple adults from the same household; seven percent include children.

The learning/educational aspect of travel is important to U.S. travelers, with about one-fifth (30.2 million adults) having taken an educational trip to learn or improve a skill, sport, or hobby in the past three years according to the TIA. Eighteen percent of travelers in the past year said that taking such a trip was the main purpose of their travel. Overall, educational travelers are more likely than total U.S. travelers to be male (56%), younger (average 39 years), college graduates (49%), have a professional or managerial occupation (38%), have children in the household (51%), have a higher annual household income ($75,000 average [mean] annual household income), and are less likely to be married.

Federal agencies and organizations with an interest in the recreation and tourism industry and its effects on the economy and the environment include agencies within the Department of Commerce (DOC) such as the National Oceanic and Atmospheric Administration (NOAA), including the National Ocean Service (NOS), National Weather Service (NWS), National Marine Fisheries and National Environmental Satellite Data and Information Service (NESDIS). The Environmental Protection Agency (EPA) and the Department of the Interior's National Forest Service have also commissioned studies on various aspects of the recreation and tourism industry.

U.S. Department of Commerce has a direct interest in recreation and tourism through the Tourism Industries

International Trade Administration (ITA). The DOC also gathers economic data and reports on the condition and status of a wide range of activities and conditions. This baseline data reflects the state of the nation and its overall economic health. NOAA's National Climate Data Center (NCDC) 'Climate Indices for the Economy' program aims to enhance the understanding of the effects of weather and climate on socioeconomic sectors in the U.S.

The Tourism Policy Council (TPC) is an interagency committee established by law to ensure U.S. tourism interests are considered in Federal decision-making. Coordination of Federal activities and policies affecting tourism development need to remain steady and effective to maintain and grow the U.S. market share and fulfill tourism's economic potential that will further community development, economic empowerment, welfare-to-work, and global competitiveness. In 1995, the TPC defined a revised role for the Federal government in tourism development, emphasizing coordination among Federal agencies. The Strategy set out 52 recommendations, developed by the TPC with input fr m the U.S. travel and tourism industries.

The White House Conference on Travel and Tourism (WHCTT) comprised representatives primarily from industry personnel of President Clinton's Cabinet, the Senate, the House, and state and local governments. They identified 10 top priorities for the U.S. in tourism development. There were also many other supporting recommendations. This National Strategy, entitled National Travel and Tourism Strategy of the White House Conference on Travel and Tourism, set out the goal of a public/private partnership that would draw on the strengths of both sectors in business, international commerce, employment, and revenue-generation . TPC member organizations have made efforts to implement the WHCTT recommendations of TPC agencies working individually, with each other, and with the private sector.

The EPA's mission is primarily to protect human health and to safeguard the natural environment (air, water, and land). The EPA, as well as having an interest in the impacts of business and industry on the environment, also encourages environmentally sustainable business practices. It recognizes that while business and industry can affect weather, climate, and ocean conditions, business and industry are, at the same time, largely dependent on weather, climate, and ocean conditions for their well-being. The EPA has also undertaken research into the recreation and tourism industry and its effects on the environment and worked to promote 'ecotourism' under its 'Being a Responsible Traveler' scheme.

State and local authority agencies concerned with recreation and tourism include economic development councils, chambers of commerce, tourist agencies, and local convention and visitor bureaus. The tourism sector is one of the economic areas in which the U.S. has a balance of trade surplus, literally "tourists bring in money". Some States are more aware of the economic benefits of tourism than others. The State of Illinois has (unusually) a $45 million budget, mostly for advertising and promotion of tourism in the State, and this is considered as making a return on the investment; Illinois does not regard expenditure on recreation and tourism as "corporate welfare" as many states do. It is almost impossible to account accurately for the economic benefits tourists bring in; for example, not all restaurant sales in a 'tourist' area are attributable to travel and tourism as only a percentage of sales may be tourist-based. In the U.S. tourism is a $580 billion industry in direct spending, plus indirect jobs ("people grow potatoes, which are used in hotel meals"). If these fringe aspects are taken into account, then the industry is worth trillions of dollars.

Coastal Resources

Coastal tourism and recreation in the United States comprise the largest and fastest-growing sector of the U.S. service industry, accounting for 85% of all tourism-related revenues. Coastal communities depend on healthy coastal ecosystems and clean coastal waters for their survival. However, rapidly growing coastal populations, increasing numbers of visitors (180 million annually), and unsustainable coastal development are resulting in the degradation of water quality and destruction of the habitats that are the main attractions of coastal areas. Although tourism and recreation-related development are major factors determining the use and management of U.S. ocean and coastal resources, this sector has not been the focus of policy, management, planning, and resource allocation . Beaches are dynamic landscapes which respond and change with every tide, swell, and season.

In 1990, Caribbean tourism earned US $8.9 billion and employed over 350,000 people. Divers and other special-interest tourists account for over one-fifth or more of this total. A 1981 Island Resources Foundation cost benefit study of the Virgin Islands National Park found that benefits (US $23.3 million, of which US $20 million were indirect) were more than ten times larger than costs (US $2.1 million), which illustrates the economic benefits of marine protected areas.

In the United States alone, coral reefs support millions of jobs. Every year, they contribute billions of dollars in U.S. economic activity from tourism, fisheries, and recreation. U.S. coral reef ecosystems support billions of dollars in tourism annually, over $1.2 billion each year in the Florida Keys alone. Diving tours, fishing trips, hotels, restaurants, and other businesses close to the reefs provide millions of jobs and support many regional economies in the U.S. and developing countries. In Hawaii, gross revenues generated from just a single, half square mile coral reef reserve are estimated to be over $8.6 million each year. Fifty percent of all federally managed U.S. fisheries species depend on coral reefs and associated seagrass and mangrove habitats for part of their life cycle. The annual dockside value of commercial U.S. fisheries from coral reefs is over $100 million. The annual value of reef-dependent recreational fisheries probably exceeds $100 million per year.

Coastal protection is a key value. Coral reefs buffer adjacent shorelines from wave action and thereby prevent erosion, property damage, and loss of life. They further protect the highly productive mangrove fisheries and wetlands along the coast, as well as ports and harbors and the economies they support. Globally, about half a billion people live within 60 miles of a coral reef and benefit from its production and protection .

Tourism can be an environmentally friendly way of generating income from coral reef ecosystems but only when resort development and operation are carefully controlled. Unlimited collecting, sport fishing, and accidental damage by waders, swimmers, and boat anchors can all degrade the reefs that earn tourist dollars. Allowing sewage and other wastes from tourist facilities to pollute reefs, or siting resorts so that beach erosion increases, can be even more degrading to the health of the reef than the direct damage caused by visitors. There is increasing concern about rising sea levels having very serious consequences for nations situated on low, coral reef archipelagos.

The International Coral Reef Symposium (ICRS) was held in Panama in 1996. A project which is specifically designed to provide centralized access to information from these and other coral reef programs is ReefBase: the International Database on Coral Reefs. This project of the International Center for Living Aquatic Resources Management (ICLARM) seeks to gather a broad range of information about the status of the world's reefs from papers, reports, and inputs from monitoring projects. The project includes an activity of the World Conservation Monitoring Center to digitize maps of coral reefs and to make them available through the database. The ReefBase project serves as a medium of information exchange for scientists and as a conduit of useful information to coastal planners and managers.

Degradation of coral reef ecosystems would have significant impact on world food sources, long-term negative economic impacts on fishery and tourist industries, and a devastating effect on millions of people around the world for whom coral reefs represent the primary source of livelihood . The development and implementation of integrated coastal zone management strategies to effectively manage coral reef ecosystems are necessary. These strategies should address human activities in the coastal watershed and marine areas and involve combinations of a number of integrated actions. These include public education (including education in the use of traditional forms of reef tenure and management and education on sustainable use practices); community development; economic incentives and alternative income generation; global or regional legal instruments used in an efficient manner as well as strengthened for the conservation and sustainable use of coral reef ecosystems; management of tourism and recreational activities (e.g., education programs, installation of mooring buoys); management of land-based activities and coastal development, e.g., using environmental impact assessments (EIA), wise siting of facilities; and coral reef ecosystem monitoring, mapping, database creation, and restoration. Combining these management techniques is critical for success. If used alone, these techniques tend to be ineffective over the long term. They must be strongly supported at scales ranging from the village to nation, and often at the regional scale as well. They must be oriented toward long-term sustainability of reef resources and designed to be adaptive to different cultures/governments and changing situations without compromising effectiveness.

Throughout the world's coastal oceans, observations of harmful algal blooms (HABs), such as accumulations of microscopic species of algae or the larger, multicellular species, are being reported with increasing frequency. Often, these events are accompanied by severe impacts to coastal resources, local economies, and public health. Some species recur in the same geographic regions each year, while others are episodic, leading to the unexpected deaths of local fish, shellfish, mammals, and birds. Only about 50 of the thousands of known algal species actually produce toxins. Some of these toxins have direct and deleterious effects on local plants and animals; others have indirect effects on organisms by changing local environmental conditions .

All HABs were once referred to as "red tides" because of the color imparted by algae suspended in the water, but the description has since become a misnomer because not all HABs are red (some may be brown, yellow, or green), and some may not discolor the water at all. Accumulations can be so high as to cover the bottom of a region, excluding other biota as well as creating an environment in which high oxygen consumption and the associated anoxic conditions accompany decomposition of the accumulated or displaced biomass. The detrimental effects of a harmful algal bloom can range from cell and tissue damage to organism mortality and can be caused by a number of mechanisms, including toxin production, predation, particle irritation, induced starvation, and localized anoxic conditions.

As a result, a bloom may affect many living organisms of the coastal ecosystem, from zooplankton to fish larvae to people. In 1995, a federal interagency program known as ECOHAB (Ecology and Oceanography of HABs) was initiated to support HAB research in the United States . NOAA has research grants to study the causes and consequences of harmful algal blooms, including outbreaks of toxic Pfiesteria and similar organisms in mid-Atlantic coastal waters. The grants are part of NOAA's coordination of a national interagency response to increased incidents of these blooms.

The increasing frequency, duration, and geographical distribution cannot be explained entirely by improved monitoring or attention from the scientific community. In the past HABs have had adverse economic impacts on the aquaculture industry, human health, coastal economies, and subsistence shellfish harvesters. The threat of paralytic shellfish poisoning (PSP) or "red tide" has prompted routine closures of both commercial and recreational shellfish harvesting as well as finfish aquaculture operations in some coastal states. Past closures have resulted in large-scale losses for the industry and bankruptcies in some cases. HAB occurrences also affect consumer perceptions of the safety of uncontaminated shellfish and finfish. This reduces the demand for shellfish in general and affects the fishing industry even in areas where there is no algal contamination. HABs may have significant impacts on coastal economies. The uncertainty associated with the potential of toxic algal outbreaks has adversely affected investment in coastal aquaculture. Bans on recreational harvests affect local economies that depend on recreational shellfish harvesters for at least some of their income.

In addition, the social costs of HABs, their impact on coastal economies and their effect on consumer perceptions are considerable and could underestimate the total cost associated with HABs. Wessells et. al estimated that domoic acid contamination of mussels from Prince Edward Island had a significant impact on reducing the demand for uncontaminated mussels . These results point to the need for accurate public information on the nature and extent of algal contamination to ensure that public perception of the risks associated with shellfish is accurate (misperceptions lead to considerable economic losses). Greater investment in monitoring and testing efforts and improved communication of these monitoring data to the public could help bolster public confidence in the safety of the shellfish supply.

The incidence of HABs along the North American coast is greater than in other shellfish-producing regions of the world. Frequent closures of U.S. aquaculture operations due to the threat of HABs create uncertain product flow and hamper the ability of U.S. producers to compete in a global market. Competitive disadvantage of U.S. producers can result from a reduction in the supply of both shellfish and farmed finfish, a reduction in the demand for U.S. shellfish products, or both. Both consumers and producers of shellfish incur economic losses. The cost to the aquaculture industry is measured by the annual reduction in producer surplus attributable to HABs. This estimate reflects two economic impacts of HABs: a supply effect and a demand effect. Although fisheries closures have a large negative impact on coastal economies, and on communities that depend on these fisheries for subsistence fishing, there are substitution effects, which, if ignored, may result in an overestimation of the impact of HABs on the economy of a state or region.

Recreational shellfish harvesting may have many other substitutes. People may choose to go on a hike in the mountains (or to another uncontaminated beach) instead of going on a recreational trip to a HAB-contaminated beach. To the extent that there are substitutes available for shellfish harvesting as a recreational activity, the overall impact of these closures on the state's economy may be small. However, coastal regions bear a disproportionately large burden of the loss while other regions of each state may stand to gain from beach closures. Also, while harvesting bans in any one year may affect the shellfish industry in that year, they provide an opportunity for the ecosystem to regenerate. Typically, years in which shellfishing is prohibited are followed by years of record harvest of shellfish. Any economic assessment of the cost of harvesting bans must also take into account their benefits in terms of increasing the stock of shellfish in succeeding years.

The Pacific region is the most economically important fishery region in the United States, both in terms of landed seafood and also dollar value. It leads all other regions in both the number of seafood processing plants (27% of all seafood plants) and also in the number of people employed (about 33% of all people employed) in the seafood industry. Alaska has the largest, most productive fishery in the United States, contributing 54% to the total U.S. landings. With an annual revenue of approximately $3 billion, commercial fishing is second only to oil as Alaska's most important industry. The fishing industry is Alaska's largest employer supplying over 10% of Alaska's jobs, while seafood processing supplies 63% of the employment to the manufacturing sector .

Although the finfish and crab fisheries are enormous, PSP hinders expansion into underutilized shellfish fisheries. Even in regions of the state where PSP does not generally occur, regulatory requirements for testing increase the costs and financial risks of investing in new fisheries and prevent maximization of income from existing shellfish harvest. Estimates of Alaska's sustained annual harvest of bivalve shellfish are over 50 million pounds.

The magnitude of the economic impacts caused by PSP varies for each shellfish fishery based on remoteness, dispersion of the fishery, history of PSP toxicity in the region, and the value of the final product. Similar effects of PSP blooms are felt in other quarters of the fishing industry, such as in the harvesting of oysters and crabs, with similar economic consequences. Global warming and other climate change events are also believed to be associated with extreme weather events that have had a significant effect on HAB by dramatically altering the flow of nutrients in the marine ecosystem. HABs constitute a negative marine side effect associated with human activities in both agricultural and industrial activities.

6

Tourism Marketing: Current Trends

Tourism consists of a highly complex system of activities and services with numerous regional to global interrelationships into other economic and social areas . Accordingly, a large number of players are involved in tourism activities in the various sectors and at just about every physical level. If sustainable tourism is to be developed to achieve a specific effect, it presupposes a fundamental understanding of the complexity and characteristics of the global tourism system.

Drawing from tourism benefits for the host region, assumes the application of free-market mechanisms for ecological and social purposes. This implies accepting the logic of a system mainly carried by private enterprise, in which competitiveness and operational profitability are both the core purpose and at the same time the prerequisite for its very ability to function. Administrations of environmental protection areas, government-run institutions, NGOs and local communities that want to partake actively in tourism, therefore, will have to begin thinking in these terms as well.

Tourism takes place on several physical levels, ranging from the place or country of origin to the destination. This means that training a few local guides, building lodgings and printing information brochures will not suffice on its own. The entire service chain of a journey, which often crosses national boundaries, must function in order to develop tourism in a particular area. Because there is no possibility for the traveller to get to visit the destination before the decision of buying the journey.

In the tourism industry, a marketing strategy includes many factors that influence the marketing effort: timing, brands, packaging, pricing, channels of distribution, product, image, advertising, selling, public relations. The tourism product includes not only the physical product and service but also planning and development, branding and packaging. Basic marketing concepts suggest that any new product development must meet the needs of some segment of the market. The original touristic offering consists of:

— natural attractions(landscapes, climate, water, beaches, wildlife, vegetation)

— cultural attractions (historic, religious or especially typical architectural monuments, traditional handicrafts or other economic forms, folklore, festivals, everyday culture, hospitality, special dishes, etc.).

The natural and cultural attractions must be rendered accessible and available in order to be utilisable for tourism. This is possible with the derived offerings, which consist of the following developments:

— Transportation facilities

— Holiday facilities (accommodations, food, shops, entertainment and other facilities necessary for tourism activities, such as hiking paths)

— Mediating facilities (travel agents, tour operators, tourist information offices).

The touristic product is a combination of the original and the derived offerings.Marketing comprises all the activities and processes used to bring buyers and sellers together, including creating, distributing, promoting, pricing and innovating ideas to facilitate satisfying exchange relationships in a dynamic environment. To compete in today's tourism marketplace with its increasing global competition, organisations of both, the public and private sectors must know who their customers are and what they want. They must also be able to communicate the availability of tourism products and services to potential customers and convince them to become actual customers.

For communities that hope to compete for their share of visitors, the marketing of a distinctive culture, attractions or outstanding amenities might be the central theme. For firms in the private sector, success may be dependant on effective marketing and selling activities of the airline, hotel chain, or tour company.

Promotion is essentially communication with the goal of changing the behaviour o the consumer, specifically to purchase a tourism product such as air travel, hotel accommodations, restaurant meals, tours, or a complete destination package. Understanding where potential buyers are in terms of readiness to buy is important in setting appropriate objectives and developing effective promotional materials.

When conservation area managers, NGOs or local administrations receive support in developing tourism products, they have to keep in mind the market demands. When marketing matches the right product or service with the right customer at the right place and the right time, the results are a profitable business and a satisfied customer. In order to market a local touristic product, the private sector must become involved, mainly tour operators and wholesalers. When designing offerings and managing tourism, their interests and operational processes must be taken into consideration. In view of sustainable tourism development, marketing and promotion should emphasise environmentally sound and socioculturally equitable behaviour on the part of the tourists and on the tourism industry in general.

As with other enterprises, the tourism industry is also dependent on certain framework conditions in order to function in a sustainable manner. The necessary conditions for implementing sustainable tourism can be subdivided as follows:

Tourism is almost impossible without these framework conditions being met. Furthermore, tourism companies depend on a climate propitious to investment as well as on industry-wide institutions (e.g. vocational training centres) and on funding within the framework of economic or tourism policies. Finally, other political, institutional, planning and financial framework conditions are necessary in order to regulate that tourism is not only economically sustainable, but also ecologically and socially sustainable as well as economic benefits for the host communities.

To secure or create important touristic framework conditions and to promote and regulate tourism, government institutions are on the one hand necessary, and private sector, community or mixed associations on the other. Small and medium enterprises (SME) in particular depend on the existence of funding and on the possibility of consulting as well as preliminary work by the government (e.g. existing infrastructure). SME tend to lose money in developing countries. In contrast, larger companies and business federations are in a better position to offset government deficits at least in part using their own means (e.g. in the areas of training, infrastructure).

Tourism expenditures create direct benefits in tourism-related services and such as accommodation, hospitality, attractions, events, and transportation, and indirect and induced benefits in other sectors such as agriculture, construction and manufacturing.

Direct benefits are realised through direct tourist expenditures for goods and services in the destination, in the form of business receipts, income, employment, and government receipts from the sectors that directly receive the tourism expenditure. In the destination areas, jobs are mainly created in accommodation, catering and other services (programmes). It is safe to say that in comparison to other modern economic sectors, tourism is relatively job intensive in relationship to volume of turnover and often, too, to the capital invested. Rough estimates of job impact of tourism in developing nations range from one to a maximum of two jobs per bed in the total tourism trade of a destination area.

Indirect benefits are generated by the circulation of the tourism expenditure in the destination through inter-business transactions in the domestic economy. For example, indirect benefits can be generated from the investment and spending by businesses which benefit directly from tourism expenditures. The direct business receipts, when re-funnelled as investments or used to purchase other goods and services from domestic suppliers (who, in turn, purchase goods and services from other domestic suppliers), stimulate income and employment in other sectors.

In addition, tourism expenditure within the destination can create induced benefits. As income levels rise due to the direct and indirect effects of the change in the level of tourism expenditure, some of the additional personal income is spent within the destination. This results in amplification of the direct impact on the creation of income and jobs in neighbourhood or economically linked areas as well, which is known as the multiplier effect.

The extent of direct and indirect effects on the creation of income and jobs in an area under consideration depends on the following factors:

— Existence of capital, entrepreneurial initiative and know-how

— Availability and qualification of workers

— Availability, quality, prices of local goods and services.

Some of the added revenues from the increase in tourism expenditures may, however, undergo leakage. Leakage refers to the process through which tourism receipts leave the destination's economy. Revenues may leak out of the local economy in the form of payment for imports or moneys saved (without reinvestment). Important payments can take several forms, such as repatriation of profits to foreign corporations and salaries to non-local managers, as well as payment for imported goods and for promotion and advertising by companies based outside the destination.

The bulk of travel traffic consists of business trips and classic "seaside tourism" in the large holiday centres. In spite of recent tendencies towards alternative travel, the latter is still the true engine of national and international tourism traffic. The natural and cultural attractions of rural areas have captured relatively little traveller interest, but it is growing. The most relevant forms of upcoming tourism alternatives are:

— *Nature tourism:* Interest lies in diverse nature, pristine at best.

— *Rural /cultural tourism:* Interest lies in special cultural manifestations in a rural context, or at least in one close to nature.

— *Scientific tourism:* Interest lies in visiting social or ecological projects and trips for professional or educational purposes.

Exact data on the world-wide demand for nature tourism is not available, but isolated figures for certain countries/ regions do exist. East Africa and South Africa (safari tourism), the Himalayan countries (mountain tourism), Southeast Asia (rain-forest tourism), the coral reefs of the Indian Ocean, the South Pacific and the Caribbean (scuba-diving tourism) and Central and South America (rain forest and mountain tourism) are the most important destinations for nature tourists in developing countries.

The exclusivness of the nature experience has a more or less important position at the root of the tourists' needs in this particular segment of the demand. Such qualities are more frequently encountered in conservation areas than elsewhere. The quantitative significance of the various demand segments are also important in order to assess the market potential of a nature tourism product.

According to growth forecasts, the "classic" ecotourist with a special interest in nature, with low demands on comfort and high environmental awareness will increasingly be part of the minority in the global nature tourism market. The number of "casual" nature tourists is far greater, i.e. those who schedule visits to nature areas often as a mere add-on to a trip and tend not to make "purist" claims when it comes to proximity to nature and the presence of other visitors. This type includes especially the bulk of domestic tourists in developing nations.

The respective needs must be taken into consideration when doing the planning. Indeed, if well managed, this type of tourism could even be a significant potential for income for nature areas within range of holiday centres.

Surveys of tourism to developing countries show a great interest amongst travellers in what they experience as exotic culture in the destination countries. As opposed to nature tourism, which can be principally conducted without the participation of the local population, intercultural encounters are the core of the journey in cultural tourism. Usually the highest possible level of cultural authenticity is also expected. In addition travellers often have a great number of different - and in part very special - interests . Cultural trips, like nature tourism, are often combined with other attractions (e.g. stays on the beach, excursions into nature areas).

Scientific and educational tourism are interesting from an economic point of view, since this type of demand features longer on-site stays and can also often be extended after the end of the actual project. Both require the active development of suited offers by the research-project executing agency or by the responsible organisation. It can grow into a lucrative source of income for the executing organisation if combined with complementary vacation offers, and create additional jobs for the local population.

The nature and cultural tourists may be characterised by a host of combined features such as above-average academic qualification, higher income and greater travel expenditures, broad travel experience, high quality-conscious and relatively open-minded to conditions in the host country or region. The bulk of the demand stems from industrialised nations. However, domestic travellers with interest in the natural beauty and cultural heritage of their own country - is gradually gaining in popularity in the threshold nations.

What distinguishes tour operators of nature and cultural tours in developing nations and operators of lodges and guesthouses from the growing trend toward concentration in the global tourism industry is the fact that they are usually highlyspecialised, small and medium enterprises that do not really have access to major financial capacities. Nevertheless, large-scale tourism enterprises are increasingly turning to nature and cultural tourism as a means to diversify their offerings. These kinds of tour operators as a rule offer excursions into villages or nature conservation areas as add-on programmes.

Even in the area of nature and cultural tourism, striving for short-term gain and non-sustainable use of touristic resources by the private sector can be observed, because of know-how-gaps in terms of environmentally sound and socially equitable management, product design and appropriate promotion.

WTO World Tourism Barometer indicate that international tourism might be close to a turning point. As the geopolitical situation has become more relaxed, conditions for international tourism are steadily improving. Various destinations, nevertheless, succeeded to report surprisingly good results. In particular some of the recently most-afflicted destinations in the Caribbean, South America and South Asia rebounded strongly. With the uncertainty due to the geopolitical situation gradually rippling away, the' perspective is switching back towards the economic prospects.

Although the world economy is still rather weak, a change for the better is expected to take place in the second half of the year. The tourism experts consulted in the framework of the WTO Panel of Tourism Experts also confirm a more positive outlook for the coming period. In order to be able to assess the evolution of tourism for the WTO World Tourism Barometer a panel of tourism experts has been established from a broad range of countries and sectors.

In the past two years international tourism has, first and foremost, been reigned by the combination of an overall weak economy and a high level of uncertainty because of the struggle against terrorism and the looming Iraq conflict. The global economic downturn following the boom and bubble of the late nineties put pressure on expenditure resulting in an increased price sensitivity in general and cost cutting on business travel in particular. The terrorist attacks of 11 September 2001 added a huge amount of uncertainty to this already difficult climate. The subsequent war on terrorism and the tension resulting from the threat of an intervention in Iraq prolonged this uncertainty even more.

For tourism these abrupt changes of conditions resulted not so much in a decrease in overall volume but, above all, shifts in demand towards trips to familiar destinations closer to home by car, coach or train instead of plane. Consumers adopted a wait-and-see attitude, with late bookings as a result. Many sectors went and are still going through a difficult time, in particular airlines and all sectors 'dependent on long-haul traffic. Other products ' or segments of the market, however, have resisted well or even benefited, such as accommodation other than hotel, special interest trips with a high motivation factor related to culture, sports, entertainment, or travel for the purpose of visiting family, friends and relatives (VFR).

This climate has also accelerated a number of changes that were already underway. Low-cost airlines kept on growing in North America, and have developed rapidly in Europe. The Internet has strengthened its role not only as a means of information but also as a means of organising and booking trips. Individual travel has proliferated, while tour operators have faced relatively hard times.

The first part of 2003 has been predominantly a continuation of this scenario with the long awaited economic recovery further delayed because of the prolonged high level of uncertainty due to the Iraq conflict. Some destinations, however, started the year with considerable growth (e.g. Caribbean, Asia, United Kingdom and South Africa), but mostly compared to rather depressed levels in the first months of 2002. The start of the war in Iraq in March caused an immediate plunge in demand, in particular of air traffic, interregional travel and travel to destinations perceived as close to the conflict zone.

Very few destinations and sectors turned out to be immune from this new setback. A significant difference, however, this time was that National Tourism Administrations, Tourism Boards and tourism businesses were much better prepared and attempted to adapt quickly to the changed conditions, primarily focussed on shifting or reducing capacity and a rigorous cost control. In this respect the emergence of SARS was much more unexpected and disrupted the affected destinations and businesses far more severely.

In response to the unfavourable climate, tourism businesses have maintained the strategy of giving priority to profitability over volume growth already put into action after 11 September 2001. The focus has been on a strict cost management, a reorientation of activities towards more profitable products and markets and a broadening of flexibility in supply in order to be able to respond quickly to the clanging desires of their clients and the evolution of the market. The offer of open or modular packages has been increased as well as the use of other accommodation than hotels. This process has been accelerated by the growing weight of advanced information and communication technology as a source of information and sales, in particular the Internet and call centres.

National Tourism Administrations (NTA) have backed the sector with action plans in several areas such as communication, promotion and marketing. In selective cases support has been given to tourist companies, with the criteria of effectiveness and in collaboration with the private sector. At the end of 2002 a good part of the NTA's, like many tourism companies, established contingency plans anticipating events that could interfere in the normal development of the sector.

The "wait-and-see" attitude of consumers induced by the looming war and by the economic prospects in most of the advanced economies, resulted in declines in the majority of European destinations in early 2003. With the start of the military intervention in March most countries dived into the minus side, with the most severe setbacks reported by Israel, Croatia, Turkey, and Cyprus, the latter two after performing rather well in January and February. Some -countries resisted the unfavourable climate better and still show positive results. The two major South European destinations, Spain and Italy, reported respectively gains of 3% in the first four months and 2% in the first three months.

The United Kingdom ended the period up to April with a 1% increase over the same period of 2002. In particular arrivals from Western European generating markets increased substantially (+6%), most likely helped by the cheaper Great Britain Pound towards the euro, amply compensating the losses in long-haul arrivals from North America (-12%) and other parts of the world (-5%). The Nordic countries Denmark, Finland, Norway and Sweden, all show weak or negative performances, in the year-to-year variation from January to March, resulting, not from an abrupt decline in March, but from general decreases since the beginning of the year. Denmark and Sweden, though, quite improved in April.

Most countries in Western, Central and Eastern, and Southern Europe are still on the minus side, noting however, that this trend can be reversed once April figures are available. This decreasing trend cannot be attributed only to the Iraq conflict, as it was already visible at the beginning of the year, showing the apparent impact of the weak economic situation in Western Europe.

In particular, Germany, accounting as the main European generating market for more than a quarter of arrivals in the majority of the countries, has given reason to worry. For the majority of European destinations wintertime is not the prime season for tourism, and the most lmportant part of the year is still to come. At the brink of the high Season a moderate optimism is expressed of a gradual recovery with late booking continuing as on of the main trend

Tourism performance in the Americas varied significantly between the North of the region and the rest of the continent. In particular, the USA has obviously been pending the Iraq conflict, fear of terrorism and the rather uncertain economic situation. The United States, Canada and Mexico suffered two-digit decreases in March. Many other destinations in the region also saw weaker results in March but far less pronounced. For the US market, the rise from yellow (elevated) to orange (high) of the US Homeland Security Threat Advisory System Color Code had an immediate and strong impact on both international and domestic travel.

The decrease reported by Mexico is mostly due to stricter formalities for cross-border traffic with the United States (representing an significant share of the volume, but only 10% of tourism receipts as it mostly relates to short-term visits). By contrast, arrivals to the interior of Mexico were up by 6% and receipts were up by 7%. Canadian results will also be influenced by the effect of the weaker US dollar *viz a viz.* the Canadian dollar as well as by SARS, although the latter will only be visible to a full extent in the months still to be reported as the WHO travel advisory lasted from 23 to 29 April.

The Caribbean is showing clear signs of resurgence, although not yet shared equally by all its destinations. Two of the major destinations, Cuba and the Dominican Republic, both comparatively lesser dependent on the US-outbound market, succeeded in recording impressive double-digit increases. The Caribbean Tourism Organization (CTO) reported that the cruise market for the Caribbean (including some Mexican and Central American ports) is generally strong, with an increase estimated at 10% in 2002.

With the significant improvement of the economic prospects in the Mercosur coun-tries, particularly in

Argentina and Brazil, travel in the region is picking up. Argentina, Chile and Peru performed well in the first months of 2003. In particular, Argentina is showing impressive results, continuing last year's trend of two-digit growth rates.

The emergence of SARS, in the second half of March, appears immediately as the main determinant in the evolution of tourism in Asia in the first months of 2003, seriously affecting not only the destinations under the World Health Organization (WHO) travel advisories, but the majority of the destinations in the region. The results posted over the first three or four months of the year are, almost without exception, negative and particularly striking in comparison to the region''s outstanding performance in 2002. The only destinations staying out of the turmoil are found in South Asia and in Oceania. India, Nepal, Maldives and Sri Lanka all report substantial increases, compensating partially for the relatively weak performance of South Asia after 11 September 2001.

After an overall good increasing trend in January and February, with most countries reporting -often double-digit growth, in March arrivals to most destinations declined abruptly. Of course part of this decrease has to be attributed to the general slack in demand due to the Iraq conflict. Although WHO issued the first official global alert concerning SARS on 12 March 2003, followed by an emergency travel advisory on 15 March, the first SARS Travel Recommendation, including the Chinese province of Guangdong and Hong Kong (China) as areas where travellers should consider postponing all but essential travel, was issued only on 2 April. Unlike in other regions, in April arrivals fell even further, with Hong Kong (China), Singapore and Taiwan losing half or more of their arrivals compared to April 2002.

Various other destinations in the region, such as Japan, the Republic of Korea, Macao (China), Australia, Thailand, Indonesia and the Philippines, although themselves not or only very limitedly affected by the virus, are also severely touched, decreasing by between 10% and 50% in April. An important factor for this has been the fact that many destinations are relatively strongly dependent on air travel through a hub in one of the affected countries. Furthermore, the lack of adequate information at the beginning of the outbreak badly aggravated uncertainty and induced a general reluctance to travel.

SARS not only seriously affected long-haul markets, but also source markets in Asia (about 80% of the total inbound in Asia and the Pacific), for instance arrivals in Australia from its second generating market Japan, fell by more than a quarter in April. Destinations in the Middle East and North Africa show a rather similar pattern, obviously reflecting the impact of the war in Iraq. All six destinations with data available for one or more months -Morocco, Tunisia, Egypt, Jordan, Qatar and Lebanon- started the year with a substantial increase in January. February followed with a more moderate increase, while March is showing sizeable drops. In April the losses are already more limited, or even a modest increase was registered as in the case of Morocco.

Economic prospects are still relatively bleak for the countries of the European Union, in particular for Germany. Intra-regional tourism demand, however, has shown to be rather resistant in volume, although expenditure is under pressure. With the disappearance of the uncertainty, expectations for the summer season are reasonable to good, but with late bookings and pressure on prices. The stronger euro might slacken inbound tourism to euro area countries, in particular the UK market might look for more economic options, and stimulate outbound tourism from euro countries (both to European destinations outside the euro area, such as Turkey, Central and Eastern Europe and the United Kingdom, and interregional, in particular Trans-Atlantic and to Mediterranean destinations in North Africa and the Middle East). Furthermore, some countries betted on domestic tourism and promoted actively.

Tourism Marketing: An Indian Scenario

A point highlighted by the First Planning Commission way back in 1955, which ranked tourism 269 th on their priority list of industries - lower than even the development of light-houses! At that time, the average number of tourists who came knocking at our door, was around 15,000.

Post-Independence, while critical issues like agriculture, infrastructure and power supply hogged the limelight, travel and tourism received step-daughterly treatment, as it was deemed a 'luxury' - affordable by only a few. Not much has changed over the last four decades, and it seemed every time the industry gained some form of momentum despite the closed and protected economy, there was something lurking in the shadows to clip its wings. The introduction of FERA put a serious crimp in foreign investment in the country and the Emergency was yet another deterrent to the tourism movement. A look at the Five Year Plans shows that in the Third Plan (1961-1966) tourism got approx 4.001 crores, which was 0.11% of the total Plan outlay.

In the Eighth Plan, (1992-1997) it was Rs 272 crores - still 0.11% of the total plan outlay. At this time, policy makers, industry representatives and opinion makers equated tourism with foreign visitors. To their way of thinking, it was the foreign visitor who occupied hotel accommodation, filled airline seats, frequented bars and restaurants and used recreation facilities. Plus, given the foreign exchange (forex) shortage, the foreign tourist was looked upon as Daddy Big-Bucks - with an almost endless supply of crisp foreign currency.

And while key aspects of Indian tourism came to be tailored to the foreign visitor, the price mechanism too, came to be tied to overseas costs. Hotel rates, food and beverages in hotels, handicrafts, etc, were priced at a level much higher than the economic standards prevalent in the country at the time. No way could our rupee-toting lads compete. Thus, for our fellow countrymen, travel was restricted to places of pilgrimage or going to one's native town to visit the family once a year. However, other South East Asian countries were on the ball soon enough when they realised the potential of tourism.

Hong Kong, Singapore and Thailand dug in the infrastructure, developed detailed tourism plans and marketed them in glorious technicolour across the world. Ironically, today, Indian outbound tourism provides a sizeable chunk of tourist inflow into these countries. From the mid-80s to the early 90s, the Indian corporate world underwent a transformation. The Old Guard - Tatas, Birlas and Godrej - saw the emergence of the newer dynasties on the block - Reliance, Essar and Mahindra. As new factories opened and the corporate kingdoms spread across the country, so did the need for roving executives, with suitably generous travel and entertainment allowances. And thus was born the corporate traveller.

Airlines and hotels didn't take long to work out that the man with the tie and briefcase was the man with the corporate expense account! Airlines introduced business or club class and the hospitality sector set up executive floors - complete with butlers geared to cater to this booming segment. The outbound segment was still in its nascent stage. The "have- suitcase-will-travel" high lasted only for so long, as the reality of getting sponsor letters from friends and family overseas set in, and the forex restrictions of USD$ 500 as one's basic travel quota (BTQ) once every two years, made travelling abroad more than a little difficult.

Naturally, this being the land of opportunity, the grey market for forex boomed - practically every large general store in well-to-do neighbourhoods had an extra drawer for their greenbacks. Low customs allowances meant that bringing items into the country from your travels - assuming you went to some place where US$500 would get you anything - meant the little man in a white uniform welcomed you on your return to the Homeland, and rubbed his hands in glee. "Red channel please" was the helpful direction he gave you as you wearily pushed your trolley towards a long and tortuous queue!

The tourism industry began to swing in the mid-90s, with the liberalisation of the economy, and with India ratifying the agreement to set up the WTO unit in India. Foreign investment in industry, foreign investment in airlines and foreign media got the country excited about the world "out there" and the guy with 50 channels at his disposal, found bikini-clad motivation on his 21 inch screen, to get out of his armchair and check out new destinations.

The alphabets 'MBA' next to a young person's name opened up the road to five-figure salaries, six-figure bonuses and stock options. Young people were raring to go where they parents hadn't been and they had the means to do it! And, more surprisingly, the Indian traveller began to get excited about touring around his own country and the trend for domestic tourism was firmly set. The last decade of the last century alone, saw an increase by more than 100 million travellers in the domestic tourism segment - from 63.8 million visitors in 1990, to 176 million in 1999.

On a broader scale though, finding accurate figures and statistics is something of a problem even today, and in the absence of centrally appointed and vigilant monitoring body, one can only make estimates. Immigration figures based on disembarkation cards are unreliable as they make little distinction between visitors coming only to India or backtracking from Nepal or other neighbouring countries. Also, a large number of arrivals stay with family friends and do not contribute much to the forex kitty.

Forex earnings have been accepted by the tourism industry, being the surer criterion of the quality and number of tourists country is attracting. A study by FICCI, in 1994, showed that the overall forex earnings from tourism had been static around US$ 1.2 - 1.4bn. In 1989, our earnings in forex were Rs ,2103 crores, which rose to Rs 3,990 crores in 1993. But one were to take into account the devaluation that the rupee had been facing against the dollar at the time, then the net dollar earnings had virtually remained stagnant.

Tracking tourism in the domestic sector is even more difficult this is still an unorganised sector, with individuals making their own arrangements or availing of the services of small outfits. Post-September 11, the tourism industry in India has shown resilience with Indian travellers opting to look inwards to domestic tourism or to explore other destinations such as Australia and New Zealand. The Kargil conflict, the current Iraq war and the new flu on the loose in South East Asia, have also dealt serious blows to the global tourism industry.

Despite this litany of international crises, today, it is an accepted fact that tourism is the fastest growing industry in the world; a creator of wealth and business opportunities, an income multiplier, a catalyst for employment and preserver of the environment. An investment of Rs 10 lakhs in tourism, creates 89 jobs, as against 45 in agriculture, and 13 in manufacturing for the same investment.

The current budget has finally granted the tourism industry "infrastructure" status, and an increase in plan outlay to Rs 225 crore. The international airports in the four metros are to be upgraded to world-class standards and six comprehensive tourism circuits will be developed to help promote tourism. The lack of a centralised government apex body to give it the tourism industry focus and direction, is still a cause for serious concern.

At present, the central ministry of tourism's functions are limited to marketing India overseas and providing meagre financial support to state governments for the creation of tourism facilities. Most of the important issues relating to tourism are deciding elsewhere. The Ministry of Civil Aviation controls aviation policy as well as the administration of airports. The Ministry of Home Affairs/External Affairs decides the visa regime, and the Ministry of Finance supervises the fiscal policy for investment in the tourism sector and of course the all-important tax structure. It is left to the private sector to run between the ministries to bring about any radical reforms.

The more significant findings of the many reports done for the international travel and tourism industry show that the focus of the industry is gradually shifting from Europe and N America to east/South Asia and the Pacific. A research forecast by the World Travel and Tourism Council pegs tourism industry growth at 4.5% over the next ten years. Turkey is expected to be the fastest growing travel and tourism economy over the next 10 years at a rate of 10.2%, while India will have a growth of 9.7%. This buoyant outlook also reflects a possibility of the creation of nearly 7 million jobs over the next 10 years.

Using 2001 data, India's tourism industry is ranked no 111 out of 114 countries surveyed by the World Travel and Tourism Council. The measure is the "human tourism index" which equally weights two measures—firstly the ratio of the total population in relation to international arrivals and departures and secondly the ratio between the sum of international tourism receipts and expenditure to GDP. Bangladesh, Iran and Algeria rank lower than India. Currently the Indian tourism industry is a $3bn industry representing 0.6% of GDP.

If the Indian tourism industry is to attract and retain capital, the country must first pass this test. Rapprochement with Pakistan is likely to be a step in the right direction. Domestic and international tourists will only use a country's facilities if the infrastructure is up to it and if the government spends its monies in the right ways on tourism development. So a key role for government is to make the country a more attractive place for tourism capital than it is today and than alternative countries.

The World Bank believes the Indian government is less effective than governments in competitor countries such as China and Thailand. According to their "Government Effectiveness Index", India is ranked 83 out of 159 countries. Another of government's roles is to improve the country's infrastructure; to make the country a more attractive place for domestic and international tourists than it is today and than alternative countries. The data suggests that India suffers from a relatively poor infrastructure. The World

Bank measures the level of infrastructure development, as the combination of three quantities:

1) the total length of roads in a country compared with the expected length of roads,
2) the percentage of the population with access to improved sanitation facilities, and
3) the percentage of the population with access to improved drinking water.

India is ranked 89 out of 118; China is ranked 93, Thailand is ranked 48 and South Africa is 27. Now look at what the Indian government commits in direct resources to the infrastructure of the tourism industry. The World Travel and Tourism Council estimates that Indian government expenditure on tourism amounts to 32.5 million rupees, only one per cent of total government spend. Proportionate to the opportunity, this is very low. Last month's announcement that Moody's, the credit rating agency, has upgraded the country's sovereign foreign-currency debt to investment grade, must surely reflect the progress that is being made. India is now on a par with such countries as Russia, Kazakhstan, Croatia and El Salvador. It opens the door for a new class of international investor to invest in Indian debt and equities. And, it's likely to cut the further the cost of borrowing for Indian companies issuing debt overseas.

There is a need for an open skies policy by the government - the opportunity for the country is so great that any benefit gained from protectionism of state assets such as airlines pales into insignificance. In many countries the state has got out of, or is getting out, owning and managing tourism assets and evolving to a role in which government uses tax revenues to support the industry in different ways.

In India, railways, airports and bus services are of a poor standard and require investment. If leisure and business travellers are to be encouraged to consider India as their destination of choice then these need to be improved.

International flights arrive and depart in the early hours of the morning. This is not a tourism friendly policy. The airports are fitted with landing assistance systems for limited visibility take-offs and landings but not for zero visibility. All these elements need to be updated.The government and others can learn from external benchmarking - of travel and tourism government departments, people, education facilities, facility and programmes.

In Indian's tourism industry there are few economies where domestic tourism is not the biggest element of the industry, and India is no exception. But the scale of domestic tourism is staggering. The statistics show that domestic tourist flows are 100 times bigger than inbound international arrivals. Indeed if one compares Indian domestic tourism with the world's total cross border tourism one finds that Indian domestic population flows are equivalent to an amazing third of the total cross border flows in all, yes all, of the rest of the world. Each of fifteen states receives more domestic tourists than the country does international arrivals.

Now some of these flows will be religious in nature but it by no means accounts for this volume. Everyone's first priority should be domestic tourism. Building the infrastructure to enable these movements of people safely, addressing the water quality, sanitation systems, roads, railways and airports, air traffic control, bus systems and railways - all the governmental paraphernalia that enables, that encourages, the population to stay away from home.

The industry's obligation then is to put in place a wide range of facilities to meet the travellers' needs. One star to five star hotels, restaurants with menus at all price points that are safe to eat in, travel packages to suit all pockets, products to satisfy the business traveller and the leisure traveller, the individual and the group.

There is an opportunity, indeed almost an obligation, for state and federal governments to encourage through fiscal incentives, sale of government land banks and everything else possible, the development by private enterprise of a new generation of mid market, budget and economy hotels. And by extension, opportunities for very high returns on capital for those investors who first develop the right product in the right location at the right cost and then operate a branded product to meet the current and future needs of this large domestic market. Domestic tourism offers a great marketing opportunity; there is huge domestic demand and apparent spare capacity. So what are the sales and marketing gurus doing to convert this opportunity into cash flow? What

The general level of hygiene in the kitchens is poor due to a lack of capital investment and outdated equipment. Also the application of hazard analysis and critical control points and other techniques to assist good practice is little used. The industry must address this. International arrivals peaked in 2000 with good growth from South Asia and the Americas but post 9/11 demand stalled. Demand is dominated by leisure travellers -business and professional visitors are half the number of five years ago. By segment one can summarise that there is a small upper market; these tourists are looking for an experience and will typically take a tour that involves multiple destinations. This product is very difficult to buy by the customer and so they are dependent on finding an in-country travel agent to make the arrangements.

It's difficult in absolute terms and it's difficult relative to similar products and experiences in other competitive countries. Clearly it is constrained - constrained by the patience of the market to accept that the product is difficult to buy and constrained by the number and competencies of the travel agents. So there is a limit to how far this market will grow without fundamental change in the way it is packaged and sold. The mass mid market is served by destinations such as Goa and Kerala; there are very few operators selling such destinations. This is the market that is clearly constrained by the lack of product. Finally there is the low and economy inbound market dominated by students on gap year experiences.

Many countries, not least the USA and UK, have addressed this large market with targeted product and this may well be an opportunity for India. The other side of international tourism is outbound tourism - usually using the same infrastructure—airports, tour operators, and aeroplanes - as inbound tourists. If the government is to encourage inbound tourism, it needs the capacity that services outbound tourism. In 2001, 2.3 million Indians travelled overseas. In the three years 1999-02, outbound tourism grew 28%. At a time that in-bound tourism grew just 3%. Singapore, USA, Bahrain and UK are the four key destinations. This aspect of tourism is likely to be largely aspirational, and is influenced by the media.

There are a limited number of agencies and operators and it may well be poorly addressed by end provider. It is market that deserves more attention than it is getting. Particularly as today's affluent middle classes come to regard travel as a right not a privilege. Building volumes and profits of international tourism is likely to involve re-learning the 3 c's - customers, channels and content - and being willing to relearn them continuously because the world is changing so much and so fast.

The first c is customers - what are the new and emerging markets that can be targeted. Consider one small segment - the so-called-silver market. The aging population in all countries, including India, is an obvious market. By 2030, China will have more than ¼ bn people older than 65 years old. Even a small slice of that market as an inbound market would be pretty profitable. Or take Thailand which will have more than 10m people older than 65 years old. What products and services can be assembled by the Indian tourist market to sell to this affluent neighbouring market? Some of the Indians who will be over 65 will be attracted to the same products and by 2030 there will be more than 100m. There are many other niche customer markets that could be researched and explored. Medical tourism is but one other that would merit putting supply in place to meet demand.

The second c is channels - the internet revolution of the last ten years has seen power move from intermediary to the end customer. A 42% per annum trend cannot be ignored. As a tool for intelligent shopping it has revolutionised domestic life. Yes it's driven down prices but it has also driven up brand loyalty - loyalty to those businesses that understand the net experience and respond to it. The major hotel brands receive most of their internet bookings through their own websites—and Starwood for example has publicly stated that they are planning for 70% of all reservations to be web delivered within five years.

India is the second largest country in the world, with an estimated population of one billion. India adds the equivalent of a population the size of Australia to its own population each year. Just under half of India's population is illiterate, nearly 70% are very poor, and only 30% live in urban areas. However, 2% are very rich and that is 20 million people!

A very significant number of Indians work overseas or are now employed in new technology companies with a high degree of mobility. 30% of NASA scientists, IBM and Microsoft employees are Indians and 12% of doctors in USA are of Indian origin. Mumbai is the main gateway, accounting for over 40% of travel to Britain, while Delhi, also with around 40%, has a larger proportion of visiting friends and relations (VFR) and government travel. The southern states contribute 13% and the rest, 7%.

Civil aviation facilities are likely to be upgraded in the South at a faster pace. Hyderabad and Bangalore will emerge as important gateways within 2-3 years. The speed of India's process of economic liberalisation has been adversely affected by lack of infrastructure in power, telecommunications and transport.

However these have been finally redressed. The 4 metros of Mumbai, Chennai and Kolkatta are being linked by super expressways at a cost of 4 billion rupees. Telecommunications has been privatised. Power reforms are still lagging through in the case of Enron this has turned out to be a blessing in disguise.

Travel and tourism trends

— Access to information has altered significantly due to the penetration of television and Internet throughout India. This is influencing lifestyles very rapidly as are the entry of many international consumer brands in

India and the rapid growth of the computer industry.

— 1.65 million home PCs are sold in India each year. The further likelihood of 20 million people surfing the Internet within the next five years will transform travel habits. The Internet will be increasingly used to access information and make bookings.

— Currently business and independent multipurpose travel are the primary reasons for travel. However, since businessmen and entrepreneurs generally declare their incomes to be far less than their real incomes, pure leisure travel attracts the attention of the taxman. Therefore many travellers state their purpose of travel to be business to enable them to claim the expenses as business expenses, thus reducing their tax liability.

— The increase of foreign exchange allowances up to US$ 10000 per person per year for overseas travel (this does not include airfares and on territory travel passes, which can be paid for in rupees), has meant a virtual freedom to travel. In addition, international credit cards, whose availability was restricted previously, can now be easily obtained in India. The rupee will be a free currency within 2-3 years.

Off-peak travel is likely to increase with airlines offering substantial reductions during September/October and January/March. This may offset the increased desire to visit Australia and South Africa, as the fares to these destinations are almost double outside the promotional period o The UK is emerging as a preferred place to study post Sept 11. Over 4000 students enroll each year now. First-time travellers from India usually opt for short-haul holidays to the Far East or Mauritius, followed by Europe and America. Repeat travel tends to be to a single destination.

Domestic tourism and short haul destinations have registered a sharp growth. The 20-40 age segment is increasing at 20% annually. There are a large number of young professionals in new technology companies with a high disposition to travel.

Travel market to Britain

Approximately 4/5 million people per annum travel overseas: 200,000 visit the UK. Visitors to Britain fall into three broad categories:

1. Business extenders,
2. Relatively unsophisticated but affluent entrepreneurs, and
3. Urban professional couples.

It is anticipated that even people who presently don't hold a passport will soon be embarking on overseas travel and will visit London as part of a European journey. The number of visits made by Indians to Britain in 2001 was 189,000 (7% decrease on 2000). However, the amount spent increased by 25% from £134 million in 2000 to £163 million in 2001. This is a result of the average length of stay increasing slightly to 21 days, combined with an increase in the average expenditure per day from £32.30 in 2000 to £41.40 in 2001 and a resultant increase in average expenditure per visit from £645.10 in 2000 to £861.80 in 2001.

Travel trends

— Repeat travel is high. British Airways currently has 35,000 frequent fliers from India. Of the UK visas issued in India in 2001, around 40,000 were for multiple entry visas and this constitutes mainly repeat independent travellers.

— Group leisure travel to Britain peaks from the period mid-April to end June. Visits tend to be restricted to 2/3 nights in London on a 14-day European Coach Tour, with FIT (Fully Independent Travel) extensions available to the rest of Britain. Kuoni India and Thomas Cook generated over 7,000 and 3,000 bookings respectively over this period in 2002 and, together with Cox & Kings, Raj Travels and Orbit, make up the top five producers. About 30 other agencies work actively to generate ad hoc groups. Independent and small group travel generates high yield traffic but there are not enough agencies to service this segment.

— Australia, South Africa and the Seychelles are luring away repeat travellers to Britain. Travel to the USA is increasing at a faster rate than that to Britain and Europe. Pan European Trips are giving way to travel to 1,2 or at the most 3 places.

— Trends are towards more independent travel and a greater interest in 'out of London' products, in particular Scotland, the Lake District and the Cotswolds. Families prefer to hire a mini-bus and have a one or two-centre holiday based in Central or Northern England. Vocational courses, workplace visits and business missions are also gaining in popularity. In London, staying in self-catering apartments has increased.

— A shared history, a common language (the English speaking population of India exceeds the population of Britain) and strong business and cultural ties have made many Indian travellers consider Britain as a second home. Less experienced travellers think getting a visa is difficult and that Britain is expensive and perhaps not very welcoming.

— One in three Indian visitors to Britain state business to be the main purpose of their visit. Britain continues to be a favourite stopover on an overseas trip due to its familiarity, language and food. It is also perceived as an easy place to combine business and leisure. However, India's business ties with the USA, Germany, Japan and Korea have increased at faster rates and into more visible consumer brand product areas.

— Younger people are unaware that Britain is lively, trendy and filled with culture. Nevertheless Britain's image has received a facelift with many India centric events in Britain in 2002, such as BFI's ImagineAsia, Selfridges Bollywood Promotion, Bombay Dreams, Indian Cricket Tour, success of India at the Commonwealth Games, Indian participation at the Edinburgh Festival.

More Indian professional now are working at software hubs in UK.

VisitBritain promotional activities

— Bollywood movies shot in Britain have also helped liven up Britain's image. The British Tourist Authority (BTA) has launched a Bollywood campaign highlighting the locations used in Bollywood films and aimed at encouraging Indian film-makers to film in Britain. As part of the campaign, a Bollywood Map, detailing over 20 films shot in the UK since 1990, was launched in April 2001. British films are also hugely popular, and the BTA Movie Map, promotional activity with Filmfare in India and recent promotions focusing on the film Mujsa Dosti Karoge and the musical Bombay Dreams have also been successful in generating interest.

—

— VisitBritain has a long term strategy in India -working with travel trade, media and non-tourism partners. They have been creative in overcoming poor travel trade, enthusiasm and lack of resources by forging alliances with non-tourism partners, the media, the High Commission and the British Council to raise the levels of awareness among targeted customer groups.

— Recent promotions, for example, have included a 20page travel and fashion feature in the Indian magazine Vivaha targeted at business extenders; A promotion with Intel with the Visit Britain CD loaded in 50000 computers and a contest with a grand prize being a holiday for 8 couples to the Cotswolds; a promotion with 100 Pipers Scotch Whisky at 4 clubs in Delhi to create awareness of Scotland; promotions with CNBC to capitalise on James Bond, Health Spas and Bombay Dreams; promotion with MTV, PVR cinemas exploiting the Beatles movie to focus on Liverpool; 14 page editorial in India Today Plus titled "To be a Sport" focussing on Sporting links. Most of the recent promotions entail in-kind support during the slower months and provide a very effective way of helping the British trade gain access to this huge market.

The travel trade in India remains reactive and last minute. Most travel agents in India are only ticketing agents focusing on the lower end of the market, ie first time group leisure travellers on a European tour with just 2/3 nights in London. This represents less than 10% of the total market to UK. The top 10 agents of most airlines are consolidators, operating on high volume and low margins through a network of sub-agents. There are about 30 wholesalers but their primary focus tends to be closed groups for Europe. The emergence of agencies servicing the individual traveller for their travel-related services is a relatively new phenomenon.

There are three major travel trade magazines. However, all newspapers and many magazines have extensive travel sections and one of the areas of VisitBritain's success has been working with the media.

In Tamil Nadu, Tourism Development Corporation (TTDC) concentrated on dissemination of information and implementation of schemes for the benefit of tourists. The TTDC on the other hand was assigned the job of conducting package tours and running of Hotels (Hotel Tamil Nadu). Over the years, the Tourism Industry in Tamil Nadu has registered a good growth. During such period, there was enormous scope for us to interact not only with the tourists from across the globe but also with the private travel agents, tour operators and hotel owners. During the same period, the Department of Tourism have received valuable feedback through its field offices.

On analyzing the tourism scenario, we found that the infrastructure facilities provided to the Tourists at Tourist Spots necessarily require upgradation to that of international standards. The expectations of the tourists are also very high. The provision of high standard infrastructure such as Construction of star category hotels, amusement / theme parks etc. require massive investment. Hence, the Government is of the view that the tourism industry need to be developed through private sector and the Government has to perform.September 2001, Global economic slowdown and climatic / ecological crisis severely hampered tourism activity at the global level during the last two years. It also had some impact on tourist arrivals to India.

However, the actual effect on the tourist inflow to Tamil Nadu was very negligible. Now, the Tourism Industry is slowly but steadily limping back to normalcy. France remained the most popular tourist destination in the world in the year 2002 with an arrival of 76.7 million foreign tourists. There are about 700 million Tourists world wide, who spend approximately 460 billion US Dollars on tourist activities every year. Tourism also accounts for 10% of the jobs world over. India gets only about 2.5. million foreign tourists every year.

In Tamil Nadu while 75% of the Tourists visit to enjoy their leisure, others combine with business, education, auspicious occasions, political/ religious / social Conferences, pilgrimage etc. Keeping the Tourism products in mind the Government are attempting to meet the requirements of all types of tourists. The Tourists visiting Tamil Nadu are drawn from all walks of life and from various countries across the globe, whose colour, religion, race, creed, language, expectations and food habits vary greatly. With a view to ensure a well targeted and focused attention visiting tourists are classified as follows:

Such a classification has enabled the Tourism Department to plan the itinerary, food, accommodation, transport etc to suit the specific needs of each category of tourists. It is also expected that this exercise will ultimately result in attracting more tourists and induce them to stay for a longer period in Tamil Nadu.

Tourism in India remains one of the largest foreign exchange earners, next only to gems, jewellery and garments. During 2001, the foreign exchange earned by Tourism in our country was estimated to be Rs.14,344/ Crores. Ministry of Tourism, Government of India have estimated that every Rs.10.00 lakhs invested in Tourism created 47.5 jobs. The same amount if invested in Agriculture & Manufacturing sector can create only 44.7 and 12.6 jobs respectively.

Today, the direct employment generated by Tourism is estimated to be 164.5 lakhs. Indirect employment is much higher at 223.7 lakhs. A sample survey by the World Tourism Council, which uses a methodology called " Tourism Satellite Account " concludes that jobs generated by Tourism could rise from today's 2.4% to 6.8% in ten years which means 80 lakhs new jobs. Similarly, in respect of hotel industry, it is estimated that an investment of Rs.10.00 lakhs will give direct employment to 12 persons and five rooms in a five star hotel on an average gives direct employment to eight persons.

Tourists visit Tamil Nadu throughout the year out of their sheer desire. Nature has bestowed Tamil Nadu with bountiful tourism products. To supplement these our ancestors too have given us Temples, magnificent architectures etc that serve as great tourists attractions. The tourist wealth of Tamil Nadu can be broadly classified under the following heads:-

a) Hill resorts

b) Beaches

c) Water falls

d) Dam sites

e) Zoological parks

f) Botanical/Horticulture Gardens

g) Wild life sanctuaries

h) Historical monuments/Heritage sites

i) Pilgrim Centres

j) Leisure tourism (Amusement parks/Theme parks)

k) Adventure tourism (mountaineering and boating etc)

l) Fairs and festivals

m) Monuments

The following tourist products will be developed during 2003-2004:-

a) Health tourism

b) Educational centres of excellence, information technology, technical education centres etc

c) Plantation tourism (To be promoted in Coffee/Tea estates)

d) Film industry and tourism (To be promoted through encouraging film shootings and Video recording in Tamil Nadu).

Beach Tourism

Tamil Nadu has a spectacular long coastline. Amusement Park falls, beaches, mangrove forests etc. Exploit natural resources by maintaining complete harmony with nature and without endangering the otherwise extremely fragile ecology. Introduction of trekking, boating, water sports, hang gliding etc by refining and repackaging the available products.

During the Seventh, Eighth, Nineth Five Year Plans, Ministry of Tourism, Government of India was assisting the State Governments/UT Administrations to undertake large number of small and isolated Tourism projects spread through out the length and breath of the country resulting in the resources being spread very thinly. This could not create any major impact on the development of tourism.

The Government of India will prepare the master plans for these Tourism circuits and would fully fund the schemes. Under this scheme Integrated development of one selected tourist destination will be taken up every year in each State. This scheme will be funded by Government of India on 90:10 basis. Major activities that would be undertaken under this scheme are Improvements to surroundings of destination, Illumination, Sewage facilities, wayside facilities, refurbishment of monuments, signages, Tourist Information centres etc.

Under this scheme, the Government of India will provide grant to act as a catalyst for large revenue generating projects like. Up to 2001 - 2002 financial assistance was being provided for the schemes recommended by the State Government and prioritised by Government of India. The State Government also provided matching grant for the schemes sanctioned by Government of India.

For the promotion of tourism and related activities in Nilgiris District, various schemes are being implemented under Hill Area Development Programme.

Tourism Department is providing infrastructural facilities at Tourist spots in Tamil Nadu in association with other departments. It is worth mentioning here that during the last two years the Tourism department alone spent Rs. 5.00 crores for provision of infrastructural facilities at Tourists spots in 15 Districts. One of the important schemes that will be taken up during 2003-2004 is development of Gangaikondachozhapuram in Perambalur District. It is famous for its Peruvudayar, which resembles the big temple at Thanjavur in certain aspects. This temple was built between 1023 and 1029 A.D. Hence, taking into account the importance of the place, projects for Rs. 163 lakhs have been prepared and the works have been taken up.

The tourists and hoteliers felt that the rate of luxury tax is very high (25%) in Tamil Nadu, when compared to other States. Representations were also received from several quarters seeking reduction of luxury tax. The Hon'ble Chief Minister considered the representations. In view of the personal interest taken by the Hon'ble Chief Minister, the Government of Tamil Nadu in December 2002 have.rupees two hundred but less than rupees five hundred per room per day.

Tamil Nadu is today an investor's paradise, as it boasts of certain factors, which make the climate in Tamil Nadu conducive for large scale private investments in all sectors. It has been already decided to set up Ethnic Village/ Garden of Peace near Mamallapuram and Construct Three Star Hotels at Palani, Thiruvannamalai, Nagore and Velankanni. Steps are being taken to set up Ethnic Village at Mamallapuram and Garden of Peace at Muttukadu with private participation. For construction of hotels, an advertisement calling for ' Expression of interest" from private investors has been published. These works would be expedited during 2003-2004 with facilities for Hang Gliding, Para Gliding, Para Sailing, Flight Simulator, Ballooning, Kite flying etc.

It is proposed to enhance the tourist facilities available at Mamallapuram. One such measure under consideration is to set up a sea sports park at the Beach Resort Complex of TTDC at Mamallapuram. Sea sports like wind surfing, water scooters, angling etc would be available at the sea-sports park.

With increase in health awareness, the value of alternative therapy has increased. As a result spas, alternative healing centres and therapists are now in great demand. Alternative therapy is the integrated approach with emphasis on the 5 elements which restore harmony of the body, mind, emotion and soul. The proposed spa resort at Kanniyakumari will have all the above facilities.

Ropeways are being used across the world successfully to transport men and materials over inhospitable terrain, valleys and in between mountain ranges. This is widely used at tourist spots, as a trip on the ropeway enables the tourists to get a birds-eye view of the picturesque scenic beauty several hundred metres below. In Tamil Nadu, Kanniyakumari, Udhagamandalam, Kodaikanal and Yercaud are ideal locations for setting up of ropeway. Necessary steps have already been taken for this project.

A Sound and Light Show is being conducted by this Department.Mamallapuram, Thanjavur, Kancheepuram and Kanniyakumari. ITDC, which possesses the technical know-how in this field has come forward to collaborate with Tourism Department in implementing this project. There are several factors which influence the length of stay of the tourists in Tamil Nadu. But, we consider that Entertainment facilities do play a major role in inducing the tourists to stay back, may be for a over night stay at selected Tourist spots in Tamil Nadu.

The Entertainment facilities normally, the tourists expect at a Tourist spot are Amusement parks, Theme parks, Golf club, Horse racing, Casinos, parks, Cinemas, Air/Sea adventure sports, Trekking, Mountaineering etc. It is seen that Chennai has fairly adequate entertainment facilities to engage the tourists especially on week ends. But such facilities are grossly inadequate in other parts of Tamil Nadu, which are frequented by Tourists in large numbers throughout the year. Hence, Tourism Department will take steps initially to set up Amusement / Theme parks in the District Capitals.

To begin with major tourist centres like Kancheepuram, Kanniyakumari, Thanjavur, Rameswaram and Madurai, where there is considerable movement of Tourists will be covered. Government will offer necessary guidance to private investors in setting up the amusement parks. It would be ensured that the Amusement / Theme parks are built to International standards and that they do not harm the ecology of the region.

The Government of India is currently preparing the 20 years perspective Tourism Development Plan for Tamil Nadu. The draft plan was perused by Tourism Department and remarks have been offered to Government of India. It is expected that the perspective plan will be finalised by Government of India shortly.

Marketing efforts will therefore be aimed at forcing the tourists to visit Tamil Nadu. Advertisements highlighting the tourism potentials are being released in newspapers and periodicals. The advertisements are inserted not only in the newspapers and magazines being published in the country but also in the magazines, published abroad and in in-flight magazines. Advertisements on Tamil Nadu Tourism are being inserted in Terrestrial and Satellite Televisions, websites, moving electronic display boards etc. Recently, a CD Rom on Tamil Nadu Tourism was released. Steps are being taken to prepare a new CD Rom incorporating some more details. A Touch Screen Kiosk has been installed in the advance reservation centre of TTDC at the Tourism Complex in Chennai for the benefit of the tourists.

Special Tourism information centres are also opened in most of the important Fairs and Festivals places. Advertisements in local magazines/dailies are also issued periodically. For disseminating tourism information to the tourists about the tourist attractions and facilities, publicity materials such as folders, maps, picture post cards, posters are brought out and distributed through the Tourist Offices and Tourist Information Centres.

Tourism Potential of Tamil Nadu is being popularised outside Tamil Nadu through our tourist Offices / Tourist Information centres. They are now linked with other State Tourism Departments for promotion of Tourism on reciprocal basis. As part of the steps to attract more number of tourists to Tamil Nadu, it has been proposed to print tourist folders in other Indian languages especially in Bengali, Hindi, Gujarati, Marathi, Oria, Telugu, Malayalam and Kanada.

To publicise Tamil Nadu's Tourism potential in other States, publicity campaigns were also held in Bhubaneshwar, Kolkatta, Lucknow, Mumbai, Bangalore, Hydrabad, Ahmedabad and Bhopal. It is proposed to conduct intensive publicity campaigns during 2003-2004 at Bhubaneshwar, Indore, Gujarat, Pune, Simla, Lucknow, Varanasi, Ahmedabad, Guwahati and Surat.

The Department of Tourism, to some extent utilises the services and facilities of 13 Government of India Tourist Offices abroad to promote the tourist interests of Tamil Nadu. Pamphlets and C.D. Rom on Tamil Nadu Tourism are being distributed through Government of India Tourist Offices. Tamil Nadu Tourism Development Corporation's marketing agents are functioning at London, Malaysia and Bangkok.

One of the major publicity measures undertaken by Government to attract tourists from abroad is participation in international travel marts. Important travel marts are conducted every year at London, Singapore, Berlin, Mauritius, South Africa, Malaysia, Kuwait, U.S. and

Switzerland. Tourism Department had participated in the international.more foreign languages will be considered for international publicity.During the conduct of travel mart, advertisements on Tamil Nadu Tourism products are released in foreign magazines. Advertisements are also released in In-flight magazines to target tourists from U.K. and other European countries. The publishers of foreign magazines also do their own coverage in Tamil Nadu and bring out articles on Tamil Nadu in their magazines. Tourists from abroad also log on to the website of Tamil Nadu Tourism/ Development Corporation to get information about Tamil Nadu Tourism Development Corporation's conducted tours/ hotels. Government also participated in Pravasi, Bharathya Diwas Sammelan held in January 2003 at New Delhi which provided a good opportunity to market tourism products especially among NRIs.

One of the major advantages associated with Tourism sector is its capacity to earn foreign exchange. Foreign tourists constitute the high spending group, who naturally contribute significantly in garnering foreign exchange. Hence, the Tourism Department will take steps to attract more tourists from foreign countries. TTDC's marketing agents at London, Malaysia and Bangkok are also publicising the Tourism potential of Tamil Nadu. During 2003 - 2004 our emphasis will be to tap the Tourist potential in countries like Sri Lanka, Singapore, Malaysia etc. from where there is good scope of attracting ethnic Tourists.

Appointment of marketing agents, conducting of publicity campaign, participation in major travel marts in these countries are some of the strategies proposed to be adopted in this exercise. Possibilities of mutual coordination and cooperation will be explored through the Embassies and Consulates in India and abroad. Publicity in the Neighbouring countries in vernacular languages will be carried out mainly through advertisement in print / Electronic media.

SKAL is an international organisation, established in 1937 in.all over the world will participate. This is the first time that such a major conference is being held in India and especially in Chennai. The Tourism Department has proposed to host the event in association with SKAL. It would give an excellent opportunity to showcase the culture, arts, Handicrafts, hospitality, heritage, history, costumes, etc of Tamil Nadu to an elite international gathering under one roof. .

There are 20 Tourist Offices and 21 Tourist Information Centres functioning under Tourism Department. Out of this, the Tourist Offices at Kanniyakumari, Tirunelveli, Rameswaram, Dharmapuri, Kodaikanal, Madurai, Udhagamandalam, Salem, Tiruchirapalli, Thanjavur, Poompuhar, Chidambaram, Mamallapuram and Chennai have been computerised. During 2003-2004 it is proposed to computerise the Tourist Offices at Goa, Mumbai, New Delhi, Agra, Jaipur and Tourist Information Centres at Thiruvananthapuram, Bangalore and Hyderabad.

Similarly fax machines have been installed at Tourist Offices of Mumbai, Goa, Kolkatta, New Delhi and Tourist Information Centres at Hyderabad, Thiruvananthapuram and Bangalore. During 2003-04 it is proposed to install fax machines at the Tourist Offices at Agra, Jaipur, Kanniyakumari, Tirunelveli, Rameswaram, Dharmapuri, Kodaikanal, Udhagamandalam, Salem, Tiruchirapalli, Thanjavur, Poompuhar, Chidambaram, Mamallapuram and Chennai.

After completing the Computerisation process it is proposed to connect the Tourist Offices, Tourist Information Centres, Units of Tamil Nadu Tourism Development Corporation with each other through WAN connectivity. This will ensure storage and retrieval of information instantaneously with pinpoint accuracy. Our ultimate aim is to provide the tourists with ON-LINE booking facility for Tamil Nadu Tourism Development Corporation's package tours and hotels. A sum of Rs. 50.00 lakhs has been sanctioned by Government of India for providing.The guides disseminate authentic information regarding the tourist spots, mode of travel, places for stay, shopping, types of food/dress etc.

The guides require training. Training of guides, apart from serving the tourists, will also provide excellent job opportunities to the educated unemployed youths. Hence, it is proposed to conduct Guide Training courses during 2003-2004. Tourism being essentially a hospitality oriented industry, it becomes necessary to inject professionalism in the various fields like reception, cooking, hospitality, interior decoration etc. Tamil Nadu has two Government Catering Institutes.

State Institute of Hotel Management and Catering Technology, Tiruchirappalli, was established in the year 1981. It is approved by All India Council of Technical Education, New Delhi and affiliated to Directorate of Technical Education, Government of Tamil Nadu. Until 1986, the Government of India had provided financial grants to this institute and thereafter the Government of Tamil Nadu is funding the activities of this institute with an annual grant of Rs.11.00 lakhs. The institute conducts 3 years diploma course in Catering Technology and one year certificate course in Front office and Book keeping, Food

Production, Bakery and confectionery, Food and beverage services and House keeping. Around 400 students are admitted to various courses every year. Most of them are getting the placement in the Campus interview.

Spiritual Tourism

Tamil Nadu is the land of temples. The huge temples of Tamil Nadu are artistic, sacred, historical & eventful. For example the temples at Kancheepuram, Chidambaram, Madurai, Kanniyakumari, Rameswaram, Thanjavur, Kumbakonam, Srirangam etc., the art and architecture constitutes the magnetic attraction to the tourists. As most of these temples are under the control of the Hindu Religious and Charitable Endowments (HR&CE) Department, the Tourism Department would work in close coordination with that Department to further promote religious and spiritual tourism. Government would also take steps to provide infrastructural facilities at the Pilgrim Centres wherever necessary.

Churches

The following are the important Churches which are visited by tourists in large numbers:-

1) Velankanni Church in Nagappattinam.
2) Manapadu Church in Tuticorin
3) Santhome Church in Chennai.

The Department of Tourism desires to provide basic amenities at the above places taking into consideration the number of Tourists visiting the above Churches. In the first phase a sum of Rs. 16.00 lakhs have been sanctioned with the financial assistance of Government of India/

Government of Tamilnadu for provision of Public Conveniences at Velankanni. The works are under progress.

Mosques provide basic amenities. In the first phase, a sum of Rs. 16.00 lakhs have been sanctioned with the financial assistance of Government of India / Government of Tamilnadu for Provision of Public Convenience at Nagore. The work is under progress.

Eco-Tourism

Eco-Tourism is a new concept and it is based on resources like Rivers, Forests, Sanctuaries, Wildlife etc. Tourists especially from other Countries are keen to enjoy visiting eco-friendly environs. Eco -Tourism wealth of Tamilnadu lies in Pitchavaram, Point Calimere in Muthupet which are famous for mangrove forests; Udhagamandalam, Gulf of Mannar are noted for Biosphere Resources; Kodaikanal, Udhagamandalam, Yercaud and Elagiri are popular Hill Stations. The Wild Life Sanctuary and National Park constitute the natural wealth. The sea, lakes, river, water falls, dam etc. are water resources. It is proposed to develop an Eco-Tourism circuit covering.a cost of Rs.34.45 lakhs at Kodiakkarai is also under construction.

Government of India / Government of Tamil Nadu have already sanctioned a sum of Rs.55.55 lakhs for promotion of Eco-Tourism at Pichavaram. The works are under progress. Kurusadai Islands in Ramanathapuram District is another Eco-Tourism area in Tamil Nadu. For Promotion of Eco-Tourism in Kurusadai Islands, the Government of India has sanctioned Rs.18.90 lakhs towards the purchase of glass bottom boats. These boats are being used for the benefit of tourists.

In Tamil Nadu Mamallapuram and Kanniyakumari are famous Beach Resorts. Considering the importance of development of Beach Tourism, it is proposed to identify and develop lesser known beach resorts. Accordingly, funds as detailed below have been sanctioned for the development of the following lesser known beach tourism destinations:

1) Nagapattinam Beach Rs. 18.00 lakhs
2) Thoothukudi Beach Rs. 10.25 lakhs
3) Eliots Beach, Chennai Rs. 38.43 lakhs

Hill stations

Udhagamandalam (Ooty), Kodaikanal, Yercaud and Elagiri are famous hill stations in Tamil Nadu. Tourists visit these hill stations in large numbers throughout the year. For the benefit of the tourists, package tours are organised by TTDC to visit these hill stations. Steps. Tamil Nadu has its ancient and rich heritage and a variety of living tradition and cultures spread over the state. Music, Dance and Drama form an integral part of the people of Tamil Nadu. No tourist can afford to miss a performance of the pure form of Indian classical dance- Bharatha Natyam, which has been in vogue for several centuries, unspoilt by time. For promoting cultural tourism in Tamil Nadu, the following festivals have been identified as annual events, so that foreign travel agencies can organise package tours.

Summer Festivals

Summer Festivals are being organised during May and June at Udhagamandalam, Sirumalai, Yercaud, Kodaikanal, Suruli Falls, Elagiri, Kolli Hills, Nagappattinam Beach, Valparai, Javvadhu Hills, Pachamalai, Silver Beach, Cuddalore and Panchalankurichi. Special Festivals are also conducted in memory of the first freedom fighter i.e. Veerapandiya Kattabomman at Panchalankurichi in Tirunelveli District in May every year.

Bird Sanctuaries

There are 12 Bird sanctuaries in Tamil Nadu viz.

1. Vedanthangal - Kancheepuram District
2. Karikili - Kancheepuram District
3. Pulicat - Thiruvallur District
4. Vettakudi - Sivaganga District
5. Ganjankulam - Ramanathapuram District
6. Chitrankudi - Ramanathapuram District
7. Melaselvanur / Kelaselvanur - Ramanathapuram District
8. Udhaya Marthandapuram - Thiruvarur District
9. Vadur - Nagapattinam District'
10. Kundankulam - Thirunelveli District
11. Karaivetti - Perambalur District
12 Vellode - Erode District

Birds from various countries visit these sanctuaries during seasons. Since large number of tourists visit the sanctuaries, this department would take steps to provide basic amenities in these sanctuaries.

Adventure Tourism

A rough survey has revealed that around 40% of the tourists visiting any tourist place are youths in the age group of 15 to 35 years. The youths especially, on excursion trips arranged by the educational institutions are interested in Adventure Tourism. To quench their appetite, the Tourism Department has introduced adventure water sports activities at Muttukadu and Kolavai lake. Trekking, mountaineering, rock climbing are also organised by this Department. Since, the Tourism Department now desires to extend the stay of tourists in Tamil Nadu, the promotion of Indian Medicine will go a long way in achieving our objectives. For this purpose initially it is proposed to open Rejuvenative Centres at Kolli hills, Courtallam and Mamallapuram.

Business Tourism

The Business Tourists desire to spend some time for pleasure after the completion of their business activities. Hence to induce them to visit tourist spots, it is proposed to set up temporary tourist information centers at the conference venues.

The two main objectives of provision of accommodation and operation of package tours for the visiting tourists. Subsequently, the Corporation constructed wayside amenities in the places of tourist importance. At present the following tourist amenities are being provided by the Corporation in almost all the places of tourist importance in Tamil Nadu under "Hotel Tamil Nadu " banner:-

1. Hotels
2. Youth Hostels
3. Restaurants
4. Boat Houses
5. Telescope Houses.
6. Service centre-Petrol Bunk at Mamallapuram

Youth Hostels are available for the benefit of budget tourists. Besides dormitory type of accommodation, room facilities are also available in these Youth Hostels.

The next major activity of the Corporation is to provide transport facility to the tourists. The package tours operated by the Tamil Nadu Tourism Development Corporation are extremely popular among the domestic tourists as well as the tourists from foreign countries. TTDC conducts the All India Tourist and Industrial Fair every year at Chennai.

At present there are 54 Hotels with TTDC. Good House keeping, Serving of quality food, Comfortable accommodation, Hospitality etc are very important for the Hotel Industry. The hotels have to be run profitably. TTDC having realised this, has taken steps to franchise 30 hotels and 7 restaurants. Accordingly, 10 hotels have been franchised to private parties so far.

There are more than 150 classified hotels in Tamil Nadu, enjoying star rating. The classified private hotels have approximately 9170 rooms and 1800 unclassified hotels have a total room strength of approximately 5000. At an average occupancy of 60% there is sufficient hotel accommodation in Tamil Nadu to receive 7.90 lakhs foreign tourists and 230 lakhs domestic Tourists. This comfortable accommodation position and the recent slashing of luxury tax is bound to rev up the hotel industry in Tamil Nadu.

For the first time during 2002-2003, the T.T.D.C. has launched value added Rail-cum-Road package tours in tie-up with Indian Railways Catering and Tourism Corporation from Mumbai, Kolkatta and New Delhi, wherein the tourists are provided a special package inclusive of confirmed rail tickets, comfortable travel in T.T.D.C. Hi-tech.package tours from Ahmedabad and Lucknow.

T.T.D.C. is anticipating an income of Rs.80 Lakhs and net profit of Rs.36 lakhs during the ensuing summer season of May to June by operation of these value added package tours. T.T.D.C. has executed M.O.U. with all major State Tourism Corporations. Based on the MOU, TTDC is organising special rail-cum-road tours from Lucknow and

Ahmedabad wherein these State Tourism Corporations would book the tickets for these rail tours and also render necessary services in boarding these tourists at Lucknow and Ahmedabad respectively. Steps are also being taken to organise a special value added package tour from Chennai linking Varanasi, Allahabad and Ayodhya through rail wherein Uttar Pradesh Tourism Corporation would take up the responsibility of local sight seeing for 3 days which would also include local guide service, food, accommodation etc.

Since the year 2001, the Government have initiated several measures to rationalise the expenditure under various heads. In tune with the Government Policy, the TTDC also has taken several steps in this regard. Out of the total staff strength of 958, 205 employees have already taken retirement under Voluntary Retirement Scheme till 31 st March 2003. Besides above, TTDC has also introduced several economy measures resulting in significant reduction of Rs.30.00 lakhs in the incidence of overheads like electricity charges, telephones etc.

From the year 2001, Tourism Department has embarked upon several ambitious projects, requiring high degree of skill and infusion of "State of the art" Technology right from the preparation of Master plans and techno economic feasibility studies. The executing and maintaining agencies also therefore have to ensure quality product. For handling all such technical matters a consultancy wing has been formed at T.T.D.C.

Government has sanctioned Rs.20.00 lakhs to this Consultancy Wing in 2002-2003 for preparation of Master Plan for Development of Tourism Destinations/Circuits. During 2003 - 2004, a sum of Rs. 25.00 lakhs will be provided for the above purpose. The package tours cover all the

Southern States and also States like Bihar, Uttar Pradesh, Orissa and Maharashtra. For the conduct of package tours, TTDC has 22 coaches including three AC hi-tech coaches. Several new package tours have been evolved and introduced covering dam sites, pilgrim centres, heritage centres, water falls etc. A well informed guide accompanies the tourists and the tourists are offered accommodation facilities in Hotel Tamil Nadu.

Special package tours are organised catering to the needs of.93.00 Lakhs for 2002-2003. The Fairs division has also achieved an all time high gross profits of Rs.75.00 Lakhs from the Trade Fair conducted from January 2003 to March 2003. With the significant improvement in the financial performance of T.T.D.C. during the year 20002-2003, it is anticipated that T.T.D.C. would wipe off the accumulated losses of Rs.193.00 lakhs during the current year itself.

Hitherto, TTDC had functioned more as a " Service Provider " rather than an " Service Facilitator". Earlier, TTDC itself was directly in charge of running the hotels and operating the tours, But in the coming days, the TTDC will assume the role of a service facilitator by which, it will render assistance to private entrepreneurs in meeting the requirements of tourists. The first step in this direction has been already taken with the franchising of 10 hotels to private parties. Similarly, publicity campaigns, festivals etc will be organised in future through private participation.

The Commissionerate of Tourism is headed by Commissioner of Tourism, who is assisted by a Joint Director, Three Deputy Directors, One Assistant Director, One Publication Officer, One Accounts Officer and 208 Ministerial staff members working in the Head Office and Unit Offices.

The field offices comprise of 20 Tourist Offices and 21 Tourist Information Centres whose main functions are rendering assistance to tourists in respect of their stay, food, sight seeing, shopping etc., Publicising the tourist potential of Tamil Nadu and co-ordinate with District Collector/ PWD/Local bodies etc in implementation of projects. To accelerate the growth in tourism, it is necessary to create awareness among the Public and Tourists by disseminating information. Hence, during 2001-2002 two more Tourist Offices in Jaipur and Agra were opened.

Bibliography

Briggs, S. *Successful Tourism Marketing,* Kogan Page: UK, PB, ISBN 0749421231 stlg19.95, 1997

Brunt, P. *Market Research in Travel & Tourism,* Butterworth Heinemann: UK, PB, ISBN 0750630825 stlg16.99, 1997.

Buttle, F., *Hotel and Food service marketing: A managerial approach,* Cassell: UK, HB ISBN 0304315338 stlg19.99, 1986

Cooper, C., Education and training, in S. Witt, and L. Moutinho (eds.), *Tourism Marketing and Management Handbook,* London, Prentice Hall, 1989

Foster, D.L. *Sales and Marketing for the Travel Professional,* Glencoe/McGraw Hill: UK, PB, ISBN 0026808676 stlg21.99, 1991

Gayle, D. (ed) "Tourism Marketing and Management in the Caribbean", Routledge: UK, ISBN 0415072638 HB stlg44, 1993.

Goodall, B. and Ashworth, G. (eds) "Marketing in the Tourism Industry: The Promotion of Destination Regions", ITBP: UK, HB, ISBN 0415045452 stlg45.00, 1988.

Hall, C.M., "Tourism in the Pacific Rim: Development Impacts and Markets", 2nd ed, Longman: Australia, ISBN 0582913438, 1997

Heath, E. and Wall, G., "Marketing Tourism Destinations", Wiley: UK, HB, ISBN 0471540676 stlg37.50, 1992

Kasper, C., "Recent developments in tourism research and education at the university level", in S. Witt and L. Moutinho, *Tourism Marketing and Management Handbook,* New York, Prentice Hall, 1989

Koh, K., "Designing the four-year tourism management curriculum: a marketing approach", *Journal of Travel Research,* Summer, pp. 68-72, 1995

Lavery, P., "Education and training in tourism", in S. Witt & L. Moutinho, *Tourism Marketing and Management Handbook,* New York, Prentice Hall (119-122), 1989.

Spears, D., Boger, C., and Gould, R., "Collaborative web-based project on tourism and marketing, Journal of Hospitality and Tourism Education", 10(4): 38-41, 1999.

Index